# The Faith Collection

*-Three Books in One-*

Smith Wigglesworth

ISBN: 1544990421
ISBN-13: 978-1544990422

For more information on our voiceover services
and to see our online store of Christian audio-books
go to **GodSounds.com**

OTHER BOOKS AVAILABLE BY GODSOUNDS, INC.

**Like Precious Faith**
by Smith Wigglesworth

**Divine Healing: A Gift from God**
by John G Lake

**Intimacy with Jesus: Verse by Verse from the Song of Songs**
by Madame Guyon

**A Plain Account of Christian Perfection**
by John Wesley

**Finney Gold: Words that Helped Birth Revival**
by Charles Finney

**Closer to God**
by Meister Eckhart

**The Letters of Ignatius**
by Ignatius

The printing of this book is dedicated to Smith Wigglesworth.

May his life simply be an example of what we all can obtain through faith in Christ Jesus

# BOOK 1: FAITH THAT PREVAILS

## Table of Contents

## BOOK 2: LIKE PRECIOUS FAITH

## **Table of Contents**

# BOOK 3: EVER INCREASING FAITH

## Table of Contents

Jesus Christ is King

†

Book 1:

# *Faith*
## *- That-*
# *Prevails*

# CHAPTER 1

# God-Given Faith

---

READ HEBREWS 11:1-11. I believe that there is only one way to all the treasures of God, and that is the way of faith. By faith and faith alone do we enter into a knowledge of the attributes and become partakers of the beatitudes, and participate in the glories of our ascended Lord. All His promises are Yea and Amen to them that believe.

God would have us come to Him by His own way. That is through the open door of grace. A way has been made. It is a beautiful way, and all His saints can enter in by this way and find rest. God has prescribed that the just shall live by faith. I find that all is failure that has not its base on the rock Christ Jesus. He is the only way, the truth and the life. The way of faith is the Christ way, receiving Him in His fulness and walking in Him; receiving His quickening life that filleth, moveth and changeth us, bringing us to a place where there is always an Amen in our hearts to all the will of God.

As I look into the 12th chapter of Acts, I find that the people were praying all night for Peter to come out of prison. They had a zeal but seem to have been lacking in faith. They were to be commended for their zeal in spending their time in prayer without ceasing, but their faith, evidently, did not measure up to such a marvelous answer. Rhoda had more faith than the rest of them. When the knock came to the door, she ran to it, and the moment she heard Peter's voice, she ran back again with joy saying that Peter stood before the gate. And all the people said, "You are mad. It isn't so." But she constantly affirmed that it was even so.

Zacharias and Elisabeth surely wanted a son, but even when the angel came and told Zacharias that he should have a son, he was full of unbelief. And the angel said, "Thou shalt be dumb, because thou believest not my words."

But look at Mary. When the angel came to her, Mary said, "Be it unto me according to thy word." It was her Amen to the will of God. And God wants us with an Amen in our lives, an inward Amen, a mighty moving Amen, a God-inspired Amen, which says, "It is, because God has spoken. It cannot be otherwise. It is impossible to be otherwise."

Let us examine this 5th verse, "By faith Enoch was translated that he should not see death; and was not found, because God translated him: for before his translation, he had this testimony that he pleased God."

When I was in Sweden, the Lord worked mightily. After one or two addresses the leaders called me and said, "We have heard very strange things about you, and we would like to know if they are true. We can see that God is with you, and that God is moving, and we know that it will be a great blessing to Sweden."

"Well," I said, "what is it?"

"Well," they said, "we have heard from good authority that you preach that you have the resurrection body." When I was in France I had an interpreter that believed this thing, and I found out, after I had preached once or twice through the interpreter, that she gave out her own ideas. And of course I did not know. I said to these brethren, "I tell you what my personal convictions are. I believe that if I had the testimony of Enoch I should be off. I believe that the moment Enoch had the testimony that he pleased God off he went."

I pray that God will so quicken our faith, for translation is in the mind of God; but remember that translation comes on the line of holy obedience and a walk that is pleasing to God. This was true of Enoch. And I believe that we must have a like walk with God in the Spirit, having communion with him, living under his divine smile, and I pray that God by His Spirit may so move us that we will be where Enoch was when he walked with God.

There are two kinds of faith. There is the natural faith. But the supernatural faith is the gift of God. In Acts 26:19, Paul is telling Agrippa of what the Lord said to him in commissioning him. "To open their eyes, and to turn them from darkness to light, from the power of satan unto God, that they may receive forgiveness of sins, and inheritance among them which are sanctified by faith that is in Me."

Is that the faith of Paul? No, it is the faith that the Holy Ghost is giving. It is the faith that He brings to us as we press in and on with God. I want to put before you this difference between our faith and the faith of Jesus. Our faith comes to an end. Most people in this place have come to where they have said, "Lord, I can go no further. I have gone so far and I can go no further. I have used all the faith I have, and I have just to stop now and wait."

I remember being one day in Lancashire, and going round to see some sick people. I was taken into a house where there was a young woman lying on a bed, a very helpless case. The reason had gone, and many things were manifested there which were satanic and I knew it. She was only a young woman, a beautiful child. The husband, quite a young man, came in with the baby, and he leaned over to kiss the wife. The moment he did, she threw herself over on the other side, just as a lunatic would do. That was very heart-breaking. Then he took the baby and pressed the baby's lips to the mother. Again another wild kind of thing happened. I asked one who was attending her, "Have you anybody to help?" "Oh," they said, "We have had everything." "But," I said, "have you no spiritual help?" Her husband stormed out, saying, "Help? You think that we believe in God, after we have had seven weeks of no sleep and maniac conditions."

Then a young woman of about eighteen or so just grinned at me and passed out of the door. That brought me to a place of compassion for the woman. Something had to be done, no matter what it was. Then with all my faith I began to penetrate the heavens, and I was soon out of that house, I will tell you, for I never saw a man get anything from God who prayed on the earth. If you get anything from God, you will have to pray into heaven; for it is all there. If you are living in the earth realm and expect things from heaven, they will never come. And as I saw, in the presence of God, the limitations of my faith, there came another faith, a faith that could not be denied, a faith that took the promise, a faith that believed God's Word. And from that presence, I came back again to earth, but not the same man. God gave a faith that could shake hell and anything else.

I said, "Come out of her, in the name of Jesus!" And she rolled over and fell asleep and wakened in fourteen hours perfectly sane and perfectly whole.

There is a process on this line. Enoch walked with God. That must have been all those years as he was penetrating, and going through, and laying hold, and believing and seeing and getting into such close cooperation and touch with God that things moved on earth and he began to move toward heaven. At last it was not possible for him to stop any longer. Oh, Hallelujah!

In the 15th chapter of 1st Corinthians we read of the body being "sown in weakness," to be raised in power. It seems to me that, as we are looking for translation, the Lord would have us know something of that power now, and would have us kept in that power, so that we shall not be sown in weakness.

There is one thing that God has given me from my youth up, a taste and relish for my Bible. I can say before God, I have never read a book but my Bible, so I know nothing about books. It seems to me better to get the Book of books for food for your soul, for the strengthening of your faith, and the building up of your character in God, so that all the time you are being changed and made meet to walk with God.

"Without faith it is impossible to please Him; for he that cometh to God must believe that He is, and that He is a rewarder of them that diligently seek him."

I can see that it is impossible to please Him on any line but faith, for everything that is not of faith is sin. God wants us to see that the plan of faith is the ideal and principle of God. In this connection I love to keep in my thoughts the beautiful words in the 2nd verse of the 12th chapter of Hebrews: "Looking unto Jesus, the author and finisher of our faith." He is the author of faith. God worked through Him for the forming of the world. "All things were made by Him, and without Him was not anything made that was made." And because of the exceedingly abundant joy of providing for us so great salvation, He became the author of a living faith. And through this principle of living faith, looking unto Him who is the author and finisher of our faith, we are changed into the same image from glory to glory, even by the Spirit of the Lord.

God has something better for you than you have ever had in the past. Come out into all the fulness of faith and power and life and victory that He is willing to provide, as you forget the things of the past, and press right on for the prize of His high calling in Christ Jesus.

# CHAPTER 2

## Like Precious Faith

---

READ 2 PETER 1:1-8. We are dull of comprehension because we so often let the cares of this world blind our eyes; but if we can be open to God, we shall see that He has a greater plan for us in the future than we have ever seen in the past. It is God's delight to make possible to us that which seems impossible, and when we reach a place where He alone has right of way, then all the things that have been misty and misunderstood are cleared up.

This like precious faith that Peter is writing about is a gift that God is willing to give to all of us, and I believe God wants us to receive it so that we may subdue kingdoms, work righteousness, and, if the time is come, to stop the mouths of lions. We should be able under all circumstances to triumph, because we have no confidence in ourselves, but our confidence is only in God. It is always those people who are full of faith that have a good report, that never murmur, that are in the place of victory, that are not in the place of human order but of divine order, since God has come to dwell in them.

This like precious faith is for all; but there may be some hindrance in your life that God will have to deal with. It seems to me as if I had

had a thousand road engines come over my life to break me up like a potter's vessel. There is no other way into the deep things of God but a broken spirit. There is no other way into the power of God. God will do the exceeding abundantly above all we ask or think for us when He can bring us to the place where we can say with Paul, "I live no longer, and Another, even Christ, has taken the reins and the rule."

I understand God by His Word. I cannot understand God by impressions or feelings; I cannot get to know God by sentiments. If I am going to know God, I am going to know Him by His Word. I know I shall be in heaven, but I could not build on my feelings that I am going to heaven. I am going to heaven because God's Word says it, and I believe God's Word. And "faith cometh by hearing, and hearing by the Word of God." Rom. 10:17.

In Mark 11:24 we read, "What things soever ye desire, when ye pray, believe that ye receive them, and ye shall have them." The previous verse speaks of mountains removed, difficulties cleared away. Veneering won't do. We must have reality, the real working of our God. We must know God. We must be able to go in and hold converse with God. We must also know the mind of God toward us, so that all our petitions are always on the line of His will.

As this like precious faith becomes a part of you, it will make you so that you will dare to do anything. And remember, God wants daring men, men who will dare all, men who will be strong in Him and dare to do exploits. How shall we reach this plane of faith? Let go your own thoughts, and take the thoughts of God, the Word of God. If you build yourself on imaginations you will go wrong. You have the Word of God and it is enough. A man gave this remarkable testimony concerning the Word: "Never compare this Book with other books. Comparisons are dangerous. Never think or never say that this Book contains the Word of God. It is the Word of God. It is supernatural in origin, eternal in duration, inexpressible in value, infinite in scope, regenerative in power, infallible in authority, universal in interest, personal in application, inspired in totality. Read it through. Write it down. Pray it in. Work it out. And then pass it on."

And truly the Word of God changes a man until he becomes an epistle of God. It transforms his mind, changes his character, moves him on from grace to grace, makes him an inheritor of the very nature of God. God comes in, dwells in, walks in, talks through, and sups with him who opens his being to the Word of God and receives the Spirit who inspired it.

When I was going over to New Zealand and Australia, I had many to see me off. There was an Indian doctor who was riding in the same car with me to the docks. He was very quiet and took in all things that were said on the ship. I began to preach, of course, and the Lord began to work among the people. In the second-class part of the ship there was a young man and his wife who were attendants on a lady and gentleman in the first-class. And as these two young people heard me talking to them privately and otherwise, they were very much impressed. Then the lady they were attending got very sick. In her sickness and her loneliness she could find no relief. They called in the doctor, and the doctor gave her no hope.

And then, when in this strange dilemma—she was a great Christian Scientist, a preacher of it, and had gone up and down preaching it—they thought of me. Knowing the conditions, and what she lived for, that it was late in the day, and that in the condition of her mind she could only receive the simplest words, I said to her, "Now you are very sick, and I won't talk to you about anything save this; I will pray for you in the name of Jesus, and the moment I pray you will be healed."

And the moment I prayed she was healed. That was this like precious faith in operation. Then she was disturbed. Now I could have poured in oil very soon. But I poured in all the bitter drugs possible, and for three days I had her on cinders. I showed her her terrible state, and pointed out to her all her folly and the fallacy of her position. I showed her that there was nothing in Christian Science, that it is a lie from the beginning, one of the last agencies of hell. At best a lie, preaching a lie, and producing a lie.

Then she wakened up. She became so penitent and broken-hearted. But the thing that stirred her first was that she had to go to preach the simple gospel of Christ where she had preached Christian Science. She asked me if she had to give up certain things. I won't mention the things, they are too vile. I said, "What you have to do is to see Jesus and take Jesus." When she saw the Lord in His purity, the other things had to go. At the presence of Jesus all else goes.

This opened the door. I had to preach to all on the boat. This gave me a great opportunity. As I preached the power of God fell, conviction came and sinners were saved. They followed me into my cabin one after another. God was working there.

Then this Indian doctor came. He said, "What shall I do? I cannot use medicine any more." "Why?" "Oh, your preaching has changed me. But I must have a foundation. Will you spend some time with me?" "Of course I will." Then we went alone and God broke the fallow ground. This Indian doctor was going right back to his Indian conditions under a new order. he had left a practice there. He told me of the great practice he had. He was going back to his practice to preach Jesus.

If you have lost your hunger for God, if you do not have a cry for more of God, you are missing the plan. There must come up from us a cry that cannot be satisfied with anything but God. He wants to give us the vision of the prize ahead that is something higher than we have ever attained. If you ever stop at any point, pick up at the place where you have dropped through, and begin again under the refining light and power of heaven and God will meet you. And while He will bring you to a consciousness of your own frailty and to a brokenness of spirit, your faith will lay hold of Him and all the divine resources, His light and compassion will be manifested through you, and He will send the rain.

Shall we not dedicate ourselves afresh to God? Some say, "I dedicated myself last night to God." Every new revelation brings a new dedication. Let us seek Him.

# CHAPTER 3

## Spiritual Power

---

BIBLE READING —Matthew 16.

The Pharisees and Sadducees had been tempting Jesus to show them a sign from heaven. He showed them that they could discern the signs that appeared on the face of the sky, and yet could not discern the signs of the times. He would give them no sign to satisfy their unbelieving curiosity, remarking that a wicked and adulterous generation sought after a sign, and that no sign would be given to them, but the sign of the prophet Jonah. A wicked and adulterous generation stumbles over the story of Jonah, but faith can see in that story a wonderful picture of the death, burial and resurrection of our Lord Jesus Christ.

After Jesus had departed from the Pharisees, and had come to the other side of the lake, He said to His disciples, "Take heed, and beware of the leaven of the Pharisees and of the Sadducees." The disciples began to reason among themselves; and all they could think of was that they had taken no bread. What were they to do? Then Jesus uttered these words, "O ye of little faith!" He had been so long with them, and yet they were still a great disappointment to Him, because of their lack of comprehension and of faith. They could not grasp the profound spiritual truth He was bringing to them, and could only think about having brought no bread. "O ye of little faith! Do ye not yet understand, neither remember the five loaves of the five thousand, and how many baskets ye took up? Neither the seven loaves of the four thousand, and how many baskets ye took up?"

At one time Jesus said to Peter, "What thinkest thou, Simon? of whom do the kings of the earth take custom or tribute? of their own children or of strangers?" Peter said, "Of strangers." Then Jesus said, "Then are the children free. Nevertheless, lest we should offend them, go thou to the sea, and cast a hook, and take up the fish that first cometh up; and when thou hast opened his mouth, thou shalt find a piece of money; take that, and give unto them, for me and thee." Peter had been at the fishing business all his life, but he never had caught a fish with any silver in its mouth. But the Master does not want us to reason things out—for carnal reasoning will always land us in a bog of unbelief—but just to obey. "This is a hard job," Peter may have said, as he put the bait on his hook, "but since You told me to do it, I'll try;" and he cast his line into the sea. There were millions of fish in the sea, but every fish had to stand aside and leave that bait alone, and let that fish with the piece of money in his mouth come up and take it.

A woman came to me in Cardiff, Wales, who was filled with ulceration. She had fallen in the streets twice through this trouble. She came to the meeting and it seemed as if the evil power within her purposed to kill her right there, for she fell, and the power of the devil was rending her sore. She was helpless, and it seemed as if she had expired. I cried, "O God, help this woman." Then I rebuked the evil power in the name of Jesus, and instantly the Lord healed her. She rose up and made a great to-do. She felt the power of God in her body and wanted to testify all the time. After three days she went to another place and began to testify about the Lord's power to heal. She came to me and said, "I want to tell everyone about the Lord's healing power. Have you no tracts on this subject?" I handed her my Bible and said, "Matthew, Mark, Luke, John—they are the best tracts on healing. They are full of incidents about the power of Jesus. They will never fail to accomplish the work of God if people will believe them."

There is where men lack. All lack of faith is due to not feeding on

God's Word. You need it every day. How can you enter into a life of faith? Feed on the living Christ of whom this Word is full. As you get taken up with the glorious fact and the wondrous presence of the living Christ, the faith of God will spring up within you. "Faith cometh by hearing, and hearing by the Word of God." Rom. 10:17.

Jesus asked His disciples what men were saying about Him. They told Him, "Some say that thou art John the Baptist; some, Elias; and others, Jeremias, or one of the prophets." Then He put the question, to see what they thought about it, "But whom say ye that I am?" Peter answered, "Thou art the Christ, the Son of the living God." And Jesus said to him, "Blessed art thou, Simon Bar-Jona: for flesh and blood hath not revealed it unto thee, but my Father which is in heaven." It is simple. Who do you say He is? Who is He? Do you say with Peter, "Thou art the Christ, the Son of the living God"? How can you know this? He is to be revealed. Flesh and blood does not reveal this. It is an inward revelation. God wants to reveal His Son within us and make us conscious of an inward presence. Then you can cry, "I know He is mine! He is mine! He is mine!" "Neither knoweth any man the Father, save the Son, and he to whomsoever the Son will reveal Him." Seek God until you get from Him a mighty revelation of the Son, until that inward revelation moves you on to the place where you are always steadfast, unmoveable, and always abounding in the work of the Lord.

There is a wonderful power in this revelation. "Upon this rock I will build my church; and the gates of hell shall not prevail against it. And I will give unto thee the keys of the kingdom of heaven; and whatsoever thou shalt bind on earth, shall be bound in heaven: and whatsoever thou shalt loose on earth shall be loosed in heaven." Was Peter the rock? No. A few minutes later he was so full of the devil that Christ had to say to him, "Get thee behind me, satan; thou art an offense unto me." This rock was Christ. He is the Rock and there are many scriptures to confirm this. And to everyone who knows that He is the Christ He gives the key of faith, the power to bind and the power to loose. Stablish your hearts with this fact.

I had been preaching on this line in Toronto, endeavoring to show that the moment a man believes with all his heart God puts into him a reality, a substance, a life; yea, God dwells in him, and with the new birth there comes into us a mighty force that is mightier than all the power of the enemy. A man ran out of the meeting, and when I got home that night he was there with a big, fine, tall man. This man said to me, "Three years ago my nerves became shattered. I can't sleep. I have lost my business. I have lost everything. I am not able to sleep at all and my life is one of misery." I said to him, "Go home and sleep in the name of Jesus." He turned around and seemed reluctant to go; but I said to him, "Go!" and shoved him out of the door.

The next morning he rang up on the telephone. He said to my host, "Tell him I slept all night. I want to see him at once." He came and said, "I'm a new man. I feel I have new life. And now can you get me my money back?" I said, "Everything!" He said, "Tell me how." I said, "Come to the meeting tonight and I'll tell you." The power of God was mightily present in that evening meeting, and he was greatly under conviction. He made for the altar, but fell before he got there. The Lord changed him and everything in him He is now a successful businessman. All his past failures had come through a lack of the knowledge of God No matter what troubles you, God can shake the devil out, and completely transform you. There is none like Him.

One day I was traveling in a railway train where there were two sick people in the car, a mother and her daughter. I said to them, "Look, I've something in this bag that will cure every case in the world. It has never been known to fail." They became very much interested, and I went on telling them more about this remedy that has never failed to remove disease and sickness. At last they summoned up courage to ask for a dose. So I opened my bag, took out my Bible, and read them that verse, "I am the Lord that healeth thee." It never fails. He will heal you if you dare believe Him. Men are searching everywhere today for things with which they can heal themselves, and they ignore the fact that the Balm of Gilead is within easy reach. As I talked about this wonderful Physician, the faith of both mother and daughter went out toward Him, and He healed them both, right in the train.

God has made His Word so precious that, if I could not get another copy, I would not part with my Bible for all the world. There is life in the Word. There is virtue in it. I find Christ in it; and He is the One I need for spirit, soul and body. It tells me of the power of His name and of the power of His blood for cleansing. The lions may lack and suffer hunger, but they that seek the Lord shall not want any good thing. Psalm 34:10.

A man came to me at one time, brought by a little woman. I said, "What's up with him?" She said, "He gets situations, but he fails every time. He is a slave to alcohol and nicotine poison. He is a bright, intelligent man in most things, but he goes under to those two things." I was reminded of the words of the Master, giving us power to bind and loose, and I told him to put out his tongue. In the name of the Lord Jesus Christ I cast out the evil powers that gave him the taste for these things. I said to him, "Man, you are free today." He was unsaved, but when he realized the power of the Lord in delivering him, he came to the services, publicly acknowledged that he was a sinner, and the Lord saved and baptized him. A few days later I asked, "How are things with you?" He said, "I am delivered." God has given us the power to bind and the power to loose.

In another place a woman came to me and said, "I have not been able to smell for twenty years; can you do anything for me?" I said, "You shall smell tonight." Could I give anybody that which had been lost for twenty years? Not of myself, but I remembered the Rock on which God's church is built, the Rock Christ Jesus, and His promise to give to His own the power to bind and loose. We can dare to do anything if we know we have the Word of God behind us. In the name of the Lord Jesus I loosed this woman. She ran all the way home. The table was full of good things, but she would not touch a thing. She said, "I am having a feast of smelling!" Praise the Lord for the fact that He Himself backs up his own Word and proves the truth of it in these days of unbelief and apostasy.

Another person came and said, "What can you do for me? I have had sixteen operations and have had my ear drums taken out." I said, "God has not forgotten how to make ear drums." I anointed her and prayed, asking the Lord that the ear drums should be replaced. She was so deaf that I do not think she would have heard had a cannon gone off. She was as deaf afterwards as it was possible to be. But she saw other people getting healed and rejoicing. Has God forgotten to be gracious? Was His power just the same? She came the next night and said, "I have come tonight to believe God." Take care you do not come in any other way. I prayed for her again and commanded her ears to be loosed in the name of Jesus. She believed, and the moment she believed she heard, she ran and jumped upon a chair and began to preach. Later I let a pin drop and she heard it fall. God can give drums to ears. All things are possible with God. God can save the worst.

Discouraged one, cast your burden on the Lord. He will sustain you. Look unto Him and be lightened. Look unto Him now.

# CHAPTER 4

## Paul's Pentecost

---

SAUL WAS PROBABLY the greatest persecutor that the early Christians had. We read that he made havoc of the church, entering into every house, and haling men and women, committed them to prison. At this time we find him breathing out threatenings and slaughter against the disciples of the Lord. He was on his way to Damascus for the purpose of destroying the church there. How did God deal with such a one? We should have dealt with him in judgment. God dealt with him in mercy. Oh, the wondrous love of God! He loved the saints at Damascus and the way He preserved them was through the salvation of the man who purposed to scatter and destroy them. Our God delights to be merciful and His grace is vouchsafed daily to both sinner and saint. He shows mercy to all. If we would but realize it, we are only alive today through the grace of our God.

More and more I see that it is through the grace of God that I am preserved every day. It is when we realize the goodness of God that we are brought to repentance. Here was Saul, with letters from the high priest, hastening to Damascus. He was struck down and there came to his vision a light, a light that was brighter than the sun. As he fell speechless to the ground he heard a voice saying to him, "Saul, Saul, why persecutest thou Me?" He answered, "Who art thou, Lord?" And the answer came back, "I am Jesus whom thou persecutest." And he cried, "Lord, what wilt Thou have me to do?" And the men that were with him lost their speech— they were speechless—but they led him to Damascus.

There are some people who have an idea that it is only preachers who can know the will of God. But the Lord has a disciple in Damascus, a man behind the scenes, who lived in a place where God could talk to him. His ears were open. He was one who listened in to the things from heaven. Oh, this is so much more marvelous than anything you can hear on earth. It was to this man that the Lord appeared in a vision. He told him to go down to the street called Straight and inquire for Saul. And He told him that Saul had seen in a vision a man named Ananias coming in and putting his hand on him that he might receive his sight. Ananias protested, "Lord, I have heard by many of this man, how much evil he hath done to Thy saints in Jerusalem: and here he hath authority from the chief priests to bind all that call on Thy name." But the Lord assured Ananias that Saul was a chosen vessel, and Ananias, nothing doubting, went on his errand of mercy.

The Lord had told Ananias concerning Saul, "Behold, he prayeth." Repentant prayer is always heard in heaven. The Lord never despises a broken and contrite heart. And to Saul was given this vision that was soon to be a reality, the vision of Ananias coming to pray for him that he might receive his sight.

As I was looking through my letters one day while in the city of Belfast, a man came up to me and said, "Are you visiting the sick?" He pointed me to go to a certain house and told me to go to it and there I would see a very sick woman. I went to the house and I saw a very helpless woman propped up in bed. I knew that humanly speaking she was beyond all help. She was breathing with short, sharp breaths as if every breath would be her last. I cried to the Lord and said, "Lord, tell me what to do." The Lord said to me, "Read the fifty-third chapter of Isaiah." I opened my Bible and did as I was told. I read down to the fifth verse of this chapter, when all of a sudden the woman shouted, "I am healed! I am healed!" I was amazed at this sudden exclamation and asked her to tell me what had happened. She said, "Two weeks ago I was cleaning house and I strained my heart very badly. Two physicians have been to see me, but they both told me there was no help. But last night the Lord gave me a vision. I saw you come right into my bedroom. I saw you praying. I saw you open your Bible at the fifty-third chapter of Isaiah. When you got down to the fifth verse and read the words, 'With His stripes we are healed,' I saw myself wonderfully healed. That was a vision, now it is a fact."

I do thank God that visions have not ceased. The Holy Ghost can give visions, and we may expect them in these last days. God willeth not the death of any sinner and He will use all kinds of means for their salvation. Oh, what a gospel of love!

Ananias went down to the house on Straight Street and he laid his hands on the one who had before been a blasphemer and a persecutor and he said to him, "Brother Saul, the Lord, even Jesus, that appeared unto thee in the way as thou camest, hath sent me, that thou mightest receive thy sight, and be filled with the Holy Ghost." The Lord had not forgotten his physical condition and there was healing for him. But there was something beyond this. It was the filling with the Holy Ghost. Oh, it always seems to me that the Gospel is robbed of its divine glory when we overlook this marvelous truth of the Baptism of the Holy Ghost. To be saved is wonderful, to be a new creature, to have passed from death unto life, to have the witness of the Spirit that you are born of God, all this is unspeakably precious. But whereas we have the well of salvation bubbling up, we need to go on to a place where from within us shall flow rivers of living water.

God chose Saul. What was he? A blasphemer. A persecutor. That is grace. Our God is gracious and He loves to show His mercy to the vilest and worst of men. There was a notable character in the town in which I lived who was known as the worst man in the town. He was so vile, and his language was so horrible, that even wicked men could not stand it. In England they have what is known as the public hangman who has to perform all the executions. This man held that appointment and he told me later that he believed that when he performed the execution of men who had committed murder, that the demon power that was in them would come upon him and that in consequence he was possessed with a legion of demons. His life was so miserable that he purposed to make an end of life. He went down to a certain depot and purchased a ticket. The English trains are much different from the American. In every coach there are a number of small compartments and it is easy for anyone who wants to commit suicide to open the door of his compartment and throw himself out of the train. This man purposed to throw himself out of the train in a certain tunnel just as the train coming from an opposite direction would be about to dash past and he thought this would be a quick end to his life.

There was a young man at the depot that night who had been saved the night before. He was all on fire to get others saved and purposed in his heart that every day of his life he would get someone saved. He saw this dejected hangman and began to speak to him about his soul. He brought him down to our mission and there he came under a mighty conviction of sin. For two and a half hours he was literally sweating under conviction and you could see a vapor rising up from him. At the end of two and a half hours he was graciously saved.

I said, "Lord, tell me what to do." The Lord said, "Don't leave him, go home with him." I went to his house. When he saw his wife he said, "God has saved me." The wife broke down and she too was graciously saved. I tell you there was a difference in that home. Even the cat knew the difference.

There were two sons in that house and one of them said to his mother, "Mother, what is up in our house? It was never like this before. It is so peaceful. What is it?" She told him, "Father has been saved." The other son was struck with the same thing.

I took this man to many special services and the power of God was on him for many days. He would give his testimony and as he grew in grace he desired to preach the gospel. He became an evangelist and hundreds and hundreds were brought to a saving knowledge of the Lord Jesus Christ through his ministry. The grace of God is sufficient for the vilest and He can take the most wicked of men and make them monuments of his grace. He did this with Saul of Tarsus at the very time he was breathing out threatenings and slaughter against the disciples of the Lord. He did it with Berry the hangman. He will do it for hundreds more in response to our cries.

You will notice that when Ananias came into that house he called the one-time enemy of the gospel "Brother Saul." The Lord Jesus has sent Ananias to that house to put his hands upon this newly saved brother that he might receive his sight and be filled with the Holy Ghost. You say, "But it does not say that he spoke in tongues." We know that Paul did speak in tongues; that he spoke in tongues more than all the Corinthians. In those early days they were so near the time of that first Pentecostal outpouring that they would never have been satisfied with anyone receiving the Baptism unless they received it according to the original pattern given on the Day of Pentecost. When Peter was relating what took place in the house of Cornelius at Caesarea he said, "And as I began to speak, the Holy Ghost fell on them, as on us at the beginning." Later, speaking of this incident, he said, "God, which knoweth the hearts, bear them witness, giving them the Holy Ghost, even as He did unto us; and put no difference between us and them, purifying their hearts by faith." And we know from the account of what took place at Cornelius' household that when the Holy Ghost fell "they heard them speak with tongues and magnify God." Many people think that God does make a difference between us and those at the beginning. But they have no Scripture for this. When anyone receives the gift of the Holy Ghost, there will assuredly be no difference between his experience today and that which was given on the Day of Pentecost. And I cannot believe that, when Saul was filled with the Holy Ghost the Lord made any difference in the experience that He gave him from the experience that He had given to Peter and the rest a short while before.

It was about thirty-one years ago that a man came to me and said, "Wigglesworth, do you know what is happening in Sunderland? People are being baptized in the Holy Ghost exactly the same way as the disciples were on the Day of Pentecost." I said, "I would like to go." I immediately took train and went to Sunderland. I went to the meetings and said, "I want to hear these tongues." I was told, "When you receive the Baptism in the Holy Ghost, you will speak in tongues." I said, "I have the Baptism in the Holy Ghost." One man said, "Brother, when I received the Baptism I spoke in tongues." I said, "Let's hear you." He could not speak in tongues to order, he could only speak as the Spirit gave him utterance and so my curiosity was not satisfied.

I saw these people were very earnest and I became quite hungry. I was anxious to see this new manifestation of the Spirit and I would be questioning all the time and spoiling a lot of the meetings. One man said to me, "I am a missionary and I have come here to seek the Baptism in the Holy Ghost. I am waiting on the Lord, but you have come in and are spoiling everything with your questions." I began to argue with him and our love became so hot that when we walked home he walked on one side of the road and I on the other.

That night there was to be a tarrying meeting and I purposed to go. I changed my clothes and left my key in the clothes I had taken off. As we came from the meeting in the middle of the night I found I did not have my key upon me and this missionary brother said, "You will have to come and sleep with me." But do you think we went to bed that night? Oh, no, we spent the night in prayer. We received a precious shower from above. The breakfast bell rang, but that was nothing to me. For four days I wanted nothing but God. If you only knew the unspeakably wonderful blessings of being filled with the Third Person of the Trinity, you would set aside everything else to tarry for this infilling.

I was about to leave Sunderland. This revival was taking place in the vestry of an Episcopal Church. I went to the Vicarage that day to say goodbye and I said to Sister Boddy, the vicar's wife, "I am going away, but I have not received the tongues yet." She said, "It isn't tongues you need, but the Baptism." I said, "I have the Baptism, Sister, but I would like to have you lay hands on me before I leave." She laid her hands on me and then had to go out of the room. The fire fell. It was a wonderful time as I was there with God alone. It seemed as though God bathed me in power. I was given a wonderful vision. I was conscious of the cleansing of the precious blood and cried out, "Clean! Clean! Clean!" I was filled with the joy of the consciousness of the cleansing. I saw the Lord Jesus Christ. I saw the empty cross and I saw Him exalted at the right hand of God the Father. As I was extolling, magnifying, and praising Him I was speaking in tongues as the Spirit of God gave me utterance. I knew now that I had received the real Baptism in the Holy Ghost.

I sent a telegram home and when I got there one of our boys said, "Father, I hear you have been speaking in tongues. Let's hear you." I could not speak in tongues. I had been moved to speak in tongues as the Spirit of God gave utterance at the moment I received the Baptism, but I did not receive the gift of tongues and could not speak a word. I never spoke again in tongues until nine months later when I was praying for someone, and it was then that God gave me the permanent gift of speaking in tongues.

And so Saul was filled with the Holy Ghost and in the later chapters of the Acts of the Apostles we see the result of this infilling. Oh, what a difference it makes. When I got home my wife said to me, "So you think you have received the Baptism of the Holy Ghost. Why, I am as much baptized in the Holy Ghost as you are." We had sat on the platform together for twenty years but that night she said, "Tonight you will go by yourself." I said, "All right." As I went up to the platform that night the Lord gave me the first few verses of the sixty-first chapter of Isaiah, "The Spirit of the Lord God is upon me; because the Lord hath anointed me to preach good tidings unto the meek: He hath sent me to bind up the broken-hearted, to proclaim liberty to the captives, and the opening of the prison to them that are bound." My wife went back to one of the furthermost seats in the hall and she said to herself, "I will watch it." I preached that night on the subject the Lord had given me and I told what the Lord had done for me. I told the people that I was going to have God in my life and I would gladly suffer a thousand deaths rather than forfeit this wonderful infilling that had come to me. My wife was very restless. She was moved in a new way and said, "That is not my Smith that is preaching. Lord, you have done something for him." As soon as I had finished, the secretary of the mission got up and said, "Brethren, I want what the leader of our mission has got." He tried to sit down but missed his seat and fell on the floor. There were soon fourteen of them on the floor, my own wife included. We did not know what to do, but the Holy Ghost got hold of the situation and the fire fell. A revival started and the crowds came. It was only the beginning of the flood-tide of blessing. We had touched the reservoir of the Lord's life and power. Since that time the Lord has taken me to many different lands and I have witnessed many blessed outpourings of God's Holy Spirit.

The grace of God that was given to the persecuting Saul is available for you. The same Holy Ghost infilling he received is likewise available. Do not rest satisfied with any lesser experience than the Baptism that the disciples received on the Day of Pentecost, then move on to a life of continuous receiving of more and more of the blessed Spirit of God.

# CHAPTER 5

# Ye Shall Receive Power

---

"YE SHALL RECEIVE POWER after the Holy Ghost is come upon you." The disciples had been asking whether the Lord would at that time restore again the kingdom to Israel. Christ told them that it was not for them to know the times and seasons which the Father had put in His own power, but He promised them that when they received the Holy Ghost they should receive power to witness for Him in all the world. To receive the Holy Ghost is to receive power with God, and power with men.

There is a power of God and there is a power which is of satan. When the Holy Spirit fell in the early days, a number of spiritists came to our meetings. They thought we had received something like they had and they were coming to have a good time. They filled the two front rows of our mission. When the power of God fell, these imitators began their shaking and muttering under the power of the devil. The Spirit of the Lord came mightily upon me and I cried. "Now, you devils, clear out of this!" And out they went. I followed them right out into the street and then they turned round and cursed me. There was power from below, but it was no match for the power of the Holy Ghost, and they soon had to retreat.

The Lord wants all saved people to receive power from on High—power to witness, power to act, power to live, and power to show forth the divine manifestation of God within. The power of God will take you out of your own plans and put you into the plan of God. You will be unmantled and divested of that which is purely of yourself and put into a divine order. The Lord will change you and put His mind where yours was and thus enable you to have the mind of Christ. Instead of you laboring according to your own plan, it will be God working in you and through you to do His own good pleasure through the power of the Spirit within. Someone has said that you are no good until you have your "I" knocked out. Christ must reign within, and the life in the Holy Ghost means at all times the subjection of your own will to make way for the working out of the good and acceptable and perfect will of God within.

I was holding a meeting, once, in London, and at the close a man came to me and said, "We are now allowed to hold meetings in this hall after 11 o'clock, and we would like you to come home with us. I am so hungry for God." The wife said she, too, was hungry, and so I agreed to go with them. At about 12:30 we arrived at their house. The man began stirring up the fire and said, "Now we will have a good supper." I said to them, "I did not come here for your warm fire, your supper or your bed. I came here because I thought you were hungry to get more of God." We got down to pray and at about 3:30 the Lord baptized the wife, and she spoke in tongues as the Spirit gave utterance. At about 5 o'clock I spoke to the husband and asked how he was getting on. He replied, "God has broken my iron, stubborn will." He had not received the Baptism, but God had wrought a mighty work within him.

The following day, at his business, everyone could tell that a great change had come to him. Before he had been a walking terror. The men who labored for him had looked upon him as a regular devil because of the way he had acted; but coming into contact with the power of God that night completely changed him. Before this he had made a religious profession, but he had never truly entered into the experience of the new birth until that night, when the power of God surged so mightily through his home. A short while afterwards I went to this man's home, and his two sons ran to me and kissed me, saying,

"We have a new father." Previous to this these boys had often said to their mother, "Mother, we cannot stand it in the home any longer. We will have to leave." But the Lord changed the whole situation that night as we prayed together. On the second visit the Lord baptized this man in the Holy Ghost. The Holy Spirit will reveal false positions, pull the mask off any refuge of lies and clean up and remove all false conditions. When the Holy Spirit came in, that man's house and business and he himself were entirely changed.

When the Holy Spirit comes in He comes to empower you to be an effective witness. At one time we were holding some special meetings and I was out distributing bills. I went into a shoemaker's and there was a man with a green shade over his eyes and also a cloth. My heart looked up to the Lord and I had the witness within that He was ready to change any condition. The man was crying, "Oh! Oh!! Oh!!!" I asked, "What's the trouble?" He said he was suffering with great inflammation and burning. I said, "I rebuke this condition in Jesus' name." Instantly the Lord healed him. He took off the shade and cloth and said, "Look, it is all gone."

At one time a lady wrote and asked if I could go and help her. She said that she was blind, having two blood clots behind her eyes. When I reached the house they brought the blind woman to me. We were together for some time and then the power of God fell. Rushing to the window she exclaimed, "I can see! Oh, I can see! The blood is gone, I can see." She then inquired about receiving the Holy Spirit and confessed that for ten years she had been fighting our position. She said, "I could not bear these tongues, but God has settled the whole thing today. I now want the Baptism in the Holy Ghost." The Lord graciously baptized her in the Spirit.

The Holy Spirit will come when a man is cleansed. There must be a purging of the old life. I never saw anyone baptized who was not clean within.

I remember being in a meeting at one time, where there was a man seeking the Baptism, and he looked like he was in trouble. He was very restless, and finally he said to me, "I will have to go." I said, "What's up?" He said, "God is unveiling things to me, and I feel so unworthy." I said, "Repent of everything that is wrong." He continued to tarry and the Lord continued to search his heart. These times of waiting on God for the fullness of the Spirit are times when He searches the heart and tries the reins. Later the man said to me, "I have a hard thing to do, the hardest thing I have ever had to do." I said to him, "Tell the Lord you will do it, and never mind the consequences." He agreed, and the next morning he had to take a ride of thirty miles and go with a bag of gold to a certain party with whom he dealt. This man had a hundred of cattle and he bought all his feed at a certain place. He always paid his accounts on a certain day, but one day he missed. He was always so punctual in paying his accounts that when later the people of his form went over their books, they thought they must have made a mistake in not crediting the man with the money and so they sent him a receipt. The man never intended not to pay the account, but if you defer to do a right thing the devil will see that you never do it. But when that man was seeking the Lord that night the Lord dealt with him on this point, and he had to go and straighten the thing the next morning. He paid the account and then the Lord baptized him in the Spirit. They that bear the vessels of the Lord must be clean, must be holy.

When the Holy Spirit comes He always brings a rich revelation of Christ. Christ becomes so real to you that, when, under the power of the Spirit, you begin to express your love and praise to Him, you find yourself speaking in another tongue. Oh, it is a wonderful thing! At one time I belonged to a class who believed that they had received the Baptism in the Spirit without the speaking in tongues. There are many folks like that today, but if you can go with them to a prayer meeting you will find them asking the Lord again and again to baptize them in the Spirit. Why all this asking if they really have received the Baptism? I have never heard anyone who has received the Baptism in the Holy Ghost after the original pattern asking the Lord to give them the Holy Ghost. They know of a surety that He has come.

I was once traveling from Belgium to England. As I landed I received a request to stop at a place between Harwich and Colchester. The people were delighted that God had sent me, and told me of a special case they wanted me to pray for. They said, "We have a brother here who believes in the Lord, and he is paralyzed from his loins downward. He cannot stand on his legs and he has been twenty years in this condition." They took me to this man and as I saw him there in his chair I put the question to him. "What is the greatest desire in your heart?" He said, "Oh, if I could only receive the Holy Ghost!" I was somewhat surprised at this answer, and I laid my hands on his head and said, "Receive ye the Holy Ghost." Instantly the power of God fell upon him and he began breathing very heavily. He rolled off the chair and there he lay like a bag of potatoes, utterly helpless. I like anything that God does. I like to watch God working. There he was with his great, fat body, and his head was working just as though it was on a swivel. Then to our joy he began speaking in tongues. I had my eyes on every bit of him and as I saw the condition of his legs I said, "Those legs can never carry that body." Then I looked up and said, "Lord, tell me what to do." The Holy Ghost is the executive of Jesus Christ and the Father. If you want to know the mind of God you must have the Holy Ghost to bring God's latest thought to you and to tell you what to do. The Lord said to me, "Command him in My name to walk" But I missed it, of course. I said to the people there, "Let's see if we can lift him up." But we could not lift him, he was like a ton weight. I cried, "Oh Lord, forgive me." I repented of doing the wrong thing, and then the Lord said to me again, "Command him to walk." I said to him, "Arise in the name of Jesus." His legs were immediately strengthened. Did he walk? He ran all round. A month after this he walked ten miles and back. He has a Pentecostal work now. When the power of the Holy Ghost is present, things will happen.

# CHAPTER 6

# Keeping the Vision

---

READ THE 20th CHAPTER of the Acts of the Apostles, beginning at verse 7. Humanity is a failure everywhere. But when humanity is filled with divine power, there is no such thing as failure; and we know that the Baptism of the Holy Spirit is not a failure.

There are two sides to this Baptism: the first is, that you possess the Spirit; the second is that the Spirit possesses you. This is my message at this time—being possessed by the Baptizer, and not merely possessing the Baptizer. There is no limit to the possibilities of such a life, because it has God behind it, in the midst of it, and through it. I see people from time to time very slack, cold, and indifferent; but after they get filled with the Holy Spirit they become ablaze for God. I believe that God's ministers are to be flames of fire; nothing less than flames; nothing less than mighty instruments with burning messages, with a heart full of love, with such a depth of consecration that God has taken full charge of the body and it exists only that it may manifest the glory of God. Surely, this is the ideal and the purpose of this great plan of salvation for man—that we might be filed with all the fulness of God, and become ministers of life God working mightily in us and through us to manifest His grace—the saving power of humanity.

Now let us turn to this wonderful Word of God. I want you to see the demonstration of this power in this man Paul—this man who was "born out of due time:" this Paul, who was plucked as a brand from the burning; this Paul whom God chose to be an apostle to the Gentiles. See him first as a persecutor, mad to destroy those who were bringing glad tidings to the people. See how madly he rushed those people to prison, striving to make them blaspheme that holy name. Then see this same man changed by the power of God and the Gospel of Christ; see him filled with the Holy Ghost, becoming a builder for God and a revealer of the Son of God, so that he could say, "It is no longer I that live, but Christ liveth in me." Gal. 2:20.

In the 9th chapter of Acts, we read that he was called to a special ministry. The Lord said to Ananias, "I will show him what great things he must suffer for my name's sake." I don't want you to think that this means suffering from diseases; for it means suffering persecution, suffering from slander, from strife, from bitterness, from revilings and from many other evil things; but none of these things will hurt you; rather, they will kindle the fire of the holy ambition, because the scripture says, "Blessed are they that have been persecuted for righteousness' sake: for theirs is the kingdom of heaven." Matt. 5:10. To be persecuted for Christ's sake is to be joined up with a blessed, blessed people; but, better still, it means to be united with our Lord Jesus in the closest of fellowship, the fellowship of His suffering. There is a day coming when we will rejoice greatly that we have been privileged to suffer for His name's sake.

Beloved, God wants witnesses, witnesses to the truth, witnesses to the full truth, witnesses to the fulness of redemption—deliverance from sin and deliverance from disease—by the eternal power working in them, as they are filled with life through the Spirit. God wants us to believe that we may be ministers of that kind—of glorious things wrought in us by the Holy Spirit.

See in verse 7, how Paul was lost in his zeal for his ministry, so that he "continued his speech until midnight." Then something happened that threatened to break up the meeting—a young man, becoming sleepy, fell out of the window. That was enough to break up any ordinary meeting. But this man, filled with the Spirit of God, was equal even to such an emergency even on the moment. He went down, picked up the young man, brought life back into him by the Spirit of life that was in him, then returned to the upper room and continued the meeting until break of day.

In Switzerland the people said to me, "How long can you preach to us?" I said to them, "When the Holy Ghost is upon us, we can preach forever!" When I was in San Francisco, driving down the main street one day, we came across a crowd in the street. The driver stopped and I jumped out of the car, and right across from where the tumult was, I found a boy lying on the ground apparently in the grip of death. I got down and asked, "What is amiss?" He replied in a whisper, "tramp." I put my hand underneath his back and said, "In the name of Jesus, come out." And the boy jumped up and ran away, not even stopping to say "Thank you."

So you will find out that, with the Baptism of the Holy Spirit, you will be in a position to act when you have no time to think. The power and working of the Holy Spirit is of divine origin. It is the supernatural, God thrilling and moving one with the authority and power of almightiness, and it brings things to pass that could not come to pass in any other way. I had some things of this character happen on the ship as I was crossing the ocean. I want ever to be in Paul's position—that at any time, even at midnight, in the face of anything, even death itself, God may be able to manifest His power and do what He wants to do through me. This is what it means to be possessed by the Spirit of God. My heart is thrilled with the possibility of coming into the place where Paul was. Let us read verse 19, that we may get our mind perfectly fortified with this blessed truth that God has for us.

"Serving the Lord with all humility of mind." None of us is going to be able to be a minister of this new covenant of promise in the unction and power of the Spirit without humility. It seems to me that the way to get up is to get down. It is clear to me that in the measure that the dying of the Lord is in me, the life of the Lord will abound in me. And to me, truly, a Baptism of the Holy Spirit is not the goal, but it is an inflow to reach the highest level, the holiest position that it is possible for human nature to reach by Divine power. The Baptism of the Holy Spirit is given to reveal and to make real Him in whom dwells "all the fulness of the Godhead bodily." Col. 2:9. So I see that to be baptized in the Holy Spirit means to be baptized into death, into life, into power, into fellowship with the Trinity, where the old life ceases to be, and the life of God possesses us forever.

No man can live after seeing God; and God wants us all to see Him in all His glorious, infinite sufficiency, so that we shall joyfully cease to be—that He may become our life. Thus it was that Paul could say, "It is no longer I that live, but Christ liveth in me." I believe that God wants to make real to us all this ideal of humility where we so recognize human helplessness and human insufficiency that we shall rest no more on human plans and human devices and human energy, but continually look to God for His thought, for His voice, for His power, for His all-sufficiency in all things.

Now here is another word for us. Let us read it. It is found in verse 22. "Now, behold, I go bound in spirit." Is there a possibility of the human coming into oneness with the divine will? Let me give you two other versions of Scripture. Jesus was a man of flesh and blood like ourselves; though He was the incarnation of the authority and power and majesty of heaven, yet He bore about in His body our flesh, our human weakness, being tempted in all points like as we are, yet without sin. Oh, He was so lovely! Such a perfect Saviour! Oh, that I could shout "Jesus!" so that all the world would hear. There is salvation, life, power, and deliverance through that name; but, beloved, I read in Mark 1:12, that that body was driven by the Spirit. In the fourth chapter of Luke, it says "led" by the Spirit. And now here is Paul "bound" in the spirit.

Oh, what condescension that God should lay hold of humanity and so possess it with His holiness, with His righteousness, with his truth, with His faith, that one can say: "I am bound in spirit; I have no choice; my only choice is for God; my only desire, my only ambition is the will of God; I am bound with God." Is this possible, beloved? If you look into Galatians, first chapter, you will see how wonderfully Paul rose into this state of bliss. If you look in the third chapter of the Ephesians, you will see that he recognized himself as less than the least of all saints. Then, if you'll look into the 26th chapter of Acts, you will find him saying, "I have never lost the vision, King Agrippa, I have never lost it." Then if you will look again in Galatians, you will see that, in order to keep the vision, he conferred not with flesh and blood; God laid hold of him, God bound him, God preserved him. I ought to say, however, that it is a wonderful position to be in—to be preserved by Almightiness—and we ought to see to it that we leave ourselves to God. The consequences will be all right. "Whosoever shall seek to save his life, shall lose it; and whosoever shall lose his life for my sake the same shall save it."

Now, beloved, I am out for men. It is my business to be out for men. It is my business to make everybody hungry, dissatisfied. It is my business to make people either glad or mad. I have a message from heaven that will not leave people as I find them. Something must happen after they are filled with the Holy Spirit. A man filled with the Holy Spirit is no longer an ordinary man. A man can be swept by the power of God in the first stage of the revelation of Christ so that from that moment he will be an extraordinary man. But to be filled with the Holy Spirit he has to become a free body for God to dwell in, and to use, and to manifest Himself through. So I appeal to you, you people who have received the Holy Spirit, I appeal to you to let God have His way at whatever cost; I appeal to you to keep moving on with God into an ever increasing realization of His infinite purpose in Christ Jesus for His redeemed ones until you are filled unto all the fulness of God. To remain three days in the same place would indicate that you have lost the vision. The child of God must catch the vision anew every day. Every day the child of God must be moved more and more by the Holy Ghost. The child of God must come into line with the power of heaven so that he knows that God has his hand upon him.

It is the same Jesus, the very same Jesus. He went about doing good. "God anointed Him with the Holy Ghost and with power: who went about doing good, and healing all that were oppressed of the devil; for God was with Him." Beloved, is not that the ministry God would have us see we are heir to? The mission of the Holy Ghost is to give us a revelation of Jesus and to make the Word of God life unto us as it was when spoken by the Son—as new, as fresh, as effective as if the Lord Himself were speaking. The Bride loves to hear the Bridegroom's voice! Here it is, the blessed Word of God, the whole Word, not part of it, no, no, no! We believe in the whole of it. We really have such an effectiveness worked in us by the Word of life, that day by day we are finding out that the Word itself giveth life; the Spirit of the Lord, breathing through, revealing by the Word, giving it afresh to us, makes the whole Word alive today. Amen. So I have within my hands, within my heart, within my mind, this blessed reservoir of promises that is able to do so many marvelous things. Some of you most likely have been suffering because you have a limited revelation of Jesus, of the fulness of life there is in Him.

In Oakland, Calif., we had a meeting in a large theater. God wrought in filling the place till we had to have overflow meetings. There was a rising tide of people getting saved in the meeting by rising voluntarily up and down in the place, and getting saved. And then we had a riding tide of people who needed help in their bodies, rising in faith and being healed. One of these latter was an old man 95 years of age. He had been suffering for three years, till he got to the place where for three weeks he had been taking liquids. He was in a terrible state. I got him to stand while I prayed for him; and he came back, and with radiant face, told us that new life had come into his body. He said, "I am 95 years old. When I came into the meeting, I was full of pain from cancer of the stomach. I have been so healed that I have been eating perfectly, and have no pain." Many of the people were healed in a similar way.

(After the telling of the above incident in the meeting in Wellington, New Zealand, where this address was given, a lady arose who had rheumatism in the left leg. After being prayed for, she ran the full length of the hall several times, then testified to partial healing. A young man with pain in the head was healed instantly. Another man with pain in the shoulder was healed instantly also.)

In the second chapter of Acts, you will see that when the Holy Ghost came there was such a manifestation of the power of God that it wrought conviction as the Word was spoken in the Holy Ghost. In the third chapter we read of the lame man healed at the Beautiful Gate through the power of the Spirit, as Peter and John went into the Temple. And in the fourth chapter, we read of such a wonderful manifestation of miraculous power through the Spirit that five thousand men besides women and children became believers in the Lord Jesus Christ. God gives manifestation of His Divine power, beloved, to prove that He is with us. Will you not, right now, open your heart to this wonderful God, and let Him come into your life and make of you all that His infinite love has moved Him to provide in Christ Jesus, and that His infinite power, through the Holy Ghost, has made possible to be wrought in sinful man.

Seek this vision from God, and keep it ever before you. Pray the prayer that the apostle Paul prayed for the Ephesian believers, as recorded in Ephesians 1:17, 18, 19, "That the God of our Lord Jesus Christ, the Father of glory, may give unto you a spirit of wisdom and revelation in the knowledge of Him, having the eyes of your heart enlightened, that ye may know what is the hope of His calling, what the riches of the glory of His inheritance in the saints, and what the exceeding greatness of His power to usward who believe."

# CHAPTER 7

## Present – Time Blessings

---

READ WITH ME the first twelve verses of Matthew 5, these verses that we generally call the "Beatitudes." Some tell us that Matthew 5 is a millennial chapter and that we cannot attain to these blessings at the present time. I believe that every one who receives the Baptism in the Spirit has a real foretaste and earnest of millennial blessing, but that here the Lord Jesus is setting forth present-day blessings that we can enjoy here and now.

"Blessed are the poor in spirit: for theirs is the kingdom of heaven." This is one of the richest places into which Jesus brings us. The poor have a right to everything in heaven. "Their's is." Dare you believe it? Yes, I dare. I believe, I know, that I was very poor. When God's Spirit comes in as the ruling, controlling power of the life, He gives us God's revelation of our inward poverty, and shows us that God has come with one purpose, to bring heaven's best to earth, and that with Jesus He will indeed "freely give us all things."

An old man and an old woman had lived together for seventy years. Someone said to them, "You must have seen many clouds during those days." They replied, "Where do the showers come from? You never get showers without clouds." It is only the Holy Ghost who can bring us to the place of realization of our poverty; but, every time He does it, He opens the windows of heaven and the showers of blessing fall.

But I must recognize the difference between my own spirit and the Holy Spirit. My own spirit can do certain things on natural lines, can even weep and pray and worship, but it is all on a human plane, and we must not depend on our own human thoughts and activities or on our own personality. If the Baptism means anything to you, it should bring you to the death of the ordinary, where you are no longer putting faith in your own understanding; but, conscious of your own poverty, you are ever yielded to the Spirit. Then it is that your body becomes filled with heaven on earth."

"Blessed are they that mourn: for they shall be comforted." People get a wrong idea of mourning. Over in Switzerland they have a day set apart to take wreaths to graves. I laughed at the people's ignorance and said, "Why are you spending time around the graves? The people you love are not there. All that taking of flowers to the graves is not faith at all." Those who died in Christ are gone to be with Him, "which," Paul said, "is far better."

My wife once said to me, "You watch me when I'm preaching. I get so near to heaven when I'm preaching that some day I'll be off." One night she was preaching and when she had finished, off she went. I was going to Glasgow and had said goodbye to her before she went to meeting. As I was leaving the house, the doctor and policeman met me at the door and told me that she had fallen dead at the Mission door. I knew she had got what she wanted. I could not weep, but I was in tongues, praising the Lord. On natural lines she was everything to me; but I could not mourn on natural lines, but just laughed in the Spirit. The house was soon filled with people. The doctor said, "She is dead, and we can do no more for her." I went up to her lifeless corpse and commanded death to give her up, and she came back to me for a moment. Then God said to me, "She is Mine; her work is done." I knew what He meant.

They laid her in the coffin, and I brought my sons and my daughter into the room and said, "Is she there?" They said, "No, father." I said, "We will cover her up." If you go mourning the loss of loved ones who have gone to be with Christ, I say it in love to you, you have never had the revelation of what Paul spoke of when he showed us that it is better to go than to stay. We read this in Scripture, but the trouble is that people will not believe it. When you believe God, you will say, "Whatever it is, it is all right. If Thou dost want to take the one I love, it is all right, Lord." Faith removes all tears of self-pity.

But there is a mourning in the Spirit. God will bring you to a place where things must be changed, and there is a mourning, an unutterable groaning until God comes. And the end of all real faith always is rejoicing. Jesus mourned over Jerusalem. He saw the conditions, He saw the unbelief, He saw the end of those who closed their ears to the Gospel. But God gave a promise that He should see the travail of His soul and be satisfied, and that He should see His seed. What happened on the day of Pentecost in Jerusalem was an earnest of what will be the results of His travail, to be multiplied a billionfold all down the ages in all the world. And as we enter in the Spirit into travail over conditions that are wrong, such mourning will ever bring results for God, and our joy will be complete in the satisfaction that is brought to Christ thereby.

"Blessed are the meek: for they shall inherit the earth." Moses was headstrong in his zeal for his own people, and it resulted in his killing a man. His heart was right in his desire to correct things, but he was working on natural lines, and when we work on natural lines we always fail. Moses had a mighty passion, and that is one of the best things in the world when God has control and it becomes a passion for souls to be born again; but apart from God it is one of the worst things. Paul had it to a tremendous extent, and, breathing out threatenings, he was hailing men and women to prison. But God changed it, and later we find him wishing himself accursed from Christ for the sake of his brethren, his kinsmen according to the flesh. God took the headstrong Moses and molded him into the meekest of men. He took the fiery Saul of Tarsus and made him the foremost exponent of grace. Oh, brothers, God can transform you in like manner, and plant in you a divine meekness and every other thing that you lack.

In our Sunday school we had a boy with red hair. His head was as red as fire and so was his temper. He was such a trial. He kicked his teachers and the superintendent. He was simply uncontrollable. The teachers had a meeting in which they discussed the matter of expelling him. They thought that God might undertake for that boy and so they decided to give him another chance. One day he had to be turned out, and he broke all the windows of the mission. He was worse outside than in. Some time later we had a ten-days revival meeting. There was nothing much doing in that meeting and people thought it a waste of time, but there was one result—the redheaded lad got saved. After he was saved, the difficulty was to get rid of him at our house. He would be there until midnight crying to God to make him pliable and use him for His glory. God delivered the lad from his temper and made him one of the meekest, most beautiful boys you ever saw. For twenty years he has been a mighty missionary in China. God takes us just as we are and transforms us by His power.

I can remember the time when I used to go white with rage, and shake all over with temper. I could hardly hold myself together. I waited on God for ten days. In those ten days I was being emptied out and the life of the Lord Jesus was being wrought into me. My wife testified of the transformation that took place in my life, "I never saw such a change. I have never been able to cook anything since that time that has not pleased him. Nothing is too hot or too cold, everything is just right." God must come and reign supreme in your life. Will you let Him do it? He can do it, and He will if you will let Him. It is no use trying to tame the "old man." But God can deal with him. The carnal mind will never be subjected to God, but God will bring it to the cross where it belongs, and will put in its place, the pure, the holy, the meek mind of the Master.

"Blessed are they which do hunger and thirst after righteousness: for they shall be filled." Note that word, "shall be filled." If you ever see a "shall" in the Bible make it yours. Meet the conditions and God will fulfil His word to you. The Spirit of God is crying, "Ho, every one that thirsteth, come ye to the waters, and he that hath no money: come ye, buy and eat; yea, come, buy wine and milk without money and without price." The Spirit of God will take of the things of Christ and show them to you in order that you may have a longing for Christ in His fullness, and when there is that longing, God will not fail to fill you.

See that crowd of worshipers who have come up to the feast. They are going away utterly unsatisfied, but on the last day, the great day of the feast, Jesus stands up and cries. "If any man thirst, let him come unto me and drink. He that believeth on me, as the scripture hath said, out of his belly shall flow rivers of living water." Jesus knew that they were going away without the living water, and so He directs them to the true source of supply. Are you thirsty today? The living Christ still invites you to Himself, and I want to testify that He still satisfies the thirsty soul and still fills the hungry with good things.

In Switzerland, I learned of a man who met with the assembly of the Plymouth Brethren. He attended their various meetings, and one morning, at their breaking of bread service, he arose and said, "Brethren, we have the Word, and I feel that we are living very much in the letter of it, but there is a hunger and thirst in my soul for something deeper, something more real than we have, and I cannot rest until I enter into it." The next Sunday this brother rose again and said, "We are all so poor here, there is no life in this assembly, and my heart is hungry for reality." He did this for several weeks until it got on the nerves of those people and they protested. "Sands, you are making us all miserable. You are spoiling our meetings, and there is only one thing for you to do, and that is to clear out."

That man went out of the meeting in a very sad condition. As he stood outside, one of his children asked him what was the matter, and he said, "To think that they should turn me out from their midst for being hungry and thirsty for more of God!" I did not know anything of this until afterward.

Some days later someone rushed up to Sands and said, "There is a man over here from England, and he is speaking about tongues and healing." Sands said, "I'll fix him. I'll go to the meeting and sit right up in the front and challenge him with the Scriptures. I'll dare him to preach these things in Switzerland. I'll publicly denounce him." So he came to the meetings. There he sat. He was so hungry and thirsty that he drank in every word that was said. His opposition soon petered out. The first morning he said to a friend, "This is what I want." He drank and drank of the Spirit. After three weeks he said, "God will have to do something now or I'll burst." He breathed in God and the Lord filled him to such an extent that he spoke in other tongues as the Spirit gave utterance. Sands is now preaching, and is in charge of a new Pentecostal assembly.

God is making people hungry and thirsty after His best. And everywhere He is filling the hungry and giving them that which the disciples received at the very beginning. Are you hungry? If you are, God promises that you shall be filled.

Book 2:

# *Like*
# *-Precious-*
# *Faith*

# CHAPTER 1

## Like Precious Faith

---

WHAT WOULD HAPPEN to us and to the needy world if we should get to the place where we really believed God? May God give us the desire to get to this place. Faith is a tremendous power, an inward mover. I am convinced that we have not yet seen all that God has for us, but if we shall only move on in faith we shall see the greater works.

When I was a little boy I remember asking my father for a pennyworth of something or other. He did not give it to me, so I sat down by his side and every now and again I would just quietly say, "Father!" He would appear to take no notice of me, but now and again I would touch him ever so gently and say, "Father!" My mother said to him, "Why don't you answer the child?" My father replied, "I have done so, but he won't accept my answer." Still I sat on, and occasionally I would touch him and say ever so quietly, "Father!" If he went out into the garden I followed him and occasionally I would touch his sleeve and say, "Father! Father! "Do you think I ever went away without the accomplishment of my desire? No, not once.

We need the same importunity as we go to God. We have the blessed assurance that if we ask anything according to His will He heareth us, and if we know that He hear us, whatsoever we ask, we know that we have the petitions that we desired of Him. Do you go to Him for heart purity? It is His will that you should receive, and if you ask in faith you can know that you have the petition that you desire of Him. Do you desire that Christ should dwell in your heart by faith? That is in accordance with His will. Ask and ye shall receive. Do you desire that the might of God's Spirit shall accompany your ministry? That is according to the will of God. Continue in the presence of your heavenly Father, quietly reminding Him that this is what you desire, and He will not fail to give you the exceeding abundantly above all you ask or think. He will fill you with rivers - the blessed rivers of the Spirit - and flowing from the midst of you they will be blessings to all that are around.

In the introduction to his second epistle Peter addresses "them that have obtained like precious faith with us." It is written, "They that trust in the Lord shall be as Mount Zion which cannot be removed." Have you this faith of divine origin springing up in your heart? It will make you steadfast and unmovable. This faith, this confidence, this trust in God, will have a transforming power; changing and transforming spirit, soul, and body, sanctifying the entire being.

"Faith comes by hearing, and hearing by the Word of God." It is God coming in by His Word and laying the solid foundation. Faith is like dynamite which bursts up the old life and nature by the power of God, and brings the almighty power of God into the life. This substance will diffuse through the whole being, bringing everything else into insignificance. The Word of God is formed within the temple. Jeremiah spoke of the Word as a "fire within." It is a power stronger than granite that is able to resist the mightiest pressure the devil can bring against it. Faith counts on God's coming forth to confound the enemy. Faith count son the display of God's might, when it is needful for Him to come forth in power.

In these eventful days we must not be content with a mere theory of faith, but must have this almighty and precious faith within us so that we may move from the ordinary into the extraordinary. We must expect Him to come forth in power through us for the deliverance of others. Peter spoke of it as "like precious faith." It is a like kind to that which Abraham had - the very faith of God. When Peter and John said to the lame man, Such as we have we give thee. In the name of Jesus Christ of Nazareth rise up and walk, there was a manifestation of the same faith that Abraham had. It is this like precious faith God wants us to have.

In the former days the prophets received the Holy Spirit in a certain measure, but the Holy Spirit was given to the Lord Jesus Christ without measure. Did not He give the Holy Spirit on the Day of Pentecost in this same measureless measure? That is His thought for you and me. Since I received the mighty Baptism in the Holy Spirit God has flooded my life with His power. From time to time there have been wonderful happenings - to Him be all the glory. Faith in God will bring the operation of the Spirit and we'll have the divine power flooding the human vessel and flowing out in blessing to others.

Faith is made in hard places when we are at wit's-end corner, and there seems no way out of our adversity. David said at one time, "The sorrows of death compassed made me afraid. The sorrows of hell compassed me about." He tells us, "In my distress I called upon the Lord, and cried unto my God: he heard my voice out of his temple . . . he bowed the heavens. . . and came down." Faith cries to God in the place of testing. It is in these places that God enlarges us and brings us forth into a large place, to prove Himself the God of deliverances, the One who is indeed our helper.

I remember in the year 1920 after a most distressing voyage I went straight from the ship on which I had been traveling, to a meeting. As I entered the building a man fell down across the doorway in a fit. The Spirit of the Lord was upon me and I commanded the demon to leave. Some years later I visited this same assembly, and I ventured to ask if anyone remembered the incident. A man stood up and I told him to come to the platform. He told me that on that day he had been delivered by the name of Jesus and had not had a fit since. We read in Acts 10:38 that "God hath anointed Jesus of Nazareth with the Holy Ghost and with power: who went about doing good, and healing all that were oppressed of the devil; for God was with him." God wants us to have this same anointing and same power, through the indwelling Christ and through a living faith. It was the Lord Himself who told us before He went away, "These signs shall follow them that believe. In my name they shall cast out demons . . . they shall lay hands on the sick and they shall recover." God is waiting to manifest His divine power through believers.

I remember a man coming to me suffering with cancer, who said he had been twelve years in pain. The power of the Lord was present to heal, and that night he came back to the meeting with all his sores dried up.

In this second epistle of Peter we further read, "According to his divine power hath given unto us all things that pertain unto life and godliness through the knowledge of him that hath called us to glory and virtue: whereby are given unto us exceeding great and precious promises :that by these ye might be partakers of the divine nature." Believe the record, His divine power has provided this life and godliness and virtue. Believe for the virtue of the Lord to be so manifested through your body that as men touch you they are healed. Believe for the current to go through you to others. It is amazing what can happen when some necessity arises when there is no time to pray, only to act. It is in such times of necessity that the Holy Ghost comes forth to act.

We must so live in God that the Spirit of God can operate through us. I remember being in one place where there were 6,000 people outside the building where we were preaching. Many of them were in chairs, waiting for hands to be laid on them and the prayer of faith to be offered. Oh for the virtue that flowed from Christ to touch the needy everywhere!
A woman said to Christ one time, "Blessed is the womb that bare thee, and the paps which thou hast sucked." But he answered, "Yea rather, blessed are they that hear the word of God, and keep it." It is through the hearing of the Word of God that faith comes, and faith brings the omnipotence of God to helpless souls and brings the virtue of Christ to the sick and to the needy. Do you remember how they asked the Lord, "What shall we do that we might work the works of God?" Jesus answered and said unto them, "This is the work of God that ye believe on him whom he hath sent." He further said, "The works that I do shall ye do also: and greater works than these shall ye do; because I go unto my Father." There is nothing impossible to

faith.

When I was in Orebro 12 years ago I ministered to a girl who was twelve years' old, and blind. When I last went to Orebro they told me that she had had perfect sight from that day. The Lord Himself challenges us to believe Him when He says, "Have faith in God." "Verily, I say unto you, That whosoever shall say unto this mountain, Be thou removed, and be thou cast into the sea; and shall not doubt in his heart, but shall believe that those things which he saith shall come to pass; he shall have whatsoever he saith." Did you get that? "He shall have whatsoever he saith." When you speak in faith, your desire is an accomplished thing. Our Lord further said, "Therefore I say unto you, What things soever ye desire, when ye pray, believe that ye receive them, and ye shall have them."

In one place a man said to me, "You helped a good many today, but you have not helped me." I said, "What is the trouble?' He said, "I cannot sleep, and I am losing my reason." I said to him, "Believe." And then I told him to go home and sleep, and I told him I would believe God. He went home and his wife said to him, "Well, did you see the preacher?" And he said, "He helped everyone but me." However, he fell asleep. His wife said, "I wonder if it is all right." Morning, noon, and night he was still asleep, but he woke bright and happy, rested and restored. What had brought about this restoration? Faith in God! "He shall have whatsoever he saith." Have you received this "like precious faith"? If so, deal bountifully with the oppressed. God has called us to loose the bands of wickedness, undo the heavy burden, let the oppressed go free, and break the yokes that the devil has put upon them. Pray in faith. Remember he that asketh receiveth. Ask and it shall be given you. Live for God. Keep clean and holy. Live under the unction of the Holy Spirit. Let the mind of Christ be yours so that you live in God's desires and plans. Glorify Him in the establishment of His blessing upon the people, and in seeing God's glory manifested in the midst. Amen.

# CHAPTER 2

# Immersed in the Holy Ghost

---

THE BAPTISM OF THE HOLY GHOST is a great beginning. I think the best word we can say is, "Lord, what wilt Thou have me to do?" The greatest difficulty today with us is to be held in the place where it shall be God only. It is so easy to get our own mind to work. The working of the Holy Ghost is so different. I believe there is a mind of Christ, and we may be so immersed in the Spirit that we are all the day asking, "What wilt Thou have me to do?"

This has been a day in the Holy Ghost. The last three months have been the greatest days of my life. I used to think if I could see such and such things worked I should be satisfied; but I have seen greater things than I ever expected to see, and I am more hungry to see greater things yet. The great thing at conventions is to get us so immersed in God that we may see signs and wonders in the name of the Lord Jesus; a place where death has taken place and we are not, for God has taken us. If God has taken hold of us we will be changed by His power and might. You can depend on it, the Ethiopian will be changed. I find God has a plan to turn the world upside down, where we are not.

When I have been at my wit's end, and have seen God open the door, I have felt I should never doubt God again. I have been taken to another place that was worse still. There is no place for us, and yet a place where God is, where the Holy Ghost is just showing forth and displaying His graces; a place where we will never come out, where we are always immersed in the Spirit, the glory of God being seen upon us. It is wonderful! There is a power behind the scenes that moves things. God can work in such a marvellous way....

I believe we have yet to learn what it would be with a Pentecostal Church in England that understood truly the work of intercession. I believe God the Holy Ghost wants to teach us that it is not only the people on the platform who can move things by prayer. You people, the Lord can move things through you. We have to learn the power of the breath of the Holy Ghost. If I am filled with the Holy Ghost, He will formulate the word that will come into my heart. The sound of my voice is only by the breath that goes through it. When I was in a little room at Bern waiting for my passport, I found a lot of people, but I couldn't speak to them. So I got hold of three men and pulled them unto me. They stared, but I got them on their knees. Then we prayed, and the revival began. I couldn't talk to them, but I could show them the way to talk to Someone else.

God will move upon the people to make them see the glory of God just as it was when Jesus walked in this world, and I believe the Holy Ghost will do special wonders and miracles in these last days. I was taken to see a young woman who was very ill. The young man who showed me the way said, "I am afraid we shall not be able to do much here, because of her mother, and the doctors are coming." I said, "This is what God has brought me here for," and when I prayed the young woman was instantly healed by the power of God. God the Holy Ghost says in our hearts today that it is only He who can do it. After that we got crowds, and I ministered to the sick among them for two hours.

The secret for the future is living and moving in the power of the Holy Ghost. One thing I rejoice in is that there need not be an hour or a moment when I do not know the Holy Ghost is upon me. Oh, this glorious life in God is beyond expression; it is God manifest in the flesh. Oh, this glorious unction of the Holy Ghost — that we move by the Spirit. He should be our continual life. The Holy Ghost has the last thoughts of anything that God wants to give. Glory to God for the Holy Ghost! We must see that we live in the place where we say, "What wilt Thou have me to do?" and are in the place where He can work in us to will and to do of His good pleasure.

# CHAPTER 3

## The Active Life of the Spirit – Filled Believer

---

THESE ARE THE LAST DAYS; the days of the falling away. These are days when Satan is having a great deal of power. But we must keep in mind that Satan has no power only as he is allowed.

It is a great thing to know that God is loosing you from the world, loosing you from a thousand things. You must seek to have the mind of God on all things. If you don't, you will stop His working. I had to learn that as I was on the water en route to Australia. We stopped at a place called Aden, where they were selling all kinds of ware. Among other things were some beautiful rugs and ostrich feathers in great quantities. There was a gentleman in "first class" who wanted feathers. He bought one lot and the next lot put up was too big; he did not want so many. He said to me, "Will you join me?" I knew I did not want feathers for I had no room or use for them and wouldn't know what to do with them if I got them. However, he pleaded with me to join him. I perceived it was the Spirit as clearly as anything and I said, "Yes, I will." So the feathers were knocked down for fifteen dollars. Then I found the man had no money on him. He had plenty in his cabin. I perceived it was the Spirit again, so it fell to my lot to pay for the feathers. He said to me, "I will get the money and give it to one of the stewards." I replied: "No, that is not business. I am known all over the ship. You seek me out."

The man came and brought the money. I said, "God wants me to talk to you. Now sit down." So he sat down and in ten minutes' time the whole of his life was unhinged, unraveled, broken up, so broken that like a big baby he wept and cried for salvation. It was "feathers" that did it. But you know we shall never know the mind of God till we learn to know the voice of God. The striking thing about Moses is that it took him forty years to learn human wisdom, forty years to know his helplessness, and forty years to live in the power of God. One hundred and twenty years it took to teach that man, and sometimes it seems to me it will take many years to bring us just where we can tell the voice of God, the leadings of God, and all His will concerning us.

I see that all revelation, all illumination, everything that God had in Christ was to be brought forth into perfect light that we might be able to live the same, produce the same, and be in every activity sons of God with power. It must be so. We must not limit the Holy One. And we must clearly see that God brought us forth to make us supernatural, that we might be changed all the time on the line of the supernatural, that we may every day live so in the Spirit, that all of the revelations of God are just like a canvas thrown before our eyes, on which we see clearly step by step all the divine will of God.

Any assembly that puts its hand upon the working of the Spirit will surely dry up. The assembly must be as free in the Spirit as possible, and you must allow a certain amount of extravagance when people are getting through to God. Unless we are very wise, we can easily interfere and quench the power of God which is upon us. It is an evident fact that one man in a meeting, filled with unbelief, can make a place for the devil to have a seat. And it is very true, that if we are not careful we may quench the Spirit of some person who is innocent but incapable of helping himself. "We then that are strong ought to bear the infirmities of the weak." (Romans 15:1). If you want an assembly full of life you must have one in which the Spirit of God is manifested. And in order to keep at the boiling pitch of that blessed incarnation of the Spirit, you must be as simple as babies; you must be as harmless as doves and as wise as serpents (Matthew 10:16).

I always ask God for a leading of grace. It takes grace to be in a meeting because it is so easy if you are not careful, to get on the natural side. The man who is a preacher, if he has lost the unction, will be well repaid if he will repent and get right with God and get the unction back. It never pays us to be less than always spiritual, and we must have a divine language and the language must be of God. Beloved, if you come into real perfect line with the grace of God, one thing will certainly take place in your life. You will change from that old position of the world's line where you were judging everybody, and where you were not trusting anyone, and come into a place where you will have a heart that will believe all things; a heart that under no circumstances reviles again when you are reviled.

I know many of you think many times before you speak once. Here is a great word: "For your obedience is come abroad unto all men. I am glad therefore on your behalf: but yet I would have you wise unto that which is good, and simple concerning evil" (Romans 16:19). Innocent. No inward corruption or defilement, that is full of distrusts, but just a holy, divine likeness of Jesus that dares believe that God Almighty will surely watch over all. Hallelujah! "There shall no evil befall thee, neither shall any plague come nigh thy dwelling. For He shall give his angels charge over thee, to keep thee in all thy ways" (Psalm 91:10,11). The child of God who is rocked in the bosom of the Father has the sweetest touch of heaven, and the honey of the Word is always in it.

If the saints only knew how precious they are in the sight of God they would scarcely be able to sleep for thinking of His watchful, loving care. Oh, He is a precious Jesus! He is a lovely Savior! He is divine in all His attitude toward us, and makes our hearts to burn. There is nothing like it. "Oh," they said on the road to Emmaus, "did not our heart burn within us, as He walked with us and talked with us?" (Luke 24:32). Oh beloved, it must be so today.

Always keep in your mind the fact that the Holy Ghost must bring manifestation. We must understand that the Holy Ghost is breath, the Holy Ghost is Person, and it is the most marvelous thing to me to know that this Holy Ghost power can be in every part of your body. You can feel it from the crown of your head to the soles of your feet. Oh, it is lovely to be burning all over with the Holy Ghost! And when that takes place there is nothing but the operation of the tongue that must give forth the glory and the praise.

You must be in the place of magnifying the Lord. The Holy Ghost is the great Magnifier of Jesus, the great Illuminator of Jesus. And so after the Holy Ghost comes in, it is impossible to keep your tongue still. Why, you would burst if you didn't give Him utterance. Talk about a dumb baptized soul? Such a person is not to be found in the Scriptures. You will find that when you speak unto God in the new tongue He gives you, you enter into a close communion with Him hitherto never experienced. Talk about preaching! I would like to know how it will be possible for all the people filled with the Holy Ghost to stop preaching. Even the sons and daughters must prophesy. After the Holy Ghost comes in, a man is in a new order in God. And you will find it so real that you will want to sing, talk, laugh, and shout. We are in a strange place when the Holy Ghost comes in.

If the incoming of the Spirit is lovely, what must be the onflow? The incoming is only to be an onflow. I am very interested in scenery. When I was in Switzerland I wouldn't be satisfied till I went to the top of the mountain, though I like the valleys also. On the summit of the mountain the sun beats on the snow and sends the water trickling down the mountains right through to the meadows. Go there and see if you can stop it. Just so in the spiritual. God begins with the divine flow of His eternal power which is the Holy Ghost, and you cannot stop it.

We must always clearly see that the baptism with the Spirit must make us ministering spirits.

Peter and John had been baptized only a short time. Did they know what they had? No, I defy you to know what you have. No one knows what he has in the baptism with the Holy Ghost. You have no conception of it. You cannot measure it by an human standards. It is greater than any man has any idea of, and consequently those two disciples had no idea what they had. For the first time after they were baptized in the Holy Ghost they came down to the Gate Beautiful. There they saw the man sitting who for forty years had been lame. What was the first thing after they saw him? Ministration. What was the second? Operation. What was the third? Manifestation, of course.

It could not be otherwise. You will always find that this order in the Scripture will be carried out in everybody.

I clearly see that we ought to have spiritual giants in the earth, mighty in apprehension, amazing in activity, always having a wonderful report because of their activity in faith. I find instead that there are many people who perhaps have better discernment than you, better knowledge of the Word than you, but they have failed to put it into practice, so these gifts lie dormant. I am here to help you to begin on the sea of life with mighty acts in the power of God through the gifts of the Spirit. You will find that this which I am speaking on is out of knowledge derived from a wonderful experience in many lands. The man who is filled with the Holy Ghost is always acting. You read the first verse of the Acts of the Apostles, "Jesus began both to do and teach." He began to do first, and so must we.

Beloved, we must see that the baptism with the Holy Ghost is an activity with an outward manifestation. When I was in Norway, God was mightily moving there, though I had to talk by interpretation. However, God always worked in a wonderful way. One day we met a man who stopped the three men I was with, one being the interpreter. I was walking on, but I saw he was in a dilemma, so I turned back and said to the interpreter, "What is the trouble?" "This man," he said, "is so full of neuralgia that he is almost blind and he is in a terrible state." As soon as ever they finished the conversation I said to the spirit that was afflicting him, "Come out of him in the name of Jesus." And the man said, "It is all gone! It is all gone! I am free." Ah, brothers, we have no conception of what God has for us!

I will tell you what happened in Sydney, Australia. A man with a stick passed a friend and me. He had to get down and then twist over, and the tortures on his face made a deep impression on my soul. I asked myself, "Is it right to pass this man?" So I said to my friend, "There is a man in awful distress, and I cannot go further. I must speak to him." I went over to this man and said to him, "You seem to be in great trouble." "Yes," he said, "I am no good and never will be." I said, "You see that hotel. Be in front of that door in five minutes and I will pray for you, and you shall be as straight as any man in this place." This is on the line of activity in the faith of Jesus. I came back after paying a bill, and he was there. I will never forget him wondering if he was going to be trapped, or what was up that a man should stop him in the street and tell him he should be made straight. I had said it, so it must be. If you say anything you must stand with God to make it so. Never say anything for bravado, without you have the right to say it. Always be sure of your ground, and that you are honouring God. If there is anything about it to make you anything, it will bring you sorrow. Your whole ministry will have to be on the line of grace and blessing. We helped him up the two steps, passed him through to the elevator, and took him upstairs. It seemed difficult to get him from the elevator to my bedroom, as though Satan was making the last stroke for his life, but we got him there. Then in five minutes' time this man walked out of that bedroom as straight as any man in this place. He walked perfectly and declared he hadn't a pain in his body.

Oh, brother, it is ministration, it is operation, it is manifestation! Those are three of the leading principles of the baptism with the Holy Ghost. And we must see to it that God is producing these three through us.

The Bible is the Word of God, it has the truths and whatever people may say of them they stand stationary, unmovable. Not one jot or tittle shall fail of all His good promises. His word will come forth. In heaven it is settled, on earth it must be made manifest that He is the God of everlasting power.

God wants manifestation and He wants His glory to be seen. He wants us all to be filled with that line of thought that He can look upon us and delight in us subduing the world unto Him. And so you are going to miss a great deal if you don't begin to act. But once you begin to act in the order of God, you will find that God establishes your faith and from that day starts you on the line of the promises. When will you begin?

In a place in England I was dealing on the lines of faith and what would take place if we believed God. Many things happened. But when I got away it appeared one man who worked in the colliery had heard me. He was in trouble with a stiff knee. He said to his wife, "I cannot help but think every day that that message of Wigglesworth's was to stir us to do something. I cannot get away from it. All the men in the pit know how I walk with a stiff knee, and you know how you have wrapped it around with yards of flannel. Well, I am going to act. You have to be the congregation." He got his wife in front of him. "I am going to act and do just as Wigglesworth did." He got hold of his leg unmercifully, saying, "Come out, you devils, come out! In the name of Jesus. Now, Jesus, help me. Come out, you devils, come out." Then he said, "Wife they are gone! Wife, they are gone. This is too good. I am going to act now." So he went to his place of worship and all the collier boys were there. It was a prayer meeting. As he told them this story these men became delighted. They said, "Jack, come over here and help me." And Jack went. As soon as he was through in one home he was invited to another, loosing these people of the pains they had gotten in the colliery.

Ah, brothers and sisters, we have no idea what God has for us if we will only begin! But oh, the grace we need! We may make a mishap. If you do it outside of Him, if you do it for yourself, and if you want to be some one, it will be a failure. We shall only be able to do well as we do it in the name of Jesus. Oh, the love that God's Son can put into us if we are only humble enough, weak enough, and helpless enough to know that except He does it, it will not be done! "What things soever ye desire when ye pray, believe that ye receive and ye shall have them."

Live in the Spirit, walk in the Spirit, walk in communion with the Spirit, talk with God. All leadings of the divine order are for you. I pray that if there are any who have turned to their own way and have made God second, they will come to repentance on all lines. Separate yourself from every earthly touch, and touch ideas. And God will bring you to an end of yourself. Begin with God this moment.

# CHAPTER 4

## Workers Together With God

---

INTERPREATION OF TONGUES: God has come to visit us and He has revealed Himself unto us, but He wants you to be so ready that nothing that He says will miss. He wants to build you on the foundation truth.

Are you ready this morning? What for? Because God has something better than yesterday. Higher ground, holier thoughts, more concentrated, clearer ministry - God wants us every day to be in a rising tide. It is a changing of faith. It is an attitude of the spirit. It is where God rises higher and higher.

God wants us to come into the place where we will never look back. God has no room for the man that looks back, thinks back, or acts back.

The Holy Ghost wants to get you ready for stretching yourself out to God and believe that He is a rewarder of them that diligently seek Him. You need not use vain repetition. Ask and believe.

People come with their needs, they ask, they go away still with their

needs because they do not faithfully wait to receive what God has promised them. If they ask they will get it.
Many people are missing the highest order. I went to a person who was full of the Spirit, but was all the time saying, "Glory! Glory! Glory!"

I said, "You are full of the Holy Ghost, but the Spirit cannot speak because you continually speak." He kept still then and the Spirit began speaking through him. We are altogether in the way of God. Do more believing and less begging.

I want so to change your operation in God till you will know that God is operating through you for this time and forevermore more. May the Spirit awake us to deep things today.

Are you ready? What for? That you may move and be moved by the mighty power of God that cannot be moved and so chastened and built up till you are in the place, it doesn't matter where the wind blows or difficulty comes, you are fixed in God.

Are you ready? What for? To come into the plan of the Most High God, believing what the Scripture says, and holding fast that which is good, believing so that no man shall take your crown.

God can so change us by His Word that we are altogether different day by day - David knew this. He said, "Thy word hath quickened me. He sent his word and healed me." How beautiful that God can make His Word abound! "I have hid thy word in my heart that I might not sin against thee."

It is absolutely infidelity and unbelief to pray about anything in the Word of God. The Word of God has not to be prayed about, the Word of God has to be received. If you will receive the Word of God, you will always be in a big place. If you pray about the Word of God the devil will be behind the whole thing. Never pray about anything which is "Thus saith the Lord." It has to be yours to build you on a new foundation of truth.

I want to turn your attention this morning to the sixth chapter of 2 Corinthians. This is a summit position for us, although there are many ground lines to be examined to see if we are rising to the summit of these glorious experiences. This is also ground work for deep heart searching. This is divine revelation of the spiritual character to us. The writer must have been immersed in this holy place.

If you turn to the first verse of Romans 12 you will see that the speaker is operated by an operation. He has been mightily under the operation on more than a surgical table. He has been cut to the very depths, till he has reached a place absolutely on the altar of full surrender. And out of the depths of it when he has got it there, now he is giving his whole life, as it were, in a nutshell.

"I beseech you, therefore, brethren, by the mercies of God, that ye present your bodies a living sacrifice, holy, acceptable unto God, which is your reasonable service" —Romans 12:1. Here in this sixth chapter of 2 Corinthians we have again a beautiful word which ought to bring us to a very great place of hearing by the hearing of faith.

"We then, as workers together with him. . ."

It is a collective thought. It is preaching to the whole Church in Christ Jesus. Paul has the Corinthians in his mind because the Corinthian church was the first church amongst the Gentiles, and he was the apostle to the Gentiles.

"We then, as workers together with him, beseech you also that ye receive not the grace of God in vain" (2 Corinthians 6:1). This is one of the mightiest words there is in the Scripture. People are getting blessed all the time, having revelation, and they go from one point to another but do not establish themselves in that thing which God has brought to them.

If you do not let your heart be examined when the Lord comes with blessing or correction, if you do not make it a stepping stone, if you do not make it a rising place, then you are receiving the grace of God in vain. People could be built far greater in the Lord and be more wonderfully established if they would move out sometimes and think over the graces of the Lord.

Grace is to be multiplied on conditions. How? In the first chapter of 2

Timothy we have these words: “the unfeigned faith that is in thee.”

Everyone in this place, the whole Church of God, has the same like precious faith within him. And if you allow this like precious faith to be foremost, utmost on everything, you will find that grace and peace are multiplied.

Just the same the Lord comes to us with His mercy and if we do not see that the God of grace and mercy is opening to us the door of mercy and utterances, we are receiving it in vain.

I thank God for every meeting. I thank God for every blessing. I thank God every time a person says to me, “God bless you, Brother!” I say, “Thank you, Brother. The Lord bless you!” I see it is a very great place to have people desirous that we shall be blessed. If we want strength in building in our spiritual character, we should never forget the blessings. When you are in prayer remember how near you are to the Lord. It is a time that God wants you to change strength there, and He wants you to remember He is with you.

When you open the sacred pages and the light comes right through and you say, “Oh, isn’t that wonderful!” thank God, for it is the grace of God that has opened your understanding.
When you come to a meeting like this, the revelation comes forth, you feel this is what you wanted, receive it as the grace of the Lord. God has brought you to a place where He might make you a greater blessing.

For he saith, “I have heard thee in a time accepted, and in the day of salvation have I succoured thee: behold, now is the accepted time; behold, now is the day of salvation” —2 Corinthians 6:2.

Two processes of salvation. He succoured you when the Spirit was moving you and when the adversary was against you, when your neighbours and friends wished it not to be and when everybody rose up in accusation against you. When you know there were fightings without and fightings within, He succoured you. He covered you till you came into salvation. And then He keeps you in the plan of His salvation.
This is the day of salvation. Being saved does not mean to say that

you were not saved, but that you are being continually changed, in the process of regeneration being made like unto God, being brought into the operation of the Spirit's power, being made like unto Him.

This is the day of salvation. He has succoured thee in a time when Satan would destroy thee, and He is with thee now.

This is the day of salvation. If we remain stationary, God has nothing for us. Everybody must see that they must be in progress. Yesterday will not do for today. I must thank God for yesterday. Tomorrow is what I am today.

Today: inspiration, divine intuition, where God is ravishing the heart, breaking forth all shorelines, getting my heart only responsive to His cry, where I live and move honoring and glorifying God in the Spirit. This is the day of visitation of the Lord. This is the great day of salvation, being moved on, into, for God.

*Interpretation of Tongues:* It is the Lord. Let Him do what seemeth Him well. It may be death, but He has life in the midst of death.

We will praise and magnify the Lord, for He is worthy to be praised!

He has succoured us, and now He is building us. Now He is changing us. Now we are in the operation of the Holy Ghost. You must every day make higher ground. You must deny yourself to get on with God. You must refuse everything that is not pure and holy and separate. God wants you pure in heart. He wants your intense desire after holiness.

"Seek ye first the kingdom of God, and his righteousness; and all these things shall be added unto you." (Matthew 6:33)

"Giving no offence in any thing, that the ministry be not blamed" (2 Corinthians 6:3).

That is lovely! Oh! The church can be built. God will break down opposing things.

If you people in Angelus Temple are in a place where you would rather see one person saved here than two people saved at Bethel

Temple, then you are altogether wrong and you need to be saved. If there is anybody here from Bethel Temple, if you would rather see one person saved in your temple than two people saved in Angelus Temple, then you are still out of order of the Spirit of the line of God and you are strangers to real holy life with God.

If your ministry is not to be blamed, how will it not be blamed? You have to live in love. See to it there is never anything comes out of your lips or by your acts that will interfere with the work of the Lord, but rather live in the place where you are helping everybody, lifting everybody, and causing everybody to come into perfect harmony. For remember, there is always a blessing where there is harmony. "One accord" is the keynote of the victory that is going to come to us all the time.

There are thousands and thousands of different churches, but they are all one in the Spirit just in the measure as they receive the life of Christ. If there is any division, it is always outside the Spirit. The spiritual life in the believer never has known dissension or break, because where the Spirit has perfect liberty, then they all agree and there is no schism in the body.

"The letter killeth, but the spirit giveth life." When there is division it is only because they take the letter instead of the Spirit. If we are in the Spirit, then we shall have life. If we are in the Spirit, we shall love everybody. If we are in the Spirit, there will be no division. There will be perfect harmony. God wants to show us that we must so live in the Spirit that the ministry is not blamed.

It is a wonderful ministry God has given to us because it is a life ministry. Pentecostal positions are spiritual positions. We recognize the Holy Ghost, but we recognize first the Spirit quickening us, saving us from every rudiment of evil power, transforming our human nature till it is in divine order. Then in that divine order we see that the Lord of Hosts can be very beautifully arranging the life till we live in the Spirit and are not fulfilling the lusts of flesh.

*Interpretation of Tongues:* Let not thy goodness be evil spoken of, but so live in the spiritual life with Christ that He is being glorified over thy body, thy soul and thy spirit, till thy very life becomes emblematic and God reigns over thee in love and peace.

I like that because I see that when the Holy Ghost has perfect charge, He lifts and lightens and unveils the truth in a new way till we grip it.

Oh! What I would be if every one of us would go away this morning with this word in our heart, “Let not your goodness be evil spoken of.” I know we all want to be good. It is not a wrong thing to desire that our goodness shall be appreciated. But we must watch ourselves because it is an evil day (although it is the day of salvation), and we must understand these days that the Lord wants to chasten and bring a people right into a full-tide position.

I believe that it is possible for God to sweep a company right into the glory before the Rapture just as well as at the Rapture. It is possible for you to be taken if others are left. May God grant unto us a very keen inward discerning of our heart’s purity. We want to go. It is far better for us to go. But it is far better for the church that we stay.

If you comprehend the truth of this word which Paul realized was true, “It is far better for me to go,” you will never take a pill nor use a plaster. You would never do anything to save you from going if you believed it was better to go. There is a definite, inward motion of the power of God for the human life to so change it till we would not lift a finger, believing it was far better to go.

Then there is another side to it. Believing that God has us for the proclamation of the Gospel, for the building of the church, we would say, “Lord, for the purpose of being a blessing further for Thy sake, and for the sake of the Church, just keep us full of life to stay”

We would not be full of disease, but we would be full of life.

So the Lord grant unto us this morning a living faith to believe.

“But in all things approving ourselves as the ministers of God, in much patience, in afflictions, in necessities, in distresses” (2 Corinthians 6:4).

Now, these afflictions are not the afflictions of the disease class. Paul is very definite on these lines. He suffered afflictions with the people. Jesus suffered afflictions with the people. There can be many afflictions within our human frame on the line of feeling the association of our spiritual acquaintance is not ripening in the life of others.

You have to so live in the Spirit that when you see the church not rising into its glory, you have affliction for the church. You are sorry and deeply distressed because the church is not capturing the vision, and there is affliction in your sorrow.

God would have us so spiritual that we could have perfect discernment of the spirit of the people. If I can in a moment discern the spirit, whether it is quickening, whether the whole church is receiving it, whether my heart is moved by this power, then I can see the declination of positions, I can see the waning of positions, and I can see faith waning, and that will cause affliction and trouble to my life.

May God give us to realize that we are so joined to the Church that we may labor to bring the Church up. Paul said he travailed in birth for people to be formed again. It was not to be saved again. But they had missed apprehension. They had missed fellowship of divine order, so he labored again that they might be brought into this deep fellowship in the Spirit.

God help us to see that we can travail for the church. Blessed is the person who can weep between the door and the altar. Blessed is the people of God that can take Angelus Temple on their hearts and weep behind, cry through till the church is formed again, till she rises in glory till the power of heaven is over her, till the spiritual acquaintance rises higher and higher, till the song lifts them to the heights.

This is the order of the church of God. The ministry be not blamed, but a higher height, a glorious truth, a blessed fidelity, higher and higher.

There is a word which needs to be in these days. I know I am speaking to people who have churches and who have a lot to do in churches. Remember this: You never lose so much as when you lose your peace. If the people see that you have lost your groundwork of peace, they know you have got outside of the position of victory. You have to possess your soul in peace.

Strange things will happen in the church, things will look as though they were all contrary, and you will feel that the enemy is busy. At that time, possess your soul in peace. Let the people know that you have acquaintance with One Who, when He was reviled, reviled not again.

Let your patience be so possessed that you can suffer anything for the church or for your friends or for your neighbors, or anyone. Remember this: We build character in others as our character is built. Just as we are pure in our thought, tender and gracious to other people, and possess our souls in patience, then the people have great desire for our fellowship in the Holy Ghost.

Now Jesus was emblematic of that line. They saw Him undisturbed. I love to think about Him. He helps me so much because He is the very essence of help.

"In necessities and distresses." This means spiritual distresses because of acquaintance with the Church. It is the Church we are dealing with here. Paul is in a place where he is breathing forth by divine appointment to the Church.

The purpose of these meetings is to gather the Church together in fidelity lines, because if five people could save Sodom and Gomorrah, five holy people in a church can hold the power of the Spirit till Light shall reign. We do not want to seek to save ourselves, but lose ourselves that we may save the Church. You cannot help distresses coming. They will come, and offenses will come, but woe unto those that cause offenses. See that you do not cause offense. See that you live in a higher tide. See that your tongue cannot move.

I wonder if you have ever seen the picture in the twenty-second chapter of Luke, "Lord, is it I?" Every one of them was so conscious of his human weaknesses that not a single one of them had a place where he could say that it would not be he.

“One of you will betray me,” Jesus said.

John was leaning on the breast of the Lord, and Peter beckoned to him and said, “Please get to know.”' He knew if anybody could get to know it would be John.

How long do you think Jesus had known? He had known at least for nearly three years. He had been with them in the room, He had been feeding them, He had been walking up and down with them, and He had never told any of them it was Judas.

The church that follows Jesus should be so sober, sober to a sensitiveness that they would not speak against another, whether it was true or not.

Jesus is the great personality I have in every way to listen and also to be provoked by His holy inward generosity and purity, and also His acquaintance with love.

What would it have done? If He had told them, everyone would have been bitter against Judas. So He saved all His disciples from being bitter against Judas for three years.

What love! Can't you see that holy divine Saviour? Every one of us today would throw ourselves at His feet. If we had a crown worth millions of money, we would say “You are worthy”. O God, give us such a holy, intense, divine acquaintance that we would rather die than grieve Thee! Oh, for an inward savor that shall make us say “A thousand deaths rather than sinning once.” O Jesus, we worship Thee! Thou art worthy!

*Interpretation of Tongues:* Into the very depths have I gone to succour thee. And in the very depths I called thee My own, and I delivered thee when thou wast oppressed and in oppression, and I brought thee out when thou wert sure to sink below the waves, and I lifted thee and brought thee into the banqueting house.

It is the mercy of the Lord. It is the love of the Lord. It is the grace of the Lord. It is the Spirit of the Lord. It is the will of the Lord.

Be ready Be alert for God. Live in the Holy Ghost. Oh, I can understand, “I would that ye all spake in tongues, but rather that ye prophesy except we have interpretation.” I pray God that we may learn the lesson how to keep ourselves so that the Spirit shall blend, the harmony shall be beautiful. There is not a person in the place that is not feeling the breath of the Almighty breathing over us. This is one of those moments when the Spirit is coming to us and saying, “Don’t forget. This is the receiving of the grace of God.” You are not to go away and forget. You are to go away and be what God intends you to be.

“In stripes, in imprisonments, in tumults, in labours, in watchings, in fastings” (2 Corinthians 6:5). How those first apostles did suffer! And how we together with them do suffer.

Sweden is a most remarkable place in many ways. When I was in Sweden the power of God was upon me, and it was there that I was apprehended for preaching these wonderful truths, talking about the deep things of God, seeing people healed on every line.

The Lutheran churches, yes, and the doctors rose up like an army against me and had special meetings with the king to try to get me out of the country; and at last, they succeeded. It was in Sweden that I was escorted out with two detectives and two policemen, because of the mighty powers of God moving amongst the people in Stockholm. But beloved, it was very lovely!

One of the nurses in the king’s household came, and she was healed of a leg trouble — I forget whether a broken thigh or a dislocated joint. She went to the king and she said, “I have been so wonderfully healed by this man. You know I am walking all right now.”

“Yes,” he said, “I know everything about him. I know all about him. Tell him to go. I do not want him turned out. If he goes out, he can come back; but if he is turned out, he cannot come back.”

I thank God I was not turned out, I was escorted out.

They went to see the policemen to see if I could have a big meeting in the park on the Whitsun Tide Monday. The policemen joined together and they said, "There is only one reason that we could refuse him, and it is on this line: if that man puts his hands upon the sick in the great park, it would take thirty more policemen to guard the situation. But if he will promise us that he will not lay his hands upon the people, then we will allow you to have the park."

They came and asked me, and I said, "Promise them. I know God is not subject to my laying hands upon the people. When the presence of the Lord is there to heal, it does not require hands. Faith is the great operation position. When we believe God all things are easy."

So they built places where I could speak to thousands of people.

I prayed, "Lord, You know. You have never been yet in any place fixed. You have the mind of all things. Show me how it can be done today without the people having hands laid upon them. Show me."

To the people I said, "All of you that would like the power of God going through you today, healing everything, put your hands up."

There was a great crowd of hands, thousands of hands went up.

"Lord, show me."

And He told me as clearly as anything to pick a person out that stood upon a rock. It was a very rocky place. So I told them all to put their hands down but this person. To her I said, "Tell all the people what are your troubles."

She began to relate her troubles. From her head to her feet she was so in pain that she felt if she did not sit down or lie down she would never be able to go on.

"Lift your hands high," I said. Then, "In the name of Jesus I rebuke from your head to your feet the evil one, and I believe He has loosed you."

Oh, how she danced and how she jumped and how she shouted!

That was the first time that God revealed to me it could be done. We had hundreds healed without touching them and hundreds saved without touching. Our God is a God of mighty power. Oh, how wonderful, how glorious and how fascinating it is that we can come into a royal place! This is a royal place. We have a great God. We have a wonderful Jesus. I believe in the Holy Ghost.

In Prison in Switzerland ". . . in imprisonments."

In Switzerland I have been put into prison twice for this wonderful work. But praise God, I was brought out all right!
The officers said to me, "We find no fault. We are so pleased. We have found no fault because you are such a great blessing to us in Switzerland."

And in the middle of the night they said, "You can go."

I said, "No. I will only go on one condition. That is that every officer there is in the place gets down on his knees and I pray with all of you." Glory to God!

Are you ready? What for? To believe the Scriptures. That is necessary. The Scripture is our foundation to build upon properly. Christ is the cornerstone. We are all in the building.

Oh! If I could let you see that wonderful city coming down out of heaven, millions, trillions beyond countless numbers, a city coming down out of heaven to be married, millions, trillions of people making the city.

Get ready for that. Claim your rights in God's order this morning. Do not give way. If you hear any spiritual breathing from anyone, believe that is your order. If you see Christ, believe He was your firstfruit. If you see Paul by the Holy Ghost penetrating your divine position, believe it is yours.

Have faith in God. Believe the Scripture is for you. If you want a high tide rising in the power of God, say, "Give me, Lord, that which I shall be short in nothing." Have a real faith. Believe that love covers you, His life flows through you, His quickening Spirit lifts you.

O God, take these people into Thy great pavilion. Lead them, direct them, preserve them, strengthen them, uphold them by Thy mighty power. Let the peace that passeth understanding. The joy of the Lord, the comfort of the Holy Ghost be with them. Amen.

# CHAPTER 5

## The Way to Overcome: Believe!

---

THE GREATEST WEAKNESS in the world is unbelief. The greatest power is the faith that worketh by love. Love, mercy, and grace are bound eternally to faith. There is no fear in love and no question as to being caught up when Jesus comes. The world is filled with fear, torment, remorse, and brokenness, but faith and love are sure to overcome. "Who is he that overcometh the world, but he that believeth that Jesus is the Son of God?" (1 John 5:5). God hath established the earth and humanity on the lines of faith. As you come into line, fear is cast out, the Word of God comes into operation and you find bedrock. The way to overcome is to believe Jesus is the Son of God. The commandments are wrapped up in it.

When there is a fidelity between you and God and the love of God is so real that you feel you could do anything for Jesus, all the promises are yea and amen to those who believe. Your life is centred there. Always overcoming what is in the world.

Who keepeth the commandments? The born of God. "Ye are of God, little children, and have overcome them: because greater is he that is in you, than he that is in the world" (1 John 4:4). They that believe, love. When did He love us? When we were in the mire. What did He say? Thy sins are forgiven thee. Why did He say it? Because He loved us. What for? That He might bring many sons into glory. His object? That we might be with Him forever. All the pathway is an education for this high vocation and calling. This hidden mystery of love to us, the undeserving! For our sins - the double blessing. "...whatsoever is born of God overcometh the world: and this is the victory...even our faith" (1 John 5:4). He who believeth — to believe is to overcome. On the way to Emmaus, Jesus, beginning from Moses and all the prophets, interpreted to them in all the Scriptures the things concerning Himself (Luke 24:27). He is the root! In Him is life. When we receive Christ, we receive God and the promises (Galatians 3:29), that we might receive the promise of the Spirit through faith. I am heir to all the promises because I believe. A great heirship! I overcome because I believe the truth. The truth makes me free.

*TONGUES AND INTERPRETATION*: "It is God who exalteth, God who maketh rich. The Lord in His mighty arms bears thee up — it is the Lord that encompasseth round about thee. When I am weak, then I am strong."

No wavering! This is the principle. He who believes is definite, and because Jesus is in it, it will come to pass. He is the same yesterday, today, and forever (Hebrews 13:8). They that are poor in spirit are heirs to all. There is no limit to the power, for God is rich to all who call upon Him. Not the will of the flesh, but of God (John 1:13). Put in your claim for your children, your families, your co-workers, that many sons may be brought to glory (Hebrews 2:10), for it is all on the principle of faith. There is nothing in my life or ambition equal to my salvation, a spiritual revelation from heaven according to the power of God, and it does not matter how many flashlights Satan sends through the human mind; roll all on the blood. Who overcomes? He who believes Jesus is the Son (1 John 5:5). God calls in the person with no credentials, it's the order of faith, He who believeth overcometh — will be caught up. The Holy Ghost gives revelation all along the line. He that is not against us is for us, and some of the most godly have not touched Pentecost yet. We must have a good heart especially to the household of faith. "...If any man love the world, the love of the Father is not in him" (1 John 2:15). The root principle of all truth in the human heart is Christ, and when grafted deeply there are a thousand lives you may win. Jesus is the way, the truth, and the life (John 14:6), the secret to every hard problem in the world.

You can't do it! Joseph could not! Everything depends on the principles in your heart. If God dwells in us the principle is light, it comprehends darkness. If thine eye be single, thy whole body shall be full of light, breaking through the hardest thing. "Herein is our love made perfect, that we may have boldness in the day of judgment: because as he is, so are we in this world (1 John 4:17) — for faith has full capacity. When man is pure and it is easy to detect darkness, he that hath this hope purifieth himself (1 John 3:3).

*Tongues and Interpretation:* "God confirms in us faith that we may be refined in the world, having neither spot nor blemish nor any such thing. It is all on the line of faith, he that hath faith overcomes — it is the Lord Who purifieth and bringeth where the fire burns up all the dross, and anoints with fresh oil; see to it that ye keep pure. God is separating us for Himself.

"...I will give you a mouth and wisdom, which all your adversaries will not be able to gainsay nor resist" (Luke 21:15). The Holy Spirit will tell you in the moment what you shall say. The world will not understand you, and you will find as you go on with God that you do not under-stand fully. We cannot comprehend what we are saved to, or from. None can express the joy of God's indwelling. The Holy Spirit can say through you the need of the moment. The world knoweth us not because it knew Him not.

"Who is he that overcometh the world, but he that believeth Jesus is the Son of God?" (1 John 5:5). A place of confidence in God, a place of prayer, a place of knowledge, that we have what we ask, because we keep His commandments and do the things that are pleasing in His sight. Enoch before his translation had the testimony, he had been well-pleasing unto God. We overcome by believing.

# CHAPTER 6

# Great Grace Upon The Church

---

"AND GREAT GRACE WAS UPON THEM ALL." Great grace is upon us when we magnify the Lord. If ever you want to see what God means when He gets a chance at His people, have a peep at the fourth chapter of Acts, and see what God did. Just because all the people shouted aloud to Him He imparted to them such blessing that every person was filled with the Holy Ghost, and I believe what God wants to do in these days is to give an inward manifestation of His divine presence within the body until the body is moved by the power of the Spirit. Beloved, we are accustomed to earthly things, but when God sends the heavenly it is beyond our understanding. Oh, to have the revelation of the mind of God! It fills my soul, the thought of it! Oh, for the kind of loosening of the body that we will never be bound again! Just filled with God!

I believe God wants us to understand something of the words of this life. What life? The manifestation of the power of Jesus in the human body, a divine life, a divine power, a quickening, thrilling energy given to you. I was baptized with the Holy Ghost in 1907. If anyone had said to me: "Now, Wigglesworth, you will see such and such things," it would have been beyond my human comprehension, but the tide has risen for fifteen years, and it is still rising. Thank God, there has never been a black day, nor a blank day.

When I think about the first Church, how God favored her, how He burst thru her, how He definitely spoke, how He transformed Christians and made them move with the power of apostles, that wherever they went they transformed lives. God did such wonderful things, and when I think of it, I think, that we should have something far in advance, and say: "Look up; your redemption draweth nigh!" I want to take a perspective of what they were, and we must be. I am inwardly convinced of the power that awaits us, the installation of God's movement right in our hearts.

I notice in the first Church it wasn't possible for a lie to live, and I want you to keep in mind that there is a time coming when nothing of uncleanness will be able to remain in His little flock. The first Church was so pure God overshadowed it; He nursed it, brought it thru, and He has His hand upon us at this time. How do we know? The Lord hath laid the foundation which is an immovable foundation. It is built upon the prophets; it is built upon the apostles; it is built upon the Word of God, and the church will yet come into the fullness of the manifestation of the body of Christ.

God will keep His Word. The church will be ready like a bride adorned for her husband; the gifts will be a ministry clothed upon; the graces will adorn the believer, and will be far beyond anything we have seen.

Now, Ananias and Sapphira were, I believe, baptized believers. I have a firm conviction in my heart that God in the first outpouring of the Spirit did His work so beautifully that those three thousand who were pricked in their hearts met the condition of the Bible pattern. Peter said unto them: "Repent, believe, be baptized and ye shall receive the gift of the Holy Ghost." They obeyed and we have reason to believe they received the Holy Ghost. I cannot conceive of anything else but that the Early Church all received the outpouring of the Holy Ghost. And I believe today that we should press home to every soul the necessity of meeting the conditions and being filled with the Holy Ghost. Then I notice here in this fifth chapter of Acts that God had the particular oversight of the Church. I love to think of this. They gave of their substance, they gave willingly; they laid it down at the apostles' feet, and they were so eager to give that they began selling their property, and brought the proceeds to the apostles. Now there were two people who had sold the land who began to talk over the thing at home, and this was the sense of their argument: "This thing may go down; it may leak out. If we give it all, we shall lose it all and have nothing left," and so they reserved for themselves a portion, but they missed it. Listen: God never wants anything from you but a spontaneous heart gift, and anyone who gives spontaneously to God will always get a big cup full. God is never in any man's debt.

I notice the moment God visited this people in showing up this sin and bringing death to Ananias and Sapphira, it instantly brought a tremendous fear over all the church, a fear that brought an answer. There is a fear that brings an answer. Were they afraid of God? No, it was something better than that. When they saw that God was there in judgment upon them they turned with a holy fear, with a reverence. It sobered things and the people began to see that God was zealous for them. There are two kinds of fear, one that is afraid of God, and another fear that loves God, and that was the fear that came over them, the fear of grieving God, which the Lord wants us to have. Oh, to fear Him in such a way that you would rather be shot than to grieve Him! That is it. This came over the people, and when it came, another thing happened. "No one durst join themselves to them." That was a wonderful time. May God so sanctify His church that no one durst come near without unless he means business. Brother, did God have a hand in your plan? Did you join this people because you felt they were a choice people, or did you have the constraining power of God upon you?

I see more and more in this glorious life of God, that there is a pure whiteness to be achieved, there is a pure sonship without fear and the saints of God shall rise in such confidence until they will remove what people think are mountains, till they will subdue what you call kingdoms.

I have had some wonderful times in Belfast, and in fact all over Ireland. I was in Belfast one day and a young man came to me and said: "Brother Wigglesworth, I am very much distressed," and he told me why. They had an old lady in their assembly who used to pray heaven down upon them. She had an accident. Her thigh was broken and they took her away to the infirmary. They put her in a plaster cast and she was in that condition for five months. Then they broke the cast and lifted her on to her feet and asked her to walk. She fell again and broke her leg in another place. And they found out that the first break had never knit together. They brought her home and laid her on the couch and the young man asked me to go and pray for her. When I got into the house I asked: "Do you believe that God can heal you?" She said "Yes. When I heard you had come to the city I thought, 'This is my chance to be healed.' An old man, her husband, was sitting in a chair, had been sitting there for four years; helpless. And he said, "I do not believe. I will not believe. She was the only help I had. She has been taken away with a broken leg, and they have brought her back with her leg broken twice. How can I believe God?"

I turned to her and said: "Now is it all right?" "Yes," she said, "it is all right." The right leg was broken in two parts. Physicians can join up bones beautifully, and make them fit together, but if God doesn't come in with His healing power, there is no physician that can heal them. As soon as the oil was placed upon her head and hands laid on, instantly down the right limb there was a stream of life, and she knew it. She said: "I am healed." I said: "If you are healed, you do not need anybody to help you." She went out. She took hold of the mantle shelf above her head and pulled herself up and walked all around the room. She was perfectly healed.

The old man said: "Make me walk." I said: "You old sinner, repent." Then he began: "You know, Lord, I didn't mean it." I really believe he was in earnest, and to show you the mercy and compassion of God, the moment I laid hands upon him, the power of God went thru him and he rose up after four years being stiff and walked around the room. That day both he and his wife were made whole. Do you not believe now that God has a plan in all these things? I want you to realize that what God wants to do in us and thru us in these days is to blend us together, give us one heart and one mind. They were all of one heart and one mind, and they had such faith that the shadow of Peter worked a transformation in their bodies. Of course, it was God that did the healing. But as Peter came along I can see the people moved by his presence. Beloved, we have one in the meeting tonight who is a million times mightier than Peter. His touch will set you free.

It is the living virtue! “Go speak to the people the words of this life,” the life of the Son of God, the quickener by the Word.

The first outpouring was of the Spirit, and the latter is to be the fullness of the Spirit. When God’s mighty power shakes the foundation and purifies, there is a transformation. The Lord is the life, and where the life of the Spirit and the Word are together they bring forth an issue of transforming and quickening until the man is made like Jesus. Jesus is the first fruits. It is lovely to think that God sent Him in the likeness of sinful flesh, and for sin condemned sin in the flesh. Then we are here tonight with a clear conception of this thing, that the life of Jesus has come into our flesh and delivered us from the power of darkness and disease, from bitterness and covetousness, idolatry and lust; from the corruption of the present evil world, by the same Spirit, the same life.

I believe the Lord would have me take you to a moment in my life. I was having some meetings in Belfast, and this is the rising tide of what I believe was the move of the Spirit in a certain direction, to show the greatness of that which was to follow. Night after night the Lord had led me on certain lines of truth. There was so much in it that one felt they could not give up, and every night until ten o’clock we were opening up the Word of God. They came to me and said: “Brother, we have been feasting and are so full we are ready for a burst of some kind. Don’t you think it is time to call an altar service?” I said I knew that God was working and the time would come when the altar service would be called, but we would have to get the mind of the Lord upon it. There was nothing more said. They began early in the afternoon to bring the sick people. We never had a thing said about it. The meeting came and every seat was taken up, the window sills were filled and every nook and corner. The glory of God filled the place. It was the easiest thing in the world to preach; it came forth like a river, and the power of God rested mightily. There were a lot of people who had been seeking the baptism for years. Sinners were in the meeting, and a number of sick people. What happened? God hears me say this: There was a certain moment in that meeting when every sick person was healed, every lame person was healed, and every sinner saved, and it all took place in five minutes. There comes into a meeting sometimes something we cannot understand, and it is amazing how things happen.

When I was on the ship there was a man who had trained all his life, as it were, to be a physician. He got to be eminent and was looked up to as one of the leading physicians, an Indian. He had been over to England to lecture, and was going back on the ship on which I was traveling. When the Christian Science lady got healed she saw the captain and told him what God had done. The Captain arranged a meeting and I had a fine chance to preach to all on the ship. The Indian doctor was there and he was struck with what happened. At the close of the meeting people decided for Christ; some people followed me into my stateroom, where God healed them. This Indian doctor came to me. "I am done," he said. "I have no spirit left. You must talk to me." For two hours we talked and God dealt with him. He stood before me. "I will never have any more medicine," he said. "God has saved me." That physician saw the power of God and recognized it. You ask, What is that? That is where God plans a life in a moment, thru one act. God wants the way into our lives. He wants to transform you by His grace. He wants to make you know that you are only here to be filled with His power and His presence for His glory. The "seed of the woman" must "bruise the serpent's head."

Now, beloved, the Acts of the Apostles were written to prove to us that the power and manifestation of God were to be continuous. Have you read about the scattering of these people at Jerusalem, how God was with them? Do not be afraid of persecution. I am never at my best until I am in a conflict, and until I have a fight with the enemy. They think I am rather unmerciful in my dealing with the sick, but I have no mercy for the devil and get him out at any cost. I resist him with all the power that is within me. God wrought mightily thru the persecution which came upon the church, and He could do the same today under similar circumstances.

# CHAPTER 7

# Greater Works Than These

---

I WANT ALL YOU PEOPLE to have a good time, all to be at ease, all to be without pain, I want all to be free.
There is a man here with great pain in his head, I am going to lay my hands on him in the name of Jesus and he shall tell you what God has done, I believe that would be the right thing to do, before I begin to preach to you, to help this poor man so that he shall enjoy the meeting like us, without any pain.

(The man referred to was in pain with his head wrapped up in a bandage, and after he was prayed for, he testified that he had no pain.)

I want you all to be in a place where we receive much blessing from God. It is not possible for any of you to go out with pain, if you would only believe God, the Word of God if you receive it tonight, it is life, it gives deliverance to every captive. I want to preach the Word tonight so that all the people will know; you will go with a knowledge of the deliverance of God.

I want everyone to receive a blessing at the commencement of the meeting, no one person need to live out of the plan of God. If you have pain in your knee, if you believe when you stand up, as sure as you are there, you will be free. I believe the Word of God. God has promised if we will believe we can have whatsoever we ask.

We want you to have it changed. The present tense tunes are better than future tense tunes. If you get a full salvation you will have a present tense tune. It is a good thing to be able to hope for sometimes… but it is a better thing to have it.

I used to hope and trust I would be baptised in the Holy Ghost, but when I spoke in Tongues…no! When He spoke, then I knew I was baptised. Before, I used to hope it would be so. You cannot move a fact by an argument. When you get baptized in the Holy Ghost, the Spirit speaks through you, then you know it is done - You Know the Comforter has come. Has He come to you? Has the Comforter come to you?

You must have Him, you must be filled with the Spirit, you must have an overflowing, because Jesus says, after you have received the Holy Ghost ye shall have Power. We want you to have power.

Let us look at the Scriptures. "Verily, verily I say that whatsoever you ask the Father in my name, I will do it, that the Father may be glorified in the Son. If ye shall ask anything in my name I will do it" – I WILL DO IT, who says it? JESUS, that blessed Jesus, that lovely Jesus, that incarnation from heaven, that blessed Son of God. How He wants to bless, how He saves to the uttermost, no one spoke like He spoke. How? "Come unto me all ye that are weary and heavy laden and I will give you rest." Hear what Jesus says – "I come not into the world to condemn the world, but that the world through me might be saved." How beautiful. Jesus wants us all to be saved. Did you ever look at Him in His sympathy. Just take a vision of Him on Mount Olives and looking over Jerusalem weeping and saying, "Oh Jerusalem, Oh Jerusalem how often would I have gathered thee, and you would not." Shall it not be said of the people in Colombo, in Ceylon. "How often would I have gathered thee as a hen gathered the chickens under her wings, and you would not." Will you hear what He said. "WHATSOEVER YE SHALL ASK IN MY NAME I WILL DO IT." What do you want, how much do you want, do you want anything. Are you thirsty, are you hungry, "Come unto me all that thirst and I will give you water of life." Are you hungry, "..he that eateth the flesh and drinketh the blood of the Son of man shall live for ever."

Do you want to live forever. Jesus who saves to the uttermost, He heals, He helps all that come to Him.

How many are coming for healing? How many for salvation? Listen – "Whatsoever ye ask in my name I will do it", the Word of the living God, The Son of God. How beautifully God speaks of Him – "This is my beloved Son" and yet He gave Himself for us, He gave Himself as ransom for us, Amen.

How many are going to receive Him? Take the Water of Life freely. You may say, "how can I take Him?" Believe on the Lord Jesus Christ and you shall be saved. "What is it to believe?" "He that heareth my Word and believeth on Him that sent me hath everlasting life."

Who are the people that followed Jesus – they that love Him in their hearts. Do you love Him in your hearts. From this day if you do love Him you will begin to hate all kinds of sin and you will love all kinds of righteousness, that is the secret. The man that says he loves God and loves the world – he is a liar. God says the truth is not in him. If a man loves the world the love of the Father is not in him, and you can tell tonight whether you love God or not. Do you love the world, then the love of the father is not in you. If you hate the world, then the love of the Lord Jesus is in you. Hallelujah.

I want to make you love Him. Is He worth loving? What has He done? He bought salvation. He died to deliver. The wages of sin is death. The gift of God is eternal life.

I leave it with you. Will you love Him? Will you serve Him? Will you? He knows it He understands.

There's no one that loves me like Jesus. There's no one that knows me like Him. He knows all your sickness. He knows all your sickness. There's no one that knows me like Him.

That's why He says, “Come unto me.” He knows you are needy.

I want you to be blessed now, I find I get blessed as I ask, in the street, everywhere. If you find me in the street or anywhere, if I am alone, I shall be talking to God. I make it my business to talk to God all the time. If I wake in the night, I make it my business to pray, and that’s the reason I believe that God keeps me right, always right, always ready. I believe that God the Holy Ghost keeps us living in communion with God.

I want you to begin now, begin talking to God.

PRAYER.

John 14:12. Jesus was the way and the truth, and therefore all that Jesus said was true. Jesus said, “Truly, truly, if you believe greater works than these shall ye do because I go to the father.” Has He gone? If I told you earthly things and left them - now I tell you heavenly things. The son of man is down, the son of man is up. The greatest and one of the deepest truths possible for the believer.

Do you see this Electric Light. That light is receiving power from the dynamo, it has a receiver and transmitter. The power house may be a mile or two away, the wires that are conveying the current to and from are covered. Where you are getting the light is bare wire, the juice is passing through the bare wire and gives you the light.

To bring it to you tonight to understand the life in Christ. Jesus sends the light, and life through, and it illuminates the life then returns and just as you are holy inside, the revelation of God is made manifest and the life becomes full of illumination. My life is from Him, my life receives back to Him, and I am kept by the life of God.

I touch them and instantly they change. The Life of the Son of God goes through and passes on. I live by the faith of the Son of God.

He that believeth on Me - he that believeth. The devils believe and tremble. People follow Scripture as if it had nothing to do with it. The Scripture may be Life or letter. My spirit - my Word - What is the

Word? It is spirit and life giving when we believe. What is believing? Believing is the asking of the divine life that God gives to Him. Who desires? Everyone in this place can have Divine Life.

We do not believe in baptismal regeneration. You cannot be saved by riches. Jesus says ye must be born again... The new birth comes through faith in the Lord Jesus Christ, and you can be saved in the field as well as in a church - it is the heart. When the heart desires after righteousness, God makes Himself known; so we want you to be saved by the Blood tonight. Someone says, "I want to be saved.." Shall I bring you to the Word? "He that asketh receiveth". Who says? - Jesus says. He that asks receives.

If I ask Him to receive me, will He say me nay, not till earth and not till heaven pass away.

Salvation is of the Lord. No man can save you, no man can heal you. If any one has been healed in these meetings it is the Lord that has healed them.

I would not take it under any circumstances that I can heal anybody, but I believe His Word – "He that believeth on me greater works than these shall he do because I go to my Father." He is lovely, Lovely Jesus.

He knows it all, He knows it all, My Father knows it all, The bitter tears how fast they fall, He knows, my Father knows it all.

Is not He lovely, if You get saved tonight you will have another song

He knows it all, He knows it all, My father knows it all The joy that comes that overflows He knows, my Father knows it all.

Before I was baptised in the Holy Ghost, there were many songs I used to sing as they were written. God began a change; and He changed many songs. I believe God wants to change the Song in your heart. He changed this song for me.

This is how it is sung,

Oh then it will be glory for me It will be glory for me.
But God changed it,

Oh it is now Glory for me. It is now glory for me,
As now by His grace I can look on His face,
Now it is glory,
Glory for me.

# CHAPTER 8

## The Power of Christ's Resurrection

---

THAT I MAY KNOW HIM, and the power of his resurrection, and the fellowship of his sufferings, being made conformable unto his death...I count not myself to have apprehended: but this one thing I do, forgetting those things which are behind, and reaching forth unto those things which are before, I press toward the mark for the prize of the high calling of God in Christ Jesus. -Philippians 3:10,13-14

What a wonderful Word! This surely means to press on to be filled with all the fulness of God. If we leak out here we shall surely miss God, and shall fail in fulfilling the ministry He would give us.

The Lord would have us preach by life, and by deed, always abounding in service; living epistles, bringing forth to men the knowledge of God. If we went all the way with God, what would happen? What should we see if we would only seek to bring honor to the name of our God? Here we see Paul pressing in for this. There is no standing still. We must move on to a fuller power of the Spirit, never satisfied that we have apprehended all, but filled with the assurance that God will take us on to the goal we desire to reach, as we press on for the prize ahead.

Abraham came out from Ur of the Chaldees. We never get into a new place until we come out from the old one. There is a place where we leave the old life behind, and where the life in Christ fills us and we are filled with His glorious personality.

On the road to Damascus, Saul of Tarsus was apprehended by Christ. From the first he sent up a cry, "Lord, what wilt thou have me to do?" He desired always to do the will of God, but here he realized a place of closer intimacy, a place of fuller power, of deeper crucifixion. He sees a prize ahead and every fiber of his being is intent on securing that prize. Jesus Christ came to be the firstfruits; the firstfruits of a great harvest of like fruit, like unto Himself. How zealous is the farmer as he watches his crops and sees the first shoots and blades. They are the earnest of the great harvest that is coming. Paul here is longing that the Father's heart shall be satisfied, for in that first resurrection the Heavenly Husbandman will see a firstfruits harvest, firstfruits like unto Christ, sons of God made conformable to the only begotten Son of God.

You say, "I am in a needy place." It is in needy places that God delights to work. For three days the people that were with Christ were without food, and He asked Philip, "From whence shall we buy bread that these may eat?" That was a hard place for Philip, but not for Jesus, for He knew perfectly what He would do. The hard place is where He delights to show forth His miraculous power. And how fully was the need provided for. Bread enough and to spare!

Two troubled, baffled travelers are on the road to Emmaus. As they communed together and reasoned, Jesus Himself drew near, and He opened up the Word to them in such a way that they saw light in His light. Their eyes were holden that they could not recognize who it was talking with them. But, oh how their hearts burned within as He opened up the Scripture to them. And at the breaking of bread He was made known to them. Always seek to be found in the place where He manifests His presence and power.

The resurrected Christ appeared to Peter and a few more of them early one morning on the shore of the lake. He prepared a meal for the tired, tried disciples. This is just like Him. Count on His presence.

Count on His power. Count on His provision. He is always there just where you need Him.

Have you received Him? Are you to be found "in Him"? Have you received His righteousness, which is by faith? Abraham got to this place, for God gave this righteousness to him because he believed, and as you believe God He puts His righteousness to your account. He will put His righteousness right within you. He will keep you in perfect peace as you stay your mind upon Him and trust in Him. He will bring you to a rest of faith, to a place of blessed assurance that all that happens is working for your eternal good.

Here is the widow's son on the road to burial. Jesus meets that unhappy procession. He has compassion on that poor woman who is taking her only son to the cemetery. His great heart had such compassion that death had no power - it could not longer hold its prey. Compassion is greater than suffering. Compassion is greater than death. O God, give us this compassion! In His infinite compassion Jesus stopped that funeral procession and cried to that widow's son, "Young man, I say unto thee, Arise." And he who was dead sat up, and Jesus delivered him to his mother.

Paul got a vision and revelation of the resurrection power of Christ, and so he was saying, "I will not stop until I have laid hold of what God has laid hold of me for." For what purpose has God laid hold of us? To be channels for His power. He wants to manifest the power of the Son of God through you and me. God helps us to manifest the faith of Christ, the compassion of Christ, the resurrection power of Christ.

One morning about eleven o'clock I saw a woman who was suffering with a tumor. She could not live through the day. A little blind girl led me to the bedside. Compassion broke me up and I wanted that woman to live for the child's sake. I said to the woman, "Do you want to live?" She could not speak. She just moved her finger. I anointed her with oil and said, "In the name of Jesus." There was a stillness of death that followed; and the pastor, looking at the woman, said to me, "She is gone."

When God pours in His compassion it has resurrection power in it. I carried that woman across the room, put her against a wardrobe, and held her there. I said, "In the name of Jesus, death, come out." And soon her body began to tremble like a leaf. "In Jesus' name, walk," I said. She did and went back to bed.

I told this story in the assembly. There was a doctor there and he said, "I'll prove that." He went to the woman and she told him it was perfectly true. She said, "I was in heaven, and I saw countless numbers all like Jesus. Then I heard a voice saying, 'Walk, in the name of Jesus.'"

There is power in the name of Jesus. Let us apprehend it, the power of His resurrection, the power of His compassion, the power of His love. Love will break the hardest thing - there is nothing it will not break.

# CHAPTER 9

# Preparation for the Second Coming of the Lord

---

I AM CONSCIOUS TODAY that God has a design for us greater than our thoughts even or our language, and so I am not frightened of on the line of the spiritual exaggeration, shall I say. I dare believe that God will help me say things to you that shall inspire you to beginning dare to believe God.

Up to this present time the Lord's word is for us, "Hitherto ye have asked nothing." Surely you people that have been asking great things from God for a long time would be amazed if you entered into it with clear knowledge that it is the Master, it is Jesus, who has such knowledge of the mightiness of the power of the Father, of the joint union with Him, that nothing is impossible for you to ask. Surely it is He only Who could say "Hitherto you have asked nothing."

So God means me to press you another step forward. Begin to believe on extravagant asking, believing that God is pleased when you ask large things.

If you will only dispose of yourself in a short time —for it is nothing but yourself that will hinder you — dispose of your human mind, dispose of your human measure, dispose of your strength and dispose of all you have — it is a big word for me to say — and let inspiration take whole charge of you, bring you out of yourself into the power of God, it may be today that God shall so transform you into another man as you have never been before.

*Interpretation of Tongues:* Only the divine mind has divine thought to meet human order for knowing us from the beginning and understanding us as a Father and pitying us as children, He begins with the blade and the ear and the full corn in the ear so that we might know that He won't take us out of our death but He will transform us moment by moment till we can come into full stature of the mind and thought and prayer and act.

Hallelujah! God is on the throne.

Now beloved in the Lord, I come to you this morning to inspire you to dare believe that this day is for you as a beginning of days. You have never passed this way before. So I bring you to another day of passing over any heights, passing through mists or darkness, dare believe that the cloud is upon thee, shall break with an exceeding reward of blessing.

Don't be afraid of clouds. They are all earthly. Never be afraid of an earthly thing. You belong to a higher order, a divine order, a spiritual order. Then believe that God wants you to soar high this morning.
*Interpretation of Tongues:* Fear not to enter in, for the Lord thy God has thee now in preparation. He is proving thee and He is chastising thee, but His hand is not heavy upon thee as thou mayest think, for He is gentle and entreating to bring thee into the desired place of thy heart's affections.

Be still and know that I am God. It is I and I alone that openeth to thee the good treasure. Oh, to be still that my mind be so unsurfeited with the cares of this life that I might be able to enter into the joy and the bliss God has caused me to, for I have not passed this way hitherto.

So God is going to speak to us about entering into something we have not entered into before.

The thoughts of this morning message are primary to the message of the coming of the Lord. There must be a preparing place and an understanding line because of the purposes God is arranging for us. I know He is even at the door. Spiritual perception make's us know of His near return. But we must be so built on the line of truth that when He comes we are ready.

In the few days to come I am going to declare unto you the revelation of Christ to me of the readiness, and what it is, the knowledge of it, the power of it, the purpose of it, till every vestige of our human being is so filled with it, it would be impossible for us to be out of it. We shall be in the midst of it.

I have a message this morning leading up to the knowledge of His coming. It is in Peter's second epistle, the third chapter.

"Knowing this first, that there shall come in the last days scoffers, walking after their own lusts, and saying, Where is the promise of his coming? For since the fathers fell asleep, all things continue as they were from the beginning of the creation. For this they willingly are ignorant of, that by the word of God the heavens were of old, and the earth standing out of the water and in the water: whereby the world that then was, being overflowed with water, perished: but the heavens and the earth, which are now, by the same word are kept in store, reserved unto fire against the day of judgment and perdition of ungodly men. But, beloved, be not ignorant of this one thing, that one day is with the Lord as a thousand years, and a thousand years as one day. The Lord is not slack concerning his promise, as some men count slackness; but is longsuffering to us-ward, not willing that any should perish, but that all should come to repentance. But the day of the Lord will come as a thief in the night; in the which the heavens shall pass away with a great noise, and the elements shall melt with fervent heat, the earth also and the works that are therein shall be burned up. Seeing then that all these things shall be dissolved, what manner of persons ought ye to be in all holy conversation and godliness, looking for and hasting unto the coming of the day of God, wherein the heavens being on fire shall be dissolved, and the elements shall melt with fervent heat? Nevertheless we, according to his promise, look for new heavens and a new earth, wherein dwelleth righteousness. Wherefore, beloved, seeing that ye look for such things, be diligent that ye may be found of him in peace, without spot, and blameless. And account that the longsuffering of our Lord is salvation" —2 Peter 3:3-15.

I may deal with many things on the line of spiritual awakening, for this is what is needed this day. This day is a needy day of spiritual awakening, not so much as a knowledge of salvation but a knowledge of waking in salvation.

The seed of the Lord Jesus Christ is mightily in you, which is a seed of purifying, a seed of truth and knowledge, a seed of life-giving, a seed of transforming, a seed of building another person in the body till the body that bears the seed only lives to contain the body which the seed has made, until that comes forth with glorious light and power till the whole body has yielded itself to another, a fullness, a manifestation of the perfect formation of the Christ in you. This is the great hope of the future day.

I want to speak to you very exactly. All the people which are pressing into and getting ready for this glorious attained place where they shall not be found naked, where they shall be blameless, where they shall be immovable, where they shall be purified by the power of the Word of God, have within them a consciousness of the very presence of God within, changing their very nature and preparing them for a greater thing, and causing them to be ready for translation.

You will find that this thing is not now already in the world in perfection. There are millions and millions of real believers in Christ who are losing this great upward look, and in the measure they lose this upward look, they lose perfect purification. There is only perfect purification in this upward look.

When we see the day dawning, as the manifestation of the sons of God appear, just as these things come to us in light and revelation, we will find that it makes us know that everything is on the decay. Millions of people who are Christians believe this world is being purified. All the saints of God that get the real vision of this wonderful transformation of the body are seeing every day that the world is getting worse and worse and worse and ripening for judgment. And God is bringing us to a place where we which are spiritual are having, a clear vision that we must at any cost put off the works of darkness. We must be getting ourselves ready for the glorious day.

These are last days. What will be the strongest confirmation for me to bring to you of the last days?

There are in the world two classes of believers. There are believers which are disobedient, or I ought to say there are children which are saved by the power of God which are disobedient children. And there are children which are just the same saved by the power of God who all the time are longing to be more obedient.

In this great fact Satan has a great part to play. It is on this factor in these last years that some of us have been brought to great grief at the first opening of the door with brazen fact to carnality forces. And we heard the word come rushing, through all over, "new theology" that damnable, devilish, evil power that lived in some of these disobedient children, which in these last days opened the door to the next thing.

As soon as this was noised abroad everywhere, "new theology," everybody began to say, "What is new theology?" Why, new theology is exactly on the same plane as being changed from monkeys to men. What does it mean? I want to make a clear sweep of that thing this morning. There is not a man can think on those lines only on atheism. Every person that touches a thing like that is an atheist behind all he has to say.

New theology was born in infidelity. It is atheism, and it opened the door for Russellism, which is full of false prophecy. Take the book of Russellism and go into, the prophecy. What was the prophecy? In 1924 the prophecy was that the Lord had to come. Russellism is false prophecy. Russellism is exactly the perfect plan of what will make the man of sin come forth. Russellism is preparing the door for the man of sin and they are receiving open-heartedly.

They declared that He would come in 1914. I went to see a dear beloved brother of mine who was so deluded by this false prophecy that he was utterly deceived by it. I said, "You will be deceived as sure as you live."

They said, "We are so sure it is true that if we are deceived we will give up all Russellism and have nothing to do with it."

But what does false prophecy do? False prophecy always makes a way out. The moment it did not come to pass they said they were mistaken in dates. What is the devil? If it had been a true prophecy He would have come. And the Word of God says if any prophecy does not come true that prophet has to prophesy no more.

But those people were deluded by the spirit of 'this world and the devil, which is the spirit of this world, and instantly allowed themselves to be gripped again, and the same prophet came forth saying that He was going to come in 1925.

In order to cover that, what did they do? They placarded in every nation, almost, in big cities, "Millions alive that will never die." And they have been going at that now since 1925, and they are dying all the time, and their prophecy is still a cursed, evil prophecy. Still they go on.

The spirit of this age is to get you to believe a lie. If you believe a lie, you cannot believe the truth. When once you are seasoned with a lie against the Word of God, He sends you strong delusion that you shall believe a lie. Who does? God does. God is gracious over His Word. His Word is from everlasting His Word is true.

When we see those things which are coming to pass, what do we know? We know the time is at hand. The fig tree is budding for these false prophecies and these positions.

Now you see, they never stop at that. They go on to say Christ never has risen. Of course, if ever you believe a lie, if ever you turn the Word of God to some other place, you cannot believe the truth after that.

Then the last days opened the door for that false demon power which is in the world rampant everywhere, putting up the most marvelous buildings — Christian Science, which is devilish, hellish, and deceivable. I am preaching to you this morning that you shall deliver yourself from this present-day evil thing. How shall you do it? You can do it only on one line. Let the seed in. Let the seed of truth, the seed of righteousness, this power of God, this inward incorruptible.

The seed of Christ is an inward incorruptible. The new birth, the new life, is a quickening power, incorruptible, dealing with corruptible, carnal things - evil, sensuous, devilish. And when it comes to the Word of God, the seed of the Word of God is the life of the Word and you are living the life of the Word of God and are tremendously transformed all the time by the Word of the Lord.

This is the last days. You go out in the world and there is no difficulty. What are you going to do now? Is this a fact? Is this true? Aren't people today almost afraid of sending their sons to the colleges because they come out more devils than they went in? Isn't atheism right in the seat of almost all these colleges? Then what have you to do? How shall you possess your soul in peace? How shall you preserve your children? How shall you help them? You say they have to go because you want them to come out with certain letters to their names. You want them to progress in knowledge, but how shall you save your children?

Nothing but the Word can save them.

I wish all the young men in this place would read these words in the first epistle of John: "Young men...ye are strong…and have overcome the wicked one" (1 John 2:14). What by? By the Word.

They are mighty words we read in this Scripture. What does it say? The Word is holding these things, even the fires that are going to burn the world. The Word is holding them. What is the Word? The Word is the mighty power of the revelation to us of the Son of God. And the Son of God is holding all these powers today in the world, ready for the greatest conflagration that ever could be, when the heavens shall be burnt up, when the earth shall melt with fervent heat.

The Word of God is keeping these things reserved, all ready. What manner of men ought we to be in all manner of conversation in purifying ourselves.

Remember this: In heaven the glory, the revelation, the power, the presence, that which makes all heaven so full of beauty, is that time has no count. It is so lovely! A thousand years are as a day and a day as a thousand years.

*Interpretation of tongues:* All the springs are in thee, all the revelations are in the midst of thee. It is He, the mighty God! It is He, the King of kings! It is He, the Son of the living God who is in the very innermost being of thy human nature, making thee know that before these things shall come to pass thou shalt be preserved in the midst of the flame. Whatever happens, God shall cover thee with His mighty covering; and that which is in thee is incorruptible and undefiled and fadeth not away, which is reserved in the glory.

God says to us, “In patience possess thy soul.” How beautiful! Oh! How the enrichment of the presence of the power of the Most High is bursting forth upon our — what shall I say? — our human frame. Something greater than the human frame.

Knowest thou not that that which is born to thee is greater than anything formed around thee? Knowest thou not that He which has been begotten in thee, is the very God of power to preserve thee, and to bring forth light and truth and cause the vision to be made clearer?

You notice this: There is an elect of God. I know that God has in this place people who, if you would examine yourself, you would be amazed to find that you are elect of God.

People are tremendously afraid of this position because they have heard so much on this line: “Oh, you know you are the elect of God! You are sure to be all right.” There have been in England great churches which were laid out upon these things. I thank God that they are all withered. You will find if you go to England those strong people that used to hold all these things are almost withered out. Why? Because they went on to say whatever you did, if you were elect, you were right. That is wrong.

The elect of God are those that are pressing forward. The elect of God cannot hold still. They are always on the wing. Every person that has a knowledge of the elect of God realizes it is important that he press forward. He cannot endure sin nor darknesses nor shady things. The elect is so in earnest to be elect for God that he burns every bridge behind him.

"Knowing this, that first there shall be a falling away"
Knowing this, that first God shall bring into His treasury the realities of the truth and put them side by side — the false, the true, those that can be shaken in mind, and those that cannot be shaken. God wants us to be so built upon the foundation of truth that we cannot be shaken in our mind, it doesn't matter what comes.

When I was in Sydney they said, "Whatever you do, you must see this place that they built for the man, the new man coming."

Theosophy has a new man. Nothing but theosophy could have a new man. The foundation of the theosophy has always been corruptible. From the beginning it has been corruptible. In the formation of theosophy it was joined up to Bradlaw one of the greatest atheists of the day. So you can only expect theosophy to be atheism. It sprung out of atheism.

The "Man of Sin" as he comes forth will do many things. There will be many false Christs and they will be manifestations of the forthcoming of the Man of Sin, but they will all come to an end. There will be the Man of Sin made manifest.

These people are determined to have a man. They know someone has to come. We know who He is that is coming. They begin to make a man. So they find a man in India, they polish him up as much as they can, and they make him as well in appearance, but you know we are told by the Lord that there is soft clothing that goes onto wolves' backs.

We find they are going to bring this man forth in great style. When I went around the amphitheatre in Sydney that was made for this man to come, I saw as clearly as anything it was the preparation for the Man of Sin. But they do not believe that.

What will make you to know it is the Man of Sin? This: Every religious sect and creed there is in the world all joins to it. Romanism you see joined up with it. Buddhism joined with it. There is not a religion known but what is joined up to it.

Why that is exactly what the devil will have. He will have all the false religions joining right up and the Man of Sin, when he comes, will be received with great applause.

Who will be saved? Who will know the day? Who knows now the Man of Sin? Why, we feel when we touch him, when he opens his mouth, when he writes through the paper, when we see his actions — we know who he is.

What has the Man of Sin always said? Why, exactly what Russellism says. What? No hell. The devil has always said that. What does Christian Science say? No hell, no devil. They are ready for him. The devil has always said no hell, no evil. And these people are preparing, and they do not know it, for the Man of Sin.

We have to see that these days have to come before the Lord can come. There has to be a falling away. There has to be a manifestation in this day so clear, of such undeniable fact. I tell you, when they begin to build temples for the Man of Sin to come (but they don't know it), you know the day is at hand.

A person said to me, "You see, the Christian Scientists must be right — look at the beautiful buildings. Look at all the people following them."

Yes, everybody can belong to it. You can go to any brother you like, you can go to any theater you like, you can go to any race course you like, you can be mixed up with the rest of the people in your life and still be a Christian Scientist. You can have the devil right and left and anywhere, and still belong to Christian Science.

When the Man of Sin is come, he will be hailed 'on all sides. When he is manifested, who will miss him? Why the reverent, the holy, the separated. How will they miss him? Because they will not be here to greet him!

But there will be things that will happen prior to his coming that we shall know. You can tell. I am like one this morning that is moving with a liquid - holy, indispensable - real fire in my bosom, and I know it is burning and the body is not consumed. It is real fire from heaven that is making my utterances come to you to know that He is coming. He is on the way. God is going to help me tell you why you will know. You that have the breath of the Spirit, there is something now moving as I speak. As I speak, this breath of mighty, quickening, moving, changing, desirable power is making you know and it is this alone that is making you know that you will be ready.

No matter who misses it, you will be ready. It is this I want to press upon you this morning, that you will be ready. And you won't question your position. You will know. Ah! Thank God, ye are not of the night. Ye are of the day. It shall not overtake you as a thief. Ye are the children of day. You are not the night. You are not drunken. Yes, you are. There is so much intoxication from this holy incarnation that makes you feel all the time you have to have Him hold you up. Praise the Lord! Holy intoxication, inspired revelation, invocation, incessantly inwardly moving your very nature, that you know as sure as anything that you do not belong to those who are putting off the day. You are hastening unto the day, you are longing for the day.

You say "What a great day!" Why do you say it? Because the creature. Is this body the creature? No. This is the temple that holds the creature. The creature inside the temple longeth, travaileth, groaneth to be delivered, and will be delivered. It is the living creature. It is the new creature. It' is the new creation. It is the new nature. It is the new life.

What manner of men ought we to be? I am going to read it: "The Lord is not slack concerning his promise, as some men count slackness; but is longsuffering to us-ward, not willing that any should perish, but that all should come to repentance." —2 Peter 3:9.

I want you to notice this: This is not the wicked repentant. The epistles are always speaking to the saints of God. When I speak to you saints of God, you will find that my language will make you see that there is not within you one thing that has to be covered. I say it without fear of contradiction, because it is my whole life, inspired by the truth. You know that these meetings will purify you.

It is on this line that every time you hear people speak upon this — I do not mean as a theory. This is not a theory. There is a difference between a man standing before you on theory. He has chapter and verse, line upon line, precept upon precept, and he works it out upon the scriptural basis. It is wonderful, it is good, it is inspiring; but I am not there this morning. Mine is another touch. Mine is the spiritual nature showing to you that the world is ripening for judgment. Mine is a spiritual acquaintance bringing you to a place of separation, holiness unto God, that you may purify yourself and be clean, ready for the great day.

This is the day of purifying. This is the day of holiness. This is the day of separation. This is the day of waking. O God, let us wake today! Let the inner spirit wake into consciousness that God is calling us. The Lord is upon us. We see that the day is upon us. We look at the left side, we look at the right side, we see everywhere new theories. New things will not stand the light of the truth. When you see these things, you know that there must be a great falling away before the day. And it is coming. It is upon us.

Paul said he travailed in birth. Jesus did the same. John had the same. So brothers and sisters, may God bless you and make you see that this is a day of travailing for the Church of God that she might be formed so that she is ready for putting on the glorious raiment of heaven forever and forever.

Seeing then that all these things shall be dissolved, what manner of persons ought ye to be in all holy conversation and godliness, looking for and hasting unto the coming of the day of God, wherein the heavens being on fire shall be dissolved, and the elements shall melt with fervent heat?

Nevertheless we, according to his promise, look for new heavens and a new earth, wherein dwelleth righteousness. Wherefore, beloved, seeing that ye look for such things, be diligent that ye may be found of him in peace, without spot, and blameless —2 Peter 3:11-14.

Without spot! WITHOUT SPOT! Without spot and blameless!

Do you believe it? Who can do it? THE BLOOD CAN DO IT! The blood, the blood, oh the blood! The blood of the Lamb! The blood of Jesus can do it. Spotless, clean, preserved for God.

Give the devil the biggest chase of his life and say these words, "The blood of Jesus Christ, God's Son, cleanseth us from all unrighteousness."

If ever you hear a row like that in any Christian Science meeting about the blood of Jesus, go and I will tell you they are being converted. If you ever hear, tell of Russellism getting excited over the blood of Jesus, I can tell you God has dealt with them. If ever you hear about this new man in theosophy getting excited about the blood of Jesus, you can tell them from Wigglesworth that there is a new order in the world. But they have no room for the blood. And yet we see the blood is preparing us for this great day.

In the amphitheatre in Sydney, when I spoke about the blood and when I spoke about this infernal thing, the whole place was upset. You be careful when anybody comes to you with a sugar-coated pill or with a slimy tongue. They are always of the devil. The Spirit of the Lord will always deal with truth. These people never deal with truth. They always cover up the truth. "Oh, you know, we are all sons of God. We all belong to God." That is what people said when Jesus was here, and He said, "You are mistaken. You belong to the devil." And if Jesus dared say things like that, I dare.

# CHAPTER 10

## What Wilt Thou Have Me To Do?

---

READ ACTS 19. As soon as Paul saw the light from heaven above the brightness of the sun, he said, "Lord, what wilt thou have me to do?" (Acts 9:6). And as soon as he was willing to yield he was in a condition where God could meet his need; where God could display His power; where God could have the man. Oh, beloved, are you saying today, "What wilt thou have me to do?" The place of yieldedness is just where God wants us.

People are saying, "I want the baptism, I want healing, I would like to know of a certainty that I am a child of God," and I see nothing, absolutely nothing in the way except unyieldedness to the plan of God. The condition was met which Paul demanded, and instantly when he laid hands on them they were filled with the Spirit and spake in other tongues and prophesied (Acts 19:6). The only thing needed was just to be in the condition where God could come in. The main thing today that God wants is obedience. When you begin yielding and yielding to God He has a plan for your life, and you come in to that wonderful place where all you have to do is to eat the fruits of Canaan. I am convinced that Paul must have been in divine order as well as those men, and Paul had a mission right away to the whole of

Asia.

Brothers and sisters, it is the call of God that counts. Paul was in the call of God. Oh, I believe God wants to stir somebody's heart today to obedience; it may be for China or India or Africa, but the thing God is looking for is obedience.

"What wilt thou have me to do?" (Acts 9:6).

...God wrought special miracles by the hands of Paul: so that from his body were brought unto the sick handkerchiefs or aprons, and the diseases departed from them, and the evil spirits went out of them.

Acts 19:11,12

If God can have His way today, the ministry of somebody will begin; it always begins as soon as you yield. Paul had been bringing many people to prison, but God brought Paul to such a place of yieldedness and brokenness that he cried out, "What wilt thou have me to do?" (Acts 9:6). Paul's choice was to be a bondservant for Jesus Christ. Beloved, are you willing that God shall have His way today? God said, "I will shew him how great things he must suffer for my name's sake" (Acts 9:16). But Paul saw that these things were working out a far more exceeding weight of glory. You people who have come for a touch from God, are you willing to follow Him; will you obey Him?

When the prodigal son had returned and the father had killed the fatted calf and made a feast for him, the elder brother was angry and said, "...thou never gavest me a kid, that I might make merry with my friends," (Luke 15:29) but the father said to him, "...all that I have is thine" (v. 31). He could kill a fatted calf at any time. Beloved, all in the Father's house is ours, but it will come only through obedience. And when He can trust us, we will not come behind in anything.

"...God wrought special miracles by the hands of Paul" (Acts 19:11). Let us notice the handkerchiefs that went from his body; it means to say that when he touched and sent them forth, God wrought special miracles through them, and diseases departed from the sick, and evil spirits went out of them. Is it not lovely? I believe after we lay hands on these handkerchiefs and pray over them, that they should be handled very sacredly, and even as the one carries them they will bring life, if they are carried in faith to the suffering one. The very effect of it, if you only believed, would change your own body as you carried it.

A woman came to me one day and said, "My husband is such a trial to me; the first salary he gets he spends it in drink, and then he cannot do his work and comes home; I love him very much, what can be done?" I said, "If I were you I would take a handkerchief and would place it under his head when he went to sleep at night, and say nothing to him, but have a living faith." We anointed a handkerchief in the name of Jesus, and she put it under his head. Oh, beloved, there is a way to reach these wayward ones. The next morning on his way to work he called for a glass of beer; he lifted it to his lips, but he thought there was something wrong with it, and he put it down and went out. He went to another saloon, and another, and did the same thing. He came home sober. His wife was gladly surprised and he told her the story; how it had affected him. That was the turning point in his life; it meant not only giving up drink, but it meant his salvation.

God wants to change our faith today. He wants us to see it is not obtained by struggling and working and pining. "…the Father himself loveth you..." (John 16:27). "...Himself took our infirmities, and bare our sicknesses" (Matthew 8:17). "Come unto me, all ye that labour and are heavy laden, and I will give you rest" (Matthew 11:28).

Who is the man that will take the place of Paul, and yield and yield and yield, until God so possesses him in such a way that from his body virtue shall flow to the sick and suffering? It will have to be the virtue of Christ that flows. Don't think there is some magic virtue in the handkerchief or you will miss the virtue; it is the living faith in the man who lays the handkerchief on his body, and the power of God through that faith. Praise God, we may lay hold of this living faith today. "The blood has never lost its power." As we get in touch with Jesus, wonderful things will take place; and what else? We shall get nearer and nearer to Him.

There is another side to it. "...exorcists, took upon them to call over them which had evil spirits the name of the Lord Jesus, saying, 'We adjure you by Jesus whom Paul preacheth'...and the evil spirit answered and said, 'Jesus I know, and Paul I know; but who are ye?'" (Acts 19:13,15). I beseech you in the name of Jesus, especially those of you who are baptized, to awaken up to the fact that you have power if God is with you; but there must be a resemblance between you and Jesus. The evil spirit said, "…Jesus I know, and Paul I know; but who are ye?" (Acts 19:15). Paul had the resemblance.

You are not going to get it without having His presence; His presence changes you. You are not going to be able to get the results without the marks of the Lord Jesus. The man must have the divine power within himself; devils will take no notice of any power if they do not see the Christ. "Jesus I know, and Paul I know; but who are ye?" The difference between these men was they had not the marks of Christ, so the manifestation of the power of Christ was not seen.

You want power: don't take the wrong way. Don't take it as power because you speak in tongues, and if God has given you revelations along certain lines don't take that for the power; or if you have even laid hands on the sick and they have been healed, don't take that for the power. "The Spirit of the Lord is upon me..." (Luke 4:18); that alone is the power. Don't be deceived; there is a place to get where you know the Spirit is upon you, so you will be able to do the works which are wrought by this blessed Spirit of God in you, and the manifestation of His power shall be seen, and people will believe in the Lord.

What will make men believe the divine promises of God? Beloved, let me say to you today, God wants you to be ministering spirits, and it means to be clothed with another power. And this divine power, you know when it is there, and you know when it goes forth. The baptism of Jesus must bring us to have a single eye to the glory of God; everything else is wasted time and wasted energy. Beloved, we can reach it; it is a high mark but we can get to it. You ask how? "What wilt thou have me to do?" That is the plan. It means a perfect surrender to the call of God, and perfect obedience.

A dear young Russian came to England. He did not know the language, but learned it quickly and was very much used and blessed of God; and as the wonderful manifestations of the power of God were seen, they pressed upon him to know the secret of his power, but he felt it was so sacred between him and God he should not tell it, but they pressed him so much he finally said to them: "First God called me, and His presence was so precious, that I said to God at every call I would obey Him, and I yielded, and yielded, and yielded, until I realized that I was simply clothed with another power altogether, and I realized that God took me, tongue, thoughts and everything, and I was not myself but it was Christ working through me." How many of you today have known that God has called you over and over, and has put His hand upon you, but you have not yielded? How many of you have had the breathing of His power within you, calling you to prayer, and you have to confess you have failed?

I went to a house one afternoon where I had been called, and met a man at the door. He said, "My wife has not been out of bed for eight months; she is paralyzed. She has been looking so much for you to come, she is hoping God will raise her up." I went in and rebuked the devil's power. She said, "I know I am healed; if you go out I will get up." I left the house, and went away not hearing anything more about her. I went to a meeting that night, and a man jumped up and said he had something he wanted to say; he had to go to catch a train but wanted to talk first. He said, "I come to this city once a week, and I visit the sick all over the city. There is a woman I have been visiting and I was very much distressed about her; she was paralyzed and has lain on that bed many months, and when I went there today she was up doing her work." I tell this story because I want you to see Jesus.

We had a letter which came to our house to say that a young man was very ill. He had been to our Mission a few years before with a very bad foot; he had no shoe on, but a piece of leather fastened on the foot. God healed him that day. Three years after, something else came upon him. What it was I don't know, but his heart failed, and he was helpless; he could not rise or dress or do anything for himself, and in that condition he called his sister and told her to write and see if I would pray. My wife said to go, and she believed God would give me that life. I went, and when I got to this place I found the whole country was expecting me; they had said that when I came this man would be healed. I said to the woman when I arrived, "I have come." "Yes," she said, "but it is too late." "Is he alive?" I asked, "Yes, just alive," she said. I went in and put my hands upon him, and said, "Martin." He just breathed slightly, and whispered, "The doctor said if I move from this position I will never move again." I said, "Do you know the Scripture says, 'God is the strength of my heart, and my portion for ever'?" (Psalm 73:26). He said, "Shall I get up?" I said, "No."

That day was spent in prayer and ministering the Word. I found a great state of unbelief in that house, but I saw Martin had faith to be healed. His sister was home from the asylum. God held me there to pray for that place. I said to the family, "Get Martin's clothes ready; I believe he is to be raised up." I felt the unbelief. I went to the chapel and had prayer with a number of people around there, and before noon they too believed Martin would be healed. When I returned I said, "Are his clothes ready?" They said, "No." I said, "Oh, will you hinder God's work in this house?" I went in to Martin's room all alone. I said, "I believe God will do a new thing today. I believe when I lay hands on you the glory of heaven will fill the place." I laid my hands on him in the name of the Father, Son, and Holy Ghost, and immediately the glory of the Lord filled the room, and I went headlong to the floor. I did not see what took place on the bed, or in the room, but this young man began to shout out, "Glory, glory!" and I heard him say, "for Thy glory, Lord," and that man stood before me perfectly healed. He went to the door and opened it and his father stood there. He said, "Father, the Lord has raised me up," and the father fell to the floor and cried for salvation. The young woman brought out of the asylum was perfectly healed at that moment by the power of God in that house.

God wants us to see that the power of God coming upon people has something more in it than we have yet known. The power to heal and to baptize is in this place, but you must say, "Lord, what wilt thou have me to do?" You say it is four months before the harvest. If you had the eyes of Jesus you would see that the harvest is already here. The devil will say you can't have faith; you tell him he is a liar. The Holy Ghost wants you for the purpose of manifesting Jesus through you. Oh, may you never be the same again! The Holy Spirit moving upon us will make us to be like Him, and we will truly say, "Lord, what wilt thou have me to do?"

# CHAPTER 11

## Questions & Answers

---

Q: In Ephesians 6:12 does "wrestling" mean wrestling in prayer? "For we wrestle not against flesh and blood, but against principalities," etc.

A: According to 2 Corinthians 10:5, we are able to smite the enemy and bring every thought into perfect obedience to the law of Christ.

"Casting down imaginations, and every high thing that exalteth itself against the knowledge of God, and bringing into captivity every thought to the obedience of Christ."

Now is that through prayer, or how? It is quite clear to me that faith inspires you to pray but faith will command you to command. And if you are in the place of real faith when these things come up against you, you will say "Get thee behind me" no matter what it is.

Prayer is without accomplishment unless it is accompanied by faith. Jude says we can pray in the Holy Ghost. Be sure you are filled with the Spirit that you do not pray but another prays. Be sure you are filled with the life of Christ till faith rises, claims, destroys, brings down imagination and everything that opposes Christ. Faith and prayer, an act, a command.

•

Q: Which is the right way to baptize, in the name of Jesus, or the Father, Son, and Holy Ghost?

A: Always do that which causes no contention and no split. Water baptism in the name of Jesus causes more trouble than anything else, and you should never have trouble in the church, you should be at peace. The Lord said it was to be in the name of the Father, Son, and Holy Ghost, and when we keep in the right order, as He said, then there is no schism in the body.

When you go on your own line and strike out a new cord, you cause dissension and trouble. This thing has caused more trouble than anything because it has not been satisfied to go there. It has gone further and said that Jesus is the Father, Jesus is the Son, and Jesus is the Holy Ghost. If you do not keep on the right line, keep in the words where Jesus was, you will be tippled over in awful distress and darkness. Keep on the high line.

•

Q: What should be our attitude toward the coming of the Lord? Should we be enjoying His personal presence now, disregarding the time of His coming, or should we wait and anticipate His coming?

A: Do what Peter did. He hastened to the coming, and he left everything behind him to catch the gleam of it. You have to keep your mind upon it, looking unto and hastening it. It is a joy to the Church. It is that "blessed hope." It is that glorious appearing. And it will save you from any amount of things, for he that looks for that purifieth himself.

•

Q: Does a person have to go to school in order to save souls?

A: I think you will save more souls out of the school. What you have got to do is to understand that soul-saving work is never made in schools. Soul-saving work is the regenerative of the spirit, of the life, to make you eaten up with the zeal of the Lord. Soul saving is the best thing. It is the sure place, it is the right place, and I hope we are doing it when He comes.

•

Q: Is the Spirit of God within the individual that is born again? I have always thought so from the eighth chapter of Romans.

A: If you will rightly consider the truth and keep it before you, it will save you from any amount of error. The epistles are for people who are baptized in the Holy Ghost, baptized believers.

When you say, "Except you have the Spirit of Christ, you are none of His," you will find that is a perfect word right in the epistles. The new birth has within it the Spirit of Jesus, and it has the word also, "My word is spirit and life." It is not the Holy Spirit; it is the Spirit of Jesus.

The Holy Spirit is that which comes after, and is with you all the time. He was with you in revelation of conviction, but when you were filled He came inside. And after He comes inside, it is so much different from being outside.

•

Q: Did Jesus think it not robbery to be equal with God? What did He mean by saying that?

A: It meant He was equal in power, equal in authority, equal in the glory. He was perfectly one, and what His Father was, He was, perfectly joined. Yet in order for perfect obedience, that all the people should learn obedience, He left the glory, He left everything behind to save us. He had as much right to stop and say, "Father, You go," but He was willing to go and left the glory although He had the right to stop.

•

Q: If a contract were entered into by two people and broken by one party, should that be collected by law by the other party?

A: Yes, if you lived in the law. But if you lived in the Spirit, then you would not go to law with your brother. It depends upon whether you live in law or live in grace. If you live in grace, you will never go into law.

I thank God that I was in business for twenty-five years and might have picked up a lot of money, but it is still left there because I would not go to law. I do not believe in it.

But I am not a law to you people. I tell you what law is and I tell you what grace is.

•

Q: What is the seal put upon God's people?

A: The seal is the Holy Spirit. It is different from anything else. It is upon you, and the devil knows it. All the evil powers of the earth know it. You are sealed with that Holy Spirit of promise till the day of redemption. You are also baptized in the same Spirit, and that is in the epistles. But don't forget that you get a great deal in your salvation, in the new birth. Press on and get sealed with the Spirit.

All they which are in Christ will be caught up at His coming. The twenty-second chapter of Luke distinctly says that Jesus would not sit down again to break bread till the kingdom had come. Now the kingdom is in every believer, and He will not sit down till every believer is there. The kingdom is in the believer, and the kingdom will come and millions and millions of people, I am sure, will be there who never received the Holy Ghost. But they had the life of the Christ inside. When He comes Who is our life — it is not the Holy Ghost Who is the life; Christ is the life — when He comes Who is our life, then shall we go to the Life.

•

Q: Is it every Christian's privilege to have his eyes so preserved that he need never wear glasses?

A: One thing will take place with every person here. There are any number of people who have been praying ever since they were ten years old, and if praying and the life within them could have altered the situation, it would have been altered. But I see they are here today with gray hair, and white hair, meaning that the natural man decays and you cannot do what you like with it. But the supernatural man may so abound in the natural man that it never decays. It can be replaced by divine life.

There comes a time in life when at fifty or so all eyes, without exception, begin to be dim. But why? What kind of dimness? If we were living in the time of Moses we should not require glasses and we should have as good eyesight as he had. How do you know? Because those tables of stone that he carried were written on so that he could see or anybody else could see without glasses.

It doesn't mean to say that your eyes are any worse than were Moses'. It means to say that the natural man has had a change. I believe and affirm that the supernatural power can be so ministered to us that even our eyesight can be preserved right through. But I say this: Any person is a fool that professes to have faith and then gets a big printed Bible so that he will not need glasses. It presents a false position before the people. What he has got to see is if he will carry a Bible about in his hand which, as the whole of the Bible in very short space, his eyesight may require either some help or he may not be able to read correctly.

I have been preaching faith to our people for thirty years. When my daughter came back from Africa and saw her mother and myself with glasses, she was amazed. When our people saw us put glasses on the first time, they were very much troubled. They were no more troubled than we were. But I found it was far better to be honest with the people and acknowledge my place than get a Bible that was right big print and deceive the people and say that my eyesight was all right. I like to be true. My eyesight gave way at about fifty-three, and somehow God is doing something. I am now sixty-eight, and I do not want any kind of glasses different, and I am satisfied God is restoring me.

When I was seeking this way of divine healing I was stumbled because all the people that had such testimony of divine healing were wearing glasses. I said, "I cannot go on with this thing. I am stumbled every time I see the people preaching divine healing wearing glasses." And I got such a bitterness in my spirit that God had to settle me on that line — and I believe yet that I have not fully paid the price.

My eyes will be restored, but until then I will not deceive anybody. I will use glasses till I can perfectly see.

A woman came up to me one day and I noticed she had no teeth.

"Why," I said, "your mouth is very uneven. Your gums have dropped in some places and the old gums are very uneven."

"Yes," she said, "I am trusting the Lord for a new set of teeth."

"That is very good," I said. "How long have you been trusting Him for them?"

"Three years."

"Look here," I said, "I would be like Gideon: I would put the fleece out and I would tell the Lord that I would trust Him to send me teeth in ten days or money to buy a set in ten days, and whichever came first I would believe it was He."

In eight days, fifty dollars came to her from a person whom she had never been acquainted with in any way, and it bought her a beautiful set of teeth — and she looked well in them.

A person is prayed for for eyesight and as soon as he is prayed for, he believes, and God stimulates his faith, but his eyesight is about the same. "What shall I do?" he asks. "Shall I go away without my glasses?"

"Can you see perfectly?" I ask. "Do you require any help?"

"Yes. If I should go as I go now, I would stumble."

"Put your glasses on," I say. "For when your faith is perfected you will not require any glasses, and when God perfects your faith your glasses will drop off. But as long as you have need, use them."

You can take that for what you like, but I believe in common sense.

•

Q: Is it true if we believe a lie we cannot believe the truth?

A: That is not what I said. If you once believe the Word of God to be a lie, then you cannot believe the truth of the Word of God. The Word of God comes to you like life and revelation, but Satan in his spurious condition comes, as he has done with many and moved them from truth to believe in some theory of truth. They have gotten a theory of something else which is not truth and they have denied the truth to take hold of the theory. It is all theory when people have left the truth. The people that live in truth never have a theory; it is always fact.

•

Q: Because I have laid aside my Christian Science books, the people are now using what they call "malicious magnetism" against me. I know Jesus is stronger than they.

A: This is a very important thing. There are many people so under delusion and devil oppressed on these lines that they join together to damage the character of others because they do not go their way. That is the devil if nothing else is. The greatest fact about Christian Science's false position is that they are led captive by the father of liars. He has been a liar from the beginning. They have stepped out of truth and been taken in charge by this monster devil till they cannot believe the truth.

"I am 'the light of the world'; any man that walketh in me shall not be in darkness. I am the light to light every man that cometh into the world."

If you will go back to the time when you knew the light of the truth was burning through you, you will find that there you turned from that to take something else which was not light. Keep in the light and there is no power of Satan. If a hundred people came and stood around you and said to you, "We will join together to bind you that you shall be crippled," or your mind be affected, or anything, if you know you have the Light you can smile and say, "You can do nothing to me."

Never be afraid of anything. There are two things in the world: one is fear, the other faith. One belongs to the devil; the other to God. If you believe in God, there is no fear. If you sway toward any delusion of Satan, you will be brought into fear. Fear always brings bondage. There is a place of perfect love to Christ where you are always casting out all fear and you are living in the place of freedom.

Be sure that you never allow anything to make you afraid. God is for you, who can be against you?

The secret of many people going into Christian Science is a barren church that had not the Holy Ghost. Christian Science exists because the churches have a barren place because they haven't the Holy Ghost. There would be no room for Christian Science if the churches were filled with the Holy Ghost. But because the churches had nothing, then the needy people went to the devil and he persuaded them they had something, and they are coming out knowing they have got nothing only a wilderness experience.

Let us save ourselves from all this trouble by letting the Holy Ghost fill our hearts.

Will you be baptized in this faith, Baptized in the Holy Ghost? To be free indeed 'tis the power you need, Baptized in the Holy Ghost.

Don't depend on any past tense, any past momentum, but let the unction be upon you, let the presence and the power be upon you. Are you thirsty? Longing? Desiring? Then God will pour out of His treasures all you need. God wants to satisfy us with His great, abounding, holy love, imparting love upon love and faith upon faith.

The secret of all declension is refusal of the Holy Ghost. If you have fallen short, it is because you refused the Holy Ghost. Let the Holy Ghost be light in you to lighten the light which is in you, and no darkness shall befall you. You will be kept in the middle of the road.

Hasten unto the coming of the Lord. Set your house in order. Be at peace. Live at peace. Forgive and learn how to forgive.

Never bear malice. Don't hold anybody any grudge. Forgive everybody. It does not matter whether they forgive you or not, you forgive them. Live in forgiveness. Live in repentance. Live wholeheartedly. Set your house in order, for God's Son is coming to take that which is in the house.

Book 3:

# *Ever*
# *- Increasing-*
# *Faith*

# CHAPTER 1

## Have Faith in God

---

"FOR VERILY I SAY UNTO YOU, That whosoever shall say unto this mountain, Be thou removed, and be thou cast into the sea; and shall not doubt in his heart, but shall believe that those things which he saith shall come to pass; he shall have whatsoever he saith. Therefore I say unto you, What things soever ye desire when ye pray, believe that ye receive them, and ye shall have them" (Mark 11:23, 24)

These are days when we need to have our faith strengthened, when we need to know God. God has designed that the just shall live by faith. Any man can be changed by faith, no matter how he may be fettered. I know that God's word is sufficient. One word from Him can change a nation. His word is from everlasting to everlasting. It is through the entrance of this everlasting Word, this incorruptible seed, that we are born again, and come into this wonderful salvation. Man cannot live by bread alone, but must live by every word that proceedeth out of the mouth of God. This is the food of faith. "Faith cometh by hearing, and hearing by the Word of God."

Everywhere men are trying to discredit the Bible and take from it all the miraculous. One preacher says, "Well, you know, Jesus arranged beforehand to have that colt tied where it was, and for the men to say just what they did." I tell you God can arrange everything without going near. He can plan for you, and when He plans for you, all is peace. All things are possible if you will believe.

Another preacher said, "It was an easy thing for Jesus to feed the people with five loaves. The loaves were so big in those days that it was a simple matter to cut them into a thousand pieces each." But He forgot that one little boy brought those five loaves all the way in his lunch basket. There is nothing impossible with God. All the impossibility is with us when we measure God by the limitations of our unbelief.

We have a wonderful God, a God whose ways are past finding out, and whose grace and power are limitless. I was in Belfast one day and saw one of the brethren of the assembly. He said to me, "Wigglesworth, I am troubled. I have had a good deal of sorrow during the past five months. I had a woman in my assembly who could always pray the blessing of heaven down on our meetings. She is an old woman, but her presence is always an inspiration. But five months ago she fell and broke her thigh. The doctors put her into a plaster cast, and after five months they broke the cast. But the bones were not properly set and so she fell and broke the thigh again."

He took me to her house, and there was a woman lying in a bed on the right hand side of the room. I said to her, "Well, what about it now?" She said, "They have sent me home incurable. The doctors say that I am so old that my bones won't knit. There is no nutriment in my bones and they could never do anything for me, and they say I shall have to lie in bed for the rest of my life." I said to her, "Can you believe God?" She replied, "Yes, ever since I heard that you had come to Belfast my faith has been quickened. If you will pray, I will believe. I know there is no power on earth that can make the bones of my thigh knit, but I know there is nothing impossible with God." I said, "Do you believe He will meet you now?" She answered, "I do."

It is grand to see people believe God. God knew all about this leg and that it was broken in two places. I said to the woman, "When I pray, something will happen." Her husband was sitting there; he had been in his chair for four years and could not walk a step. He called out, "I don't believe. I won't believe. You will never get me to believe." I said, "All right," and laid my hands on his wife in the name of the Lord Jesus. The moment hands were laid upon her the power of God went right through her and she cried out, "I'm healed." I said, "I'm not going to assist you to rise. God will do it all." She rose and walked up and down the room, praising God.

The old man was amazed at what had happened to his wife, and he cried out, "Make me walk, make me walk." I said to him, "You old sinner, repent." He cried out, "Lord, You know I never meant what I said. You know I believe." I don't think he meant what he said; anyhow the Lord was full of compassion. If He marked our sins, where would any of us be? If we will meet the conditions, God will always meet us. If we believe, all things are possible. I laid my hands on him and the power went right through the old man's body; and those legs, for the first time in four years, received power to carry his body, and he walked up and down and in and out. He said, "O what great things God has done for us tonight!"

"What things soever ye desire, when ye pray, believe that ye receive them, and ye shall have them." Desire toward God, and you will have desires from God; and He will meet you on the line of those desires when you reach out in simple faith.

A man came to me in one of my meetings who had seen other people healed and wanted to be healed, too. He explained that his arm had been fixed in a certain position for many years and he could not move it. "Got any faith?" I asked. He said He had a lot of faith. After prayer he was able to swing his arm round and round. But he was not satisfied and complained, "I feel a little bit of trouble just there," pointing to a certain place. "Do you know what is the trouble with you?" He answered, "No." I said, "Imperfect faith." "What things soever ye desire, when ye pray, believe that ye receive them, and ye shall have them."

Did you believe before you were saved? So many people would be saved, but they want to feel saved first. There was never a man who felt saved before he believed. God's plan is always this, if you will believe, you shall see the glory of God. I believe God wants to bring us all to a definite place of unswerving faith and confidence in Himself.

Jesus here uses the figure of a mountain. Why does He say a mountain? Because, if faith can remove a mountain, it can remove anything. The plan of God is so marvelous, that if you will only believe, all things are possible.

There is one special phrase to which I want to call your attention, "And shall not doubt in his heart." The heart is the mainspring. See that young man and young woman. They have fallen in love at first sight. In a short while there is a deep affection, and a strong heart love, the one toward the other. What is a heart of love? A heart of faith. Faith and love are kin. In the measure that that young man and that young woman love one another they are true. One may go to the North and the other to the South, but because of their love they will be true to each other.

It is the same when there is a deep love in the heart toward the Lord Jesus Christ. In this new life into which God has brought us, Paul tells us that we have become dead to the law by the body of Christ, that we should be married to another, even to Him who is raised from the dead. God brings us into a place of perfect love and perfect faith. A man who is born of God is brought into an inward affection, a loyalty to the Lord Jesus that shrinks from anything impure. You see the purity of a man and woman when there is a deep natural affection between them; they disdain the very thought of either of them being untrue. I say that, in the measure that a man has faith in Jesus, he is pure. He that believes that Jesus is the Christ overcomes the world. It is a faith that works by love.

Just as we have heart fellowship with our LORD our faith cannot be daunted. We cannot doubt in our hearts. There comes, as we go on with God, a wonderful association, an impartation of His very life and nature within. As we read His Word and believe the promises that He has so graciously given to us, we are made partakers of His very essence and life. The Lord is made to us a Bridegroom, and we are His bride. His words to us are spirit and life, transforming us and changing us, expelling that which is natural and bringing in that which is divine.

It is impossible to comprehend the love of God as we think on natural lines. We must have the revelation from the Spirit of God. God giveth liberally. He that asketh, receiveth. God is willing to bestow on us all things that pertain to life and godliness. Oh, it was the love of God that brought Jesus. And it is this same love that helps you and me to believe. In every weakness God will be your strength. You who need His touch, remember that He loves you. Look, wretched, helpless, sick one, away to the God of all grace, whose very essence is love, who delights to give liberally all the inheritance of life and strength and power that you are in need of.

When I was in Switzerland the Lord was graciously working and healing many of the people. I was staying with Brother Reuss of Goldiwil and two policemen were sent to arrest me. The charge was that I was healing the people without a license. Mr. Reuss said to them, "I am sorry that he is not here just now. He is holding a meeting about two miles away, but before you arrest him let me show you something."

Brother Reuss took these two policemen down to one of the lower parts of that district, to a house with which they were familiar, for they had often gone to that place to arrest a certain woman, who was repeatedly put in the prison because of continually being engaged in drunken brawls. He took them to this woman and said to them, "This is one of the many cases of blessing that have come through the ministry of the man you have come to arrest. This woman came to our meeting in a drunken condition. Her body was broken, for she was ruptured in two places. While she was drunk, the evangelist laid his hands on her and asked God to heal her and deliver her." The woman joined in, "Yes, and God saved me, and I have not tasted a drop of'liquor since." The policemen had a warrant for my arrest, but they said with disgust, "Let the doctors do this kind of thing." They turned and went away and that was the last we heard of them.

We have a Jesus that heals the broken-hearted, who lets the captives go free, who saves the very worst. Dare you, dare you, spurn this glorious Gospel of God for spirit, soul and body? Dare you spurn this grace? I realize that this full Gospel has in great measure been hid, this Gospel that brings liberty, this Gospel that brings souls out of bondage, this Gospel that brings perfect health to the body, this Gospel of entire salvation. Listen again to this word of Him who left the glory to bring us this great salvation, "Verily I say unto you, That whosoever shall say unto this mountain, Be thou removed, . . . he shall have whatsoever he with." Whatsoever!

I realize that God can never bless us on the lines of being hardhearted, critical or unforgiving. This will hinder faith quicker than anything. I remember being at a meeting where there were some people tarrying for the Baptism-seeking for cleansing, for the moment a person is cleansed the Spirit will fall. There was one man with eyes red from weeping bitterly. He said to me, "I shall have to leave. It is no good my staying without I change things. I have written a letter to my brother-in-law, and filled it with hard words, and this thing must first be straightened out." He went home and told his wife, "I'm going to write a letter to your brother and ask him to forgive me for writing to him the way I did." "You fool!" she said. "Never mind," he replied, "this is between God and me, and it has got to be cleared away." He wrote the letter and came again, and straightway God filled him with the Spirit.

I believe there are a great many people who would be healed, but they are harboring things in their hearts that are as a blight. Let these things go. Forgive, and the Lord will forgive you. There are many good people, people that mean well, but they have no power to do anything for God. There is just some little thing that came in their hearts years ago, and their faith has been paralyzed ever since. Bring everything to the light. God will sweep it all away if you will let Him. Let the precious blood of Christ cleanse from all sin. If you will but believe, God will meet you and bring into your lives the sunshine of His love.

# CHAPTER 2

## Deliverance to the Captives

---

READ LUKE 4:1-20.

Our precious Lord Jesus has everything for everybody. Forgiveness of sin, healing of diseases and the fullness of the Spirit all come from one source from the Lord Jesus Christ. Hear Him who is the same yesterday, today and forever as He announces the purpose for which He came: "The Spirit of the Lord is upon me, because he hath anointed me to preach the gospel to the poor, he hath sent me to heal the broken-hearted, to preach deliverance to the captives, and recovering of sight to the blind, to set at liberty them that are bruised, to preach the acceptable year of the Lord."

Jesus had been baptized by John in Jordan, and the Holy Spirit had descended in a bodily shape like a dove upon Him. Being full of the Holy Ghost., He had been led by the Spirit into the wilderness, there to come off more than conqueror over the arch enemy. Then He returned in the power of the Spirit to Galilee and preached in the synagogues, and at last He came to His old home town-Nazareth, where He announced His mission in the words I have just quoted. For a brief while He ministered on the earth, and then gave His life a ransom for all. But God raised Him from the dead. And before He went to the glory He told His disciples that they too should receive the power of the Holy Ghost upon them. Thus, through them, His gracious ministry would continue. This power of the Holy Ghost was not only for a few apostles, but even for them that are afar off, even as many as our God should call (Acts 2:39) even for us in this twentieth century. Some ask, "But was not this power just for the privileged few in the first century?" No. Read the Master's great commission as recorded by Mark, and you will see it is for them that believe.

After I had received the Baptism of the Holy Ghost (and I know that I received; for the Lord gave me the Spirit in just the same way as He gave Him to the disciples at Jerusalem), I sought the mind of the Lord as to why I was baptized. One day I came home from work and went into the house and my wife asked me, "Which way did you come in?" I told her that I had come in at the back door. She said, "There is a woman upstairs and she has brought an old man of eighty to be prayed for. He is raving up there and a great crowd is outside the front door, ringing the door-bell and wanting to know what is going on in the house." The Lord quietly whispered, "This is what I baptized you for."

I carefully opened the door of the room where the man was, desiring to be obedient to what my Lord would say to me. The man was crying and shouting in distress, "I am lost! I am lost! I have committed the unpardonable sin. I am lost! I am lost!" My wife said, "Dad, what shall we do?" The Spirit of the Lord moved me to cry out, "Come out, thou lying spirit." In a moment the evil spirit went, and the man was free. Deliverance to the captives! And the Lord said to me, "This is what I baptized you for."

There is a place where God, through the power of the Holy Ghost, reigns supreme in our lives. The Spirit reveals, unfolds, takes of the things of Christ and shows them to us, and prepares us to be more than a match for Satanic forces.

When Nicodemus came to Jesus he said, "We know that thou art a teacher come from God: for no man can do these miracles that thou doest, except God be with him." Jesus said to him, "Verily, verily I say unto thee, Except a man be born again, he cannot see the kingdom of God." Nicodemus was impressed by the miracles wrought; and Jesus pointed out the necessity of a miracle being wrought with every man who would see the kingdom. When a man is born of God, he is brought from darkness to light, a mighty miracle is wrought. Jesus saw every touch by God as a miracle, and so we may expect to see miracles wrought today. It is wonderful to have the Spirit of the Lord upon us. I would rather have the Spirit of God on me for five minutes than to receive a million dollars.

Do you see how Jesus mastered the devil in the wilderness? He knew He was the Son of God and Satan came along with an "if." How many times has Satan come along to you this way? He says, "After all, you may be deceived. You know you really are not a child of God." If the devil comes along and says that you are not saved, it is a pretty sure sign that you are. When he comes and tells you that you are not healed, it may be taken as good evidence that the Lord has sent His word and healed you. The devil knows that if he can capture your thought life, he has won a mighty victory over you. His great business is injecting thoughts, but if you are pure and holy you will instantly shrink from them. God wants us to let the mind that was in Christ Jesus, that pure, holy, humble mind of Christ, be in us.

I come across people everywhere I go who are held bound by deceptive conditions, and these conditions have come about simply because they have allowed the devil to make their minds the place of his stronghold. How are we to guard against this? The Lord has provided us with weapons that are mighty through God to the pulling down of these strongholds of the enemy, and by means of which every thought shall be brought into captivity to the obedience of Christ. The blood of Jesus Christ and His mighty name are an antidote to all the subtle seeds of unbelief that Satan would sow in your minds.

In the first chapter of Acts, we see that Jesus gave commandment to the disciples that they should wait for the promise of the Father, and He told them that not many days hence they would be baptized with the Holy Ghost. Luke tells us that he had written his former treatise concerning all that Jesus began both to do and teach. The ministry of Christ did not end at the cross, but the Acts and the epistles give us accounts of what He continued to do and teach through those whom

He indwelt. And our blessed Lord Jesus is still alive, and continues His ministry through those who are filled with His Spirit. He is still healing the broken-hearted and delivering the captives through those on whom He places His Spirit.

I was traveling one day in a railway train in Sweden. At one station there boarded the train an old lady with her daughter. The old lady's expression was so troubled that I enquired what was the matter with her. I heard that she was going to the hospital to have her leg taken off. She began to weep as she told that the doctors had said there was no hope for her except through having her leg amputated. She was seventy years old. I said to my interpreter, "Tell her that Jesus can heal her." The instant this was said to her, it was as though a veil was taken off her face, it became so light. We stopped at another station and the carriage filled tip with people. There was a rush of men to board that train and the devil said, "You're done." But I knew I had the best proposition, for hard things are always opportunities to get to the Lord more glory when He manifests His power. Every trial is a blessing. There have been times when I have been pressed through circumstances and it seemed as if a dozen road engines were going over me, but I have found that the hardest things are just lifting places into the grace of God. We have such a lovely Jesus. He always proves Himself to be such a mighty Deliverer. He never fails to plan the best things for us.

The train began moving and I crouched down, and in the name of Jesus commanded the disease to leave. The old lady cried, "I'm healed. I know I'm healed." She stamped her leg and said, "I'm going to prove it." So when we stopped at another station she marched up and down, and shouted, "I'm not going to the hospital." Once again our wonderful Jesus had proven Himself a Healer of the broken-hearted, a Deliverer of one that was bound.

At one time I was so bound that no human power could help me. My wife was looking for me to pass away. There was no help. At that time I had just had a faint glimpse of Jesus as the Healer. For six months I had been suffering from appendicitis, occasionally getting temporary relief. I went to the mission of which I was pastor, but I was brought to the floor in awful agony, and they brought me home to my bed. All night I was praying, pleading for deliverance, but none came. My wife was sure it was my home call and sent for a physician. He said that there was no possible chance for me-my body was too weak. Having had the appendicitis for six months, my whole system was drained, and, because of that, he thought that it was too late for an operation. He left my wife in a state of broken-heartedness.

After he left, there came to our door a young man and an old lady. I knew that she was a woman of real prayer. They came upstairs to my room. This young man jumped on the bed and commanded the evil spirit to come out of me. He shouted, "Come out, you devil; I command you to come out in the name of Jesus!" There was no chance for an argument, or for me to tell him that I would never believe that there was a devil inside of me. The thing had to go in the name of Jesus, and it went, and I was instantly healed.

I arose and dressed and went downstairs. I was still in the plumbing business, and I asked my wife, "Is there any work in? I am all right now, and I am going to work." I found there was a certain job to be done and I picked up my tools and went off to do it. Just after I left, the doctor came in, put his plug hat down in the hall, and walked up to the bedroom. But the invalid was not there. "Where is Mr. Wigglesworth?" he asked. "Oh, doctor, he's gone out to work," said my wife. "You'll never see him alive again," said the doctor; "they'll bring him back a corpse."

Well, I'm the corpse.

Since that time, in many parts of the world, the Lord has given me the privilege of praying for people with appendicitis; and I have seen a great many people up and dressed within a quarter of an hour from the time I prayed for them. We have a living Christ who is willing to meet people on every line.

A number of years ago I met Brother D. W. Kerr and he gave me a letter of introduction to a brother in Zion City named Cook. I took his letter to Brother Cook, and he said, "God has sent you here." He gave me the addresses of six people and asked me to go and pray for them and meet him again at 12 o'clock. I got back at about 12:30 and he told me about a young man who was to be married the following Monday. His sweetheart was in Zion City dying of appendicitis. I went to the house and found that the physician had just been there and had pronounced that there was no hope. The mother was nearly distracted and was pulling her hair, and saying, "Is there no deliverance!" I said to her, "Woman, believe God and your daughter will be healed and be up and dressed in fifteen minutes." But the mother went on screaming.

They took me into the bedroom, and I prayed for the girl and commanded the evil spirit to depart in the name of Jesus. She cried, "I am healed." I said to her, "Do you want me to believe that you are healed? If you are healed, get up." She said, "You get out of the room, and I'll get up." In less than ten minutes the doctor came in. He wanted to know what had happened. She said, "A man came in and prayed for me, and I'm healed." The doctor pressed his finger right in the place that had been so sore, and the girl neither moaned nor cried. He said, "This is God." It made no difference whether he acknowledged it or not, I knew that God had worked. Our God is real in saving and healing power today. Our Jesus is just the same, yesterday, and today, and forever. He saves and heals today just as of old, and He wants to be your Saviour and your Healer.

Oh, if you would only believe God! What would happen? The greatest things. Some have never tasted the grace of God, have never had the peace of God. Unbelief robs them of these blessings. It is possible to hear and yet not conceive the truth. It is possible to read the Word and not share in the life it brings. It is necessary for us to have the Holy Ghost to unfold the Word and bring to us the life that is Christ. We can never fully understand the wonders of this redemption until we are full of the Holy Ghost.

I was once at an afternoon meeting. The Lord had been graciously with us and many had been healed by the power of God. Most of the people had gone home and I was left alone, when I saw a young man who was evidently hanging back to have a word. I asked, "What do you want?" He said, "I wonder if I could ask you to pray for me." I said, "What's the trouble?" He said, "Can't you smell?" The young fellow had gone into sin and was suffering the consequences. He said, "I have been turned out of two hospitals. I am broken out all over. I have abscesses all over me." And I could see that he had a bad breaking out at the nose. He said, "I heard you preach, and could not understand about this healing business, and was wondering if there was any hope for me."

I said to him, "Do you know Jesus?" He did not know the first thing about salvation, but I said to him, "Stand still." I placed my hands on his head and then on his loins and cursed that terrible disease in the name of Jesus. He cried out, "I know I'm healed. I can feel a warmth and a glow all over me." I said, "Who did it?" He said, "Your prayers." I said, "No, it was Jesus!" He said, "Was it He? Oh, Jesus! Jesus! Jesus, save me." And that young man went away healed and saved. Oh, what a merciful God we have! What a wonderful Jesus is ours!

Are you oppressed? Cry out to God. It is always good for people to cry out. You may have to cry out. The Holy Ghost and the Word of God will bring to light every hidden, unclean thing that must be revealed. There is always a place of deliverance when you let God search out that which is spoiling and marring your life. That evil spirit that was in the man in the synagogue cried out, "Let us alone!" It was a singular thing that the evil spirit had never cried out like that until Jesus walked into the place where he was. Jesus rebuked the thing, saying, "Hold thy peace and come out of him," and the man was delivered. He is just the same Jesus, exposing the powers of evil, delivering the captives and letting the oppressed go free, purifying them and cleansing their hearts. Those evil spirits that inhabited the man who had the legion did not want to be sent to the pit to be tormented before their time, and so they cried out to be sent into the swine. Hell is such an awful place that even the demons hate the thought of going there. How much more should men seek to be saved from the pit?

God is compassionate and says, "Seek ye the Lord while He may be found." And He has further stated, "Whosoever shall call on the name of the Lord shall be saved." Seek Him now, call on His name right now, and there is forgiveness, healing, redemption, deliverance, and everything you need for you right here and now, and that which will satisfy you throughout eternity.

# CHAPTER 3

## The Power of the Name

---

### SCRIPTURE READING- Acts 3:1-16

All things are possible through the name of Jesus. God hath highly exalted Him, and given Him the name which is above every name, that at the name of Jesus every knee should bow. There is power to overcome everything in the world through the name of Jesus. I am looking forward to a wonderful union through the name of Jesus. There is none other name under heaven given among men, whereby we must be saved.

I want to instill into you a sense of the power, the virtue and the glory of that name. Six people went into the house of a sick man to pray for him. He was an Episcopalian vicar, and lay in his bed utterly helpless, without even strength to help himself. He had read a little tract about healing and had heard about people praying for the sick, and sent for these friends, who, he thought, could pray the prayer of faith. He was anointed according to James 5:14, but, because he had no immediate manifestation of healing, he wept bitterly. The six people walked out of the room, somewhat crestfallen to see the man lying there in an unchanged condition.

When they were outside, one of the six said, "There is one thing we might have done. I wish you would all go back with me and try it." They went back and all got together in a group. This brother said, "Let us whisper the name of Jesus." At first when they whispered this worthy name nothing seemed to happen. But as they continued to whisper, "Jesus! Jesus! Jesus!" the power began to fall. As they saw that God was beginning to work, their faith and joy increased; and they whispered the name louder and louder. As they did so the man arose from his bed and dressed himself. The secret was just thus, those six people had gotten their eyes off the sick man, and they were just taken up with the Lord Jesus Himself, and their faith grasped the power that there is in His name. O, if people would only appreciate the power that there is in this name, there is no telling what would happen.

I know that through His name and through the power of His name we have access to God. The very face of Jesus fills the whole place with glory. All over the world there are people magnifying that name, and O, what a joy it is for me to utter it.

One day I went up into the mountain to pray. I had a wonderful day. It was one of the high mountains of Wales. I heard of one man going up this mountain to pray, and the Spirit of the Lord met him so wonderfully that his face shone like that of an angel when he returned. Every one in the village was talking about it. As I went up to this mountain and spent the day in the presence of the Lord, His wonderful power seemed to envelop and saturate and fill me.

Two years before this time there had come to our house two lads from Wales. They were just ordinary lads, but they became very zealous for God. They came to our mission and saw some of the works of God. They said to me, "We would not be surprised if the Lord brings you down to Wales to raise our Lazarus." They explained that the leader of their assembly was a man who had spent his days working in a tin mine and his nights preaching, and the result was that he had collapsed, gone into consumption, and for four years he had been a helpless invalid, having to be fed with a spoon.

While I was up on that mountain top I was reminded of the

transfiguration scene, and I felt that the Lord's only purpose in taking us into the glory was to fit us for greater usefulness in the valley.

Tongues and Interpretation; "The living God has chosen us for His divine inheritance, and He it is who is preparing us for our ministry, that it may be of God and not of man."

As I was on the mountain top that day, the Lord said to me, "I want you to go and raise Lazarus." I told the brother who accompanied me of this, and when we got down to the valley, I wrote a postcard: " When I was up on the mountain praying today, God told me that I was to go and raise Lazarus." I addressed the postcard to the man in the place whose name had been given to me by the two lads. When we arrived at the place we went to the man to whom I had addressed the card. He looked at me and said, "Did you send this?" I said, "Yes." He said, "Do you think we believe in this? Here, take it." And he threw it at me.

The man called a servant and said, "Take this man and show him Lazarus." Then he said to me, "The moment you see him you will be ready to go home. Nothing will hold you." Everything he said was true from the natural viewpoint. The man was helpless. He was nothing but a mass of bones with skin stretched over them. There was no life to be seen. Everything in him spoke of decay.

I said to him, "Will you shout? You remember that at Jericho the people shouted while the walls were still up. God has like victory for you if you will only believe." But I could not get him to believe. There was not an atom of faith there. He had made up his mind not to have anything.

It is a blessed thing to learn that God's word can never fail. Never hearken to human plans. God can work mightily when you persist in believing Him in spite of discouragements from the human standpoint. When I got back to the man to whom I had sent the post-card, he asked, "Are you ready to go now?"

I am not moved by what I see. I am moved only by what I believe. I know this-no man looks at appearances if he believes. No man considers how he feels if he believes. The man who believes God has it. Every man who comes into the Pentecostal condition can laugh at all things and believe God. There is something in the Pentecostal work that is different from anything else in the world. Somehow, in Pentecost, you know that God is a reality. Wherever the Holy Ghost has right of way, the gifts of the Spirit will be in manifestation; and where these gifts are never in manifestation, I question whether He is present. Pentecostal people are spoiled for anything else than Pentecostal meetings. We want none of the entertainments that the churches are offering. When God comes in He entertains us Himself. Entertained by the King of kings and Lord of lords! O, it is wonderful.

There were difficult conditions in that Welsh village, and it seemed impossible to get the people to believe. "Ready to go home?" I was asked. But a man and a woman there asked us to come and stay with them. I said, "I want to know how many of you people can pray." No one wanted to pray. I asked if I could get seven people to pray with me for the poor man's deliverance. I said to the two people who were going to entertain us, "I will count on you two, and there is my friend and myself, and we need three others." I told the people that I trusted that some of them would awaken to their privilege and come in the morning and join us in prayer for the raising of Lazarus. It will never do to give way to human opinions. If God says a thing, you are to believe it.

I told the people that I would not eat anything that night. When I got to bed it seemed as if the devil tried to place on me everything that he had placed on that poor man in the bed. When I awoke I had a cough and all the weakness of a tubercular patient. I rolled out of bed on to the floor and cried out to God to deliver me from the power of the devil. I shouted loud enough to wake everybody in the house, but nobody was disturbed. God gave victory, and I got back into bed again as free as ever I was in my life. At 5 o'clock the Lord awakened me and said to me, "Don't break bread until you break it round My table." At 6 o'clock He gave me these words, "And I will raise him up." I put my elbow into the fellow who was sleeping with me. He said, "Ugh!" I put my elbow into him again and said, "Do you hear? The Lord says that He will raise him up."

At 8 o'clock they said to me, "Have a little refreshment." But I have found prayer and fasting the greatest joy, and you will always find it so when you are led by God. When we went to the house where Lazarus lived there were eight of us altogether. No one can prove to me that God does not always answer prayer. He always does more than that. He always gives the exceedingly abundant above all we ask or think.

I shall never forget how the power of God fell on us as we went into that sick man's room. O, it was lovely! As we circled round the bed I got one brother to hold one of the sick man's hands and I held the other; and we each held the hand of the person next to us. I said, "We are not going to pray, we are just going to use the name of Jesus." We all knelt down and whispered that one word, "Jesus! Jesus! Jesus!" The power of God fell and then it lifted. Five times the power of God fell and then it remained. But the person who was in the bed was unmoved. Two years previous someone had come along and had tried to raise him up, and the devil had used his lack of success as a means of discouraging Lazarus. I said, "I don't care what the devil says; if God says he will raise you up it must be so. Forget everything else except what God says about Jesus."

The sixth time the power fell and the sick man's lips began moving and the tears began to fall. I said to him, "The power of God is here; it is yours to accept it." He said, "I have been bitter in my heart, and I know I have grieved the Spirit of God. Here I am helpless. I cannot lift my hands, nor even lift a spoon to my mouth." I said, "Repent, and God will hear you." He repented and cried out, "O God, let this be to Thy glory." As he said this the virtue of the Lord went right through him.

I have asked the Lord to never let me tell this story except as it was, for I realize that God cannot bless exaggerations. As we again said, "Jesus! Jesus! Jesus!" the bed shook, and the man shook. I said to the people that were with me, "You can all go down stairs right away. This is all God. I'm not going to assist him." I sat and watched that man get up and dress himself. We sang the doxology as he walked down the steps. I said to him, "Now tell what has happened."

It was soon noised abroad that Lazarus had been raised up and the people came from Llanelly and all the district round to see him and hear his testimony. And God brought salvation to many. This man told right out in the open air what God had done, and as a result many were convicted and converted. All this came through the name of Jesus, through faith in His name, yea, the faith that is by Him gave this sick man perfect soundness in the presence of them all.

Peter and John were helpless, were illiterate, they had no college education. They had been with Jesus. To them had come a wonderful revelation of the power of the name of Jesus. They had handed out the bread and fish after Jesus had multiplied them. They had sat at the table with Him and John had often gazed into His face. Peter had often to be rebuked, but Jesus manifested His love to Peter through it all. Yea, He loved Peter, the wayward one. O, He's a wonderful lover! I have been wayward, I have been stubborn, I had an unmanageable temper at one time, but how patient He has been. I am here to tell you that there is power in Jesus and in His wondrous name to transform anyone, to heal anyone.

If you will see Him as God's Lamb, as God's beloved Son who had laid upon Him the iniquity of us all, if only you will see that Jesus paid the whole price for our redemption that we might be free, you can enter into your purchased inheritance of salvation, of life and of power.

Poor Peter, and poor John! They had no money! But they had faith, they had the power of the Holy Ghost, they had God. You can have God even though you have nothing else. Even though you have lost your character you can have God. I have seen the worst men saved by the power of God.

I was one day preaching about the name of Jesus and there was a man leaning against a lamp-post, listening. It took a lamp-post to enable him to keep on his feet. We had finished our open-air meeting, and the man was still leaning against the post. I asked him, "Are you sick?" He showed me his hand and I saw beneath his coat, he had a silver handled dagger. He told me that he was on his way to kill his unfaithful wife, but that he had heard me speaking about the power of the name of Jesus and could not get away. He said that he felt just helpless. I said, "Get you down." And there on the square, with people passing up and down, he got saved.

I took him to my home and put on him a new suit. I saw that there was something in that man that God could use. He said to me the next morning, "God has revealed Jesus to me; I see that all has been laid upon Jesus." I lent him some money, and he soon got together a wonderful little home. His faithless wife was living with another man, but he invited her back to the home that he had prepared for her. She came: and, where enmity and hatred had been before, the whole situation was transformed by love. God made that man a minister wherever he went. There is power in the name of Jesus everywhere. God can save to the uttermost.

There comes before me a meeting we had in Stockholm that I shall ever bear in mind. There was a home for incurables there and one of the inmates was brought to the meeting. He had palsy and was shaking all over. He stood up before 3,000 people and came to the platform, supported by two others. The power of God fell on him as I anointed him in the name of Jesus. The moment I touched him he dropped his crutch and began to walk in the name of Jesus. He walked down the steps and round that great building in view of all the people. There is nothing that our God cannot do. He will do everything if you will dare to believe.

Someone said to me, "Will you go to this Home for Incurables?" They took me there on my rest day. They brought out the sick people into a great corridor and in one hour the Lord set about twenty of them free.

The name of Jesus is so marvelous. Peter and John had no conception of all that was in that name; neither had the man, lame from his mother's womb, who was laid daily at the gate; but they had faith to say, "In the name of Jesus Christ of Nazareth, rise up and walk." And as Peter took him by the right hand, and lifted him up, immediately his feet and anklebones received strength, and lie went into the temple with them, walking and leaping and praising God. God wants you to see more of this sort of thing done. How can it be done? Through His name, through faith in His name, through faith which is by Him.

# CHAPTER 4

# Wilt Thou Be Made Whole?

---

READ JOHN 5:1-24

I believe the word of God is so powerful that it can transform any and every life. There is power in God's word to make that which does not appear to appear. There is executive power in the word that proceeds from His lips. The psalmist tells us, "He sent His word and healed them" (Ps. 107:20); and do you think that word has diminished in its power? I tell you nay, but God's word can bring things to pass today as of old.

The psalmist said, "Before I was afflicted I went astray; but now have I kept Thy word." And again, "It is good for me that I have been afflicted; that I might learn Thy statutes" (Ps. 119:67, 71). And if our afflictions will bring us to the place where we see that we cannot live by bread alone, but must partake of every word that proceedeth out of the mouth of God, they will have served a blessed purpose. But I want you to realize that there is a life of purity, a life made clean through the word He has spoken, in which, through faith, you can glorify God with a body that is free from sickness, as well as with a spirit set free

from the bondage of Satan.
Here they lay, a great multitude of impotent folk, of blind, halt, withered, around the pool, waiting for the moving of the water. Did Jesus heal everybody? He left many around that pool unhealed. There were doubtless many who had their eyes on the pool and who had no eyes for Jesus. There are many today who have their confidence all the time in things seen. If they would only get their eyes on God instead of on natural things, how quickly they would be helped.

The question arises, 'Is salvation and healing for all?' It is for all who will press right in and get their portion. You remember the case of that Syrophenician woman who wanted the devil cast out of her daughter. Jesus said to her, "Let the children first be filled: for it is not meet to take the children's bread, and to cast it unto the dogs." Note, healing and deliverance are here spoken of by the Master as "the children's bread"; So, if you are a child of God, you can surely press in for your portion.

The Syrophenician woman (Mark 7:24-30) purposed to get from the Lord what she was after, and she said, "Yes, Lord: yet the dogs under the table eat of the children's crumbs." Jesus was stirred as He saw the faith of this woman, and He told her, "For this saying go thy way; the devil is gone out of thy daughter." Today there are many children of God refusing their blood-purchased portion of health in Christ and are throwing it away, while sinners are pressing through and picking it up frown under the table, as it were, and are finding the cure not only for their bodies, but for their spirits and souls as well. The Syrophenician woman went home and found that the devil had indeed gone out of her daughter. Today there is bread, there is life, there is health for every child of God through His all-powerful Word.

The Word can drive every disease away from your body. It is your portion in Christ, Him who is our bread, our life, our health, our all in all. Arid though you may be deep in sin, you can come to Him in repentance, and He will forgive and cleanse and heal you. His words are spirit and life to those who will receive them. There is a promise in the last verse in Joel, "I will cleanse their blood that I have not cleansed." This is as much as to say He will provide new life within. The life of Jesus Christ, God's Son, can so purify men's hearts and minds that they become entirely transformed, spirit, soul and body.

There they are round the pool; and this man had been there a long time. His infirmity was of thirty-eight years standing. Now and again an opportunity would come, as the angel stirred the waters, but his heart would be made sick as he saw another step in and be healed before him. But one day Jesus was passing that way, and seeing him lying there in that sad condition, enquired, "Wilt thou be made whole?" Jesus said it, and His word is from everlasting to everlasting. This is His word to you, poor, tried and tested one today. You may say, like this poor impotent man, "I have missed every opportunity up till now." Never mind about that-Wilt thou be made whole?

I visited a woman who had been suffering for many years. She was all twisted up with rheumatism and had been two years in bed. I said to her, "What makes you lie here?" She said, "I've come to the conclusion that I have a thorn in the flesh." I said, "To what wonderful degree of righteousness have you attained that you have to have a thorn in the flesh? Have you had such an abundance of divine revelations that there is danger of your being exalted above measure?" She said, "I believe it is the Lord who is causing me to suffer." I said, "You believe it is the Lord's will for you to suffer, and you are trying to get out of it as quickly as you can. There are doctor's bottles all over the place. Get out of your hiding place and confess that you are a sinner. If you'll get rid of your self-righteousness, God will do something for you. Drop the idea that you are so holy that God has got to afflict you. Sin is the cause of your sickness and not righteousness. Disease is not caused by righteousness, but by sin."

There is healing through the blood of Christ and deliverance for every captive. God never intended His children to live in misery because of some affliction that comes directly from the devil. A perfect atonement was made at Calvary. I believe that Jesus bore my sins, and I am free from them all. I am justified from all things if I dare believe. He Himself took our infirmities and bare our sicknesses; and if I dare believe, I can be healed.

See this poor, helpless man at the pool. "Wilt thou be made whole?" But there is a difficulty in the way. The man has one eye on the pool and one on Jesus. There are many people getting cross-eyed this way these days; they have one eye on the doctor and one on Jesus. If you will only look to Christ and put both your eyes on Him you can be made every whit whole, spirit, soul and body. It is the word of the living God that they that believe should be justified, made free from all things. And whom the Son sets free is free indeed.

You say, "Oh, if I only could believe!" He understands. Jesus knew he had been a long time in that case. He is full of compassion. He knows that kidney trouble, He knows those corns, He knows that neuralgia. There is nothing He does not know. He only wants a chance to show Himself merciful and gracious to you. But He wants to encourage you to believe Him. If thou canst only believe, thou canst be saved and healed. Dare to believe that Jesus was wounded for your transgressions, was bruised for your iniquities, was chastised that you might have peace, and that by His stripes there is healing for you right here and now. You have failed because you have not believed Him. Cry out to Him even now, "Lord, I believe, help Thou mine unbelief."

I was in Long Beach, California, one day, and with a friend, was passing a hotel. He told me of a doctor there who had a diseased leg; that he had been suffering from it for six years, and could not get out. We went up to his room and found four doctors there. I said, "Well, doctor, I see you have plenty on, I'll call again another day." I was passing at another time, and the Spirit said, "Go join thyself to him." Poor doctor! He surely was in a bad condition. He said, "I have been like this for six years, and nothing human can help me." I said, "You need God Almighty." People are trying to patch up their lives; but you cannot do anything without God. I talked to him for awhile about the Lord, and then prayed for him. I cried, "Come out of him, in the name of Jesus." The doctor cried, "It's all gone!"

Oh, if we only knew Jesus! One touch of His mightiness meets the need of every crooked thing. The trouble is to get people to believe Him. The simplicity of this salvation is wonderful. One touch of living faith in Him is all that is required, and wholeness is your portion.

I was in Long Beach about six weeks later, and the sick were coming for prayer. Among those filling up the aisle was the doctor. I said, "What is the trouble?" He said, "Diabetes, but it will be all right tonight. I know it will be all right." There is no such thing as the Lord not meeting your need. There are no "if's" or "may's"; His promises are all "shall's." All things are possible to him that believeth. Oh, the name of Jesus! There is power in that name to meet every condition of human need.

At that meeting there was an old man helping his son to the altar. He said, "He has fits-many every day." Then there was a woman with a cancer. Oh, what sin has done! We read that, when God brought forth His people from Egypt, "there was not one feeble person among their tribes" (Ps. 105:37). No disease! All healed by the power of God! I believe that God wants a people like that today.

I prayed for the sister who had the cancer and she said, "I know I'm free and that God has delivered me." Then they brought the boy with the fits, and I commanded the evil spirits to leave, in the name of Jesus. Then I prayed for the doctor. At the next night's meeting the house was full. I called out, "Now, doctor, what about the diabetes?" He said, "It has gone." Then I said to the old man, "What about your son?" He said, "He hasn't had any fits since." We have a God who answers prayer.

Jesus meant this man at the pool to be a testimony forever. When he had both eyes on Jesus, He said to him, "Do the impossible thing. Rise, take up thy bed, and walk." Jesus called on the man with the withered hand to do the impossible-to stretch forth his hand. The man did the impossible thing-he stretched out his hand, and it was made every whit whole. And so with this impotent man-he began to rise, and he found the power of God moving within. He wrapped up his bed and began to walk off. It was the Sabbath day, and there were some of those folks around who think much more of a day than they do of the Lord; and they began to make a fuss. When the power of God is in manifestation, a protest will always come from some hypocrites. Jesus knew all about what the man was going through, and met him again; and this time He said to him, "Behold, thou art made whole: sin no more, lest a worse thing come unto thee."

There is a close relationship between sin and sickness. How many know that their sickness is a direct result of sin? I hope that no one will come to be prayed for who is living in sin. But if you will obey

God and repent of your sin and quit it, God will meet you, and neither your sickness nor your sin will remain. "The prayer of faith shall save the sick, and the Lord shall raise him up; and if he have committed sins, they shall be forgiven him."

Faith is just the open door through which the Lord comes. Do not say, "I was healed by faith." Faith does not save. God saves through that open door. Healing comes the same way. You believe, and the virtue of Christ comes. Healing is for the glory of God. I am here because God healed me when I was dying; and I have been all round the world preaching this full redemption, doing all I can to bring glory to the wonderful name of Jesus, through whom I was healed.

"Sin no more, lest a worse thing come upon thee." The Lord told us in one place about an evil spirit going out from a man. The house that he left got all swept arid garnished, but it received no new occupant. And that evil spirit, with seven other spirits more wicked than himself, went back to that unoccupied house, and the last stage of the man was worse than the first. The Lord does not heal you to go to a baseball game or to a race meet. He heals you for His glory and that from henceforth your life shall glorify Him. But this man remained stationary. He did not magnify God. He did not seek to be filled with the Spirit. And his last state became worse than the first.

The Lord would so cleanse the motive and desires of our hearts that we will seek but one thing only, and that is, His glory. I went to a certain place one day and the Lord said, "This is for My glory." A young man had been sick for along time confined to his bed in an utterly hopeless condition. He was fed only with a spoon, and was never dressed. The weather was damp, and so I said to the people of the house, "I wish you would put the young man's clothes by the fire to air." At first they would not take any notice of my request, but because I was persistent, they at last got out his clothes, and, when they were aired, I took them into his room.

The Lord said to me, "You will have nothing to do with this;" and I just lay out prostrate on the floor. The Lord showed me that He was going to shake the place with His glory. The very bed shook. I laid my hands on the young man in the name of Jesus, and the power fell in such a way that I fell with my face to the floor. In about a quarter of an hour the young man got up and walked up and down praising God. He dressed himself and then went out to the room where his father and mother were. He said, "God has healed me." Both the father and mother fell prostrate to the floor as the power of God surged through that room. There was a woman in that house who had been in an asylum for lunacy, and her condition was so bad that they were about to take her back. But the power of God healed her, too. The power of God is just the same today as of old. Men need to be taken back to the old paths, to the old-time faith, to believe God's Word and every "Thus saith the Lord" therein. The Spirit of the Lord is moving in these days. God is coming forth. If you want to be in the rising tide, you must accept all God has said.

"Wilt thou be made whole?" It is Jesus who asks it. Give Him your answer. He will hear and He will answer.

# CHAPTER 5

## I am The Lord That Healeth Thee

---

"IS ANY SICK AMONG YOU? let him call for the elders of the church; and let them pray over him, anointing him with oil in the name of the Lord: and the prayer of faith shall save the sick, and the Lord shall raise him up; and if he have committed sins, they shall be forgiven him" (James 5 :14, 15) .

We have in this precious word a real basis for the truth of healing. In this scripture God gives very definite instructions to the sick. If you are sick, your part is to call for the elders of the church; it is their part to anoint and pray for you in faith, and then the whole situation rests with the Lord. When you have been anointed and prayed for, you can rest assured that the Lord will raise you up. It is the word of God.

I believe that we all can see that the church cannot play with this business. If any turn away from these clear instructions they are in a place of tremendous danger. Those who refuse to obey, do so to their unspeakable loss.

James tells us in connection with this, "if any of you do err from the truth, and one convert him, let him know, that he which converteth the sinner from the error of his ways shall save a soul from death."

Many turn away from the Lord, as did King Asa, who sought the physicians in his sickness and consequently died; and I take it that this passage means that if one induces another to turn back to the Lord, he will save such from death and God will forgive a multitude of sins that they have committed. This scripture can also have a large application on the line of salvation. If you turn away from any part of God's truth, the enemy will certainly get an advantage over you.

Does the Lord meet those who look to Him for healing and obey the instructions set forth in James? Most assuredly. Let me tell you a story to show how He will undertake for the most extreme case.

One day I had been visiting the sick, and was with a friend of mine, an architect, when I saw a young man from his office coming down the road in a car, and holding in his hand a telegram. It contained a very urgent request that we go immediately to pray for a man who was dying. We went off in an auto as fast as possible and in about an hour and a half reached a large house in the country where the man who was dying resided. There were two staircases in that house, and it was extremely convenient, for the doctors could go up and down one, and my friend and I could go up and down the other, and so we had no occasion to meet.

I found on arrival that it was a case of this sort. The man's body had been broken, he was ruptured, and his bowels had been punctured in two places. The discharge from the bowels had formed abscesses, and blood poisoning had set in. The man's face had turned green. Two doctors were in attendance, but they saw that the case was beyond their power. They had telegraphed to London for a great specialist, and, when we arrived, they were at the railway station awaiting his arrival.

The man was very near death and could not speak. I said to his wife, "If you desire, we will anoint and pray for him." She said, "That is why I sent for you." I anointed him in the name of the Lord and asked the Lord to raise him up. Apparently there was no change. (God often hides what He does. From day to day we find that God is doing wonderful things, and we receive reports of healings that have taken place that we heard nothing about at the time of our meetings. Only last night a woman came into the meeting suffering terribly. Her whole arm was filled with poison, and her blood was so poisoned that it was certain to bring her to her death. We rebuked the thing, and she was here this morning and told us that she was without pain and had slept all night, a thing she had not done for two months. To God be all the praise. You will find He will do this kind of thing all along.)

As soon as we anointed and prayed for this brother we went down the back staircase and the three doctors came up the front staircase. As we arrived downstairs, I said to my friend who had come with me, "Friend let me have hold of your hands." We held each other's hands, and I said to him, "Look into my face and let us agree together, according to Matthew 18:19, that this man shall be brought out of this death." We laid the whole matter before God, and said, "Father, we believe."

Then the conflict began. The wife came down to us and said, "The doctors have got all their instruments out and they are about to operate." I cried, "What? Look here, he's your husband, and I tell you this, if those men operate on him, he will die. Go back and tell them you cannot allow it." She went back to the doctors and said, "Give me ten minutes." They said, "We can't afford to, the man is dying and it is your husband's only chance." She said, "I want ten minutes, and you don't touch his body until I have had them."

They went downstairs by one staircase and we went up by the other. I said to the woman, "This man is your husband, and he cannot speak for himself. It is now the time for you to put your whole trust in God and prove Him wholly true. You can save him from a thousand doctors. You must stand with God and for God in this critical hour." After that, we came down and the doctors went up. The wife faced those three doctors and said, "You shan't touch this man's body. He is my husband. I am sure that if you operate on him he will die, but he will live if you don't touch him."

Suddenly the man in the bed spoke. "God has done it," he said. They rolled back the bed clothes and the doctors examined him, and the abscesses were cut clear away. The nurse cleaned the place where they had been. The doctors could see the bowels still open and they said to the wife, "We know that you have great faith, and we can see that a miracle has taken place. But you must let us unite these broken parts and put in silver tubes, and we know that your husband will be all right after that, and it need not interfere with your faith at all." She said to them, "God has done the first thing and He can do the rest. No man shall touch him now." And God healed the whole thing. And that man is well and strong today. I can give his name and address to any who want it.

Do you ask by what power this was done? I would answer in the words of Peter, "His name, through faith in His name, made this man strong." The anointing was done in the name of the Lord. And it is written, "The LORD shall raise him up." And He provides the double cure; even if sin has been the cause of the sickness, His Word declares, "If he have committed sins, they shall be forgiven,"

You ask, "What is faith?" Faith is the principle of the Word of God. The Holy Spirit, who inspired the Word, is called the Spirit of Truth, and, as we receive with meekness the engrafted Word, faith springs in our heart-faith in the sacrifice of Calvary: faith in the shed blood of Jesus; faith in the fact that He took our weakness upon Himself, has borne our sicknesses and carried our pains, and that He is our life today.

God has chosen us to help one another. We dare not be independent. He brings us to a place where we submit ourselves to one another. If we refuse to do this, we get away from the Word of God and out of the place of faith. I have been in this place once and I trust I shall never be there again. I went one time to a meeting. I was very, very sick, and I got worse and worse. I knew the perfect will of God was for me to humble myself and ask the elders to pray for me. I put it off and the meeting finished. I went home without being anointed and prayed with, and everyone in the house caught the thing I was suffering with.

My boys did not know anything else but to trust the Lord as the family Physician, and my youngest boy, George, cried out from the attic, "Dadda, come." I cried, "I cannot come. The whole thing is from me. I shall have to repent and ask the Lord to forgive me." I made up my mind to humble myself before the whole church. Then I rushed to the attic and laid my hands on my boy in the name of Jesus. I placed my hands on his head and the pain left and went lower down;

he cried again, "Put your hands still lower." At last the pain went right down to the feet and as I placed my hand on the feet he was completely delivered. Some evil power had evidently gotten hold and as I laid my hands on the different parts of the body it left. (We have to see the difference between anointing the sick and casting out demons.) God will always be gracious when we humble ourselves before Him and come to a place of brokenness of spirit.

I was at a place one time ministering to a sick woman, and she said, "I'm very sick. I become all right for an hour, and then I have another attack." I saw that it was an evil power that was attacking her, and I learned something in that hour that I had never learned before. As I moved my hand down her body in the name of the Lord that evil power seemed to move just ahead of my hands and as I moved them down further and further the evil power went right out of her body and never returned.

I was in Havre in France and the power of God was being mightily manifested. A Greek named Felix attended the meeting and became very zealous for God. He was very anxious to get all the Catholics he could to the meeting in order that they should see that God was graciously visiting France. He found a certain bed-ridden woman who was fixed in a certain position and could not move, and he told her about the Lord healing at the meetings and that he would get me to come if she wished. She said, "My husband is a Catholic and he would never allow anyone who was not a Catholic to see me."

She asked her husband to allow me to come and told him what Felix had told her about the power of God working in our midst. He said, "I will have no Protestant enter my house." She said, "You know the doctors cannot help me, and the priests cannot help, won't you let this man of God pray for me?" He finally consented and I went to the house. The simplicity of this woman and her child-like faith were beautiful to see.

I showed her my oil bottle and said to her, "Here is oil. It is a symbol of the Holy Ghost. When that comes upon you, the Holy Ghost will begin to work, and the Lord will raise you up." And God did something the moment the oil fell upon her. I looked toward the window and I saw Jesus. (I have seen Him often. There is no painting that is a bit like Him: no artist can ever depict the beauty of my lovely Lord.) The woman felt the power of God in her body and cried, "I'm free, my hands are free, my shoulders are free, and oh, I see Jesus! I'm free! I'm free!"

The vision vanished and the woman sat up in bed. Her legs were still bound, and I said to her, "I'll put my hands over your legs and you will be free entirely." And as I put my hands on those legs covered with bed clothes, I looked and saw the Lord again. She saw Him too and cried, "He's there again. I'm free! I'm free!" She rose from her bed and walked round the room praising God, and we were all in tears as we saw His wonderful works. The Lord shall raise them up when conditions are met.

When I was a young man I always loved the fellowship of old men, and was always careful to hear what they had to say. I had a friend, an old Baptist minister who was a wonderful preacher. I spent much of my time with him. One day he came to me and said, "My wife is dying." I said, "Brother Clark, why don't you believe God? God can raise her up if you will only believe Him." He asked me to come to his house, and I looked for some one to go with me.

I went to a certain rich man who was very zealous for God, and spent much money in opening up rescue missions, and I asked him to go with me. He said, "Never you mind me. You go yourself, but I don't take to this kind of business." Then I thought of a man who could pray by the hour. When he was on his knees he could go round the world three times and come out at the same place. I asked him to go with me and said to him, "You'll have a real chance this time. Keep at it, and quit when you're through." (Some go on after they are through.)

Brother Nichols, for that was his name, went with me and started praying. He asked the Lord to comfort the husband in his great bereavement and prayed for the orphans and a lot more on this line. I cried, "O my God, stop this man." But there was no stopping him and he went on praying and there was not a particle of faith in anything he uttered. He did stop at last, and I said, "Brother Clark, it's now your turn to pray. He started, "Lord, answer the prayer of my brother and comfort me in this great bereavement and sorrow. Prepare me to face this great trial." I cried out, "My God, stop this man." The whole atmosphere was being charged with unbelief.

I had a glass bottle full of oil and I went up t0 the woman and poured the whole lot on her in the name of Jesus. Suddenly Jesus appeared, standing at the foot of the bed. He smiled and vanished. The woman stood up, perfectly healed, and she is a strong woman today.

We have a big God. We have a wonderful Jesus. We have a glorious Comforter. God's canopy is over you and will cover you at all times, preserving you from evil. Under His wings shalt thou trust. The Word of God is living and powerful and in its treasures you will find eternal life. If you dare trust this wonderful Lord, this Lord of life, you will find in Him everything you need.

So many are tampering with drugs, quacks, pills and plasters. Clear them all out and believe God. It is sufficient to believe God. You will find that if you dare trust Him, He will never fail. "The prayer of faith shall save the sick, and the LORD shall raise him up." Do you trust Him? He is worthy to be trusted.

I was one time asked to go to Weston-super-mare, a seaside resort in the West of England. I learned from a telegram that a man had lost his reason and had become a raving maniac, and they wanted me to go to pray for him. I arrived at the place, and the wife said to me, "Will you sleep with my husband?" I agreed, and in the middle of the night an evil power laid hold of him. It was awful. I put my hand on his head and his hair was like a lot of sticks. God gave deliverance-a temporary deliverance. At 6 o'clock the next morning, I felt that it was necessary that I should get out of the house for a short time.

The man saw me going and cried out, "If you leave me, there is no hope." But I felt that I had to go. As I went out I saw a woman with a Salvation Army bonnet on and I knew that she was going to their 7 o'clock prayer meeting. I said to the Captain who was in charge of the meeting, when I saw he was about to give out a hymn, "Captain, don't sing. Let's get to prayer." He agreed, and I prayed my heart out, and then I grabbed my hat and rushed out of the hall. They all thought they had a madman in their prayer meeting that morning.

I saw the man I had spent the night with, rushing down toward the sea, without a particle of clothing on, about to drown himself. I cried, “In the name of Jesus, come out of him!” The man fell full length on the ground and that evil power went out of him never to return. His wife came rushing after him, and the husband was restored to her in a perfect mental condition.

There are evil powers, but Jesus is greater than all evil powers. There are tremendous diseases, but Jesus is healer. There is no case too hard for Him. The Lion of Judah shall break every chain. He came to relieve the oppressed and to set the captive free. He came to bring redemption, to make us as perfect as man was before the fall.

People want to know how to be kept by the power of God. Every position of grace into which you are led-forgiveness, healing, deliverance of any kind, will be contested by Satan. He will contend for your body. When you are saved, Satan will come round and say, “See, you are not saved.” The devil is a liar. If he says you are not saved, it is a sure sign that you are.

You will remember the story of the man who was swept and garnished. The evil power had been swept out of him. But the man remained in a stationary position. If the Lord heals you, you dare not remain in a stationary position. The evil spirit came back to that man and found the house swept, and took seven others worse than himself, and the last state of that man was worse than the first. Be sure to get filled with God. Get the Occupier. Be filled with the Spirit.

God has a million ways of undertaking for those who go to Him for help. He has deliverance for every captive. He loves you so much that He even says, “Before they call, I will answer.” Don’t turn Him away.

# CHAPTER 6

# Himself Took Our Infirmities

---

BIBLE READING, Matt. 8:1-17.

Here we have a wonderful word. All the Word is wonderful. This blessed Book brings such life and health and peace, and such an abundance that we should never be poor any more. This Book is my heavenly bank. I find everything I want in it. I want to show you how rich you may be, that in everything you can be enriched in Christ Jesus. He has abundance of grace for you and the gift of righteousness, and through His abundant grace all things are possible. I want to show you that you can be a living branch of the living Vine, Christ Jesus, and that it is your privilege to be right here in this world what He is. John tells us, "As He is, so are we in this world." Not that we are anything in ourselves, but Christ within us is our all in all.

The Lord Jesus is always wanting to show forth His grace and love in order to draw us to Himself. God is willing to do things, to manifest His Word, and let us know in measure the mind of our God in this day and hour. There are many needy ones, many afflicted ones, but I do not think any present are half as bad as this first case that we read of in Matthew 8. This man was a leper. You may be suffering with consumption or cancers or other things, but God will show forth His perfect cleansing, His perfect healing, if you have a living faith in Christ. He is a wonderful Jesus.

This leper must have been told about Jesus. How much is missed because people are not constantly telling what Jesus will do in this our day. Probably someone had come to that leper and said, "Jesus can heal you." And so he was filled with expectation as he saw the Lord coming down the mountain side. Lepers were not allowed to come within reach of people, they were shut out as unclean. And so in the ordinary way it would have been very difficult for him to get near because of the crowd that surrounded Jesus. But as He came down from the mount He met this poor leper. Oh, this terrible disease! There was no help for him humanly speaking, but nothing is too hard for Jesus. The man cried, "Lord, if thou wilt, thou canst make me clean." Was Jesus willing? You will never find Jesus missing an opportunity of doing good. You will find that He is always more willing to work than we are to give Him an opportunity to work. The trouble is we do not come to Him, we do not ask Him for what He is more than willing to give.

And Jesus put forth His hand, and touched him, saying, "I will; be thou clean." And immediately his leprosy was cleansed. I like that. If you are definite with Him you will never go away disappointed. The divine life will flow into you and instantaneously you will be delivered. This Jesus is just the same today, and He says to you, "I will; be thou clean." He has an overflowing cup for thee, a fullness of life. He will meet you in your absolute helplessness. All things are possible if you will only believe. God has a real plan. It is so simple. Just come to Jesus. You will find Him just the same as He was in days of old.

The next case we have in this chapter is that of the centurion coming and beseeching Jesus on behalf of his servant who was sick of the palsy and grievously tormented. This man was so in earnest that he came seeking for Jesus. Notice this, that there is one thing certain, there is no such thing as seeking without finding. He that seeketh findeth. Listen to the gracious words of Jesus, "I will come and heal him." Most places that we go to there are so many people that we cannot pray for. In some places there are 200 or 300 who would like us to visit them, but we are not able to do so. But I am so glad that the Lord Jesus is always willing to come and heal. He longs to meet the sick ones. He loves to heal them of their afflictions. The Lord is healing many people today by means of handkerchiefs as you read that He healed people in the days of Paul. You can read of this in Acts 19:12.

A woman came to me in the city of Liverpool and said, "I would like you to help me. I wish you would join with me in prayer. My husband is a drunkard and every night comes into the home under the influence of drink. Won't you join me in prayer for him?" I said to the woman, "Have you a handkerchief?" She took out a handkerchief and I prayed over it and told her to lay it on the pillow of the drunken man. He came home that night and laid his head on the pillow in which this handkerchief was tucked. He laid his head on more than the pillow that night. He laid his head on the promise of God. In Mark 11 :24, we read, "What things soever ye desire when ye pray, believe that ye receive them and ye shall have them."

The next morning the man got up and called at the first saloon that he had to pass on his way to work and ordered some beer. He tasted it and said to the bartender, "You have put some poison in this beer." He could not drink it, and went on to the next saloon and ordered some more beer. He tasted it and said to the man behind the counter, "You put some poison in this beer, I believe you folks have agreed to poison me." The bartender was indignant at being thus charged. The man said, "I will go somewhere else." He went to another saloon and the same thing happened as in the two previous saloons. He made such a fuss that they turned him out. After he came out from work he went to another saloon to get some beer, and again he thought he had been poisoned and he made so much disturbance that he was thrown out. He went to his home and told his wife what had happened and said, "It seems as though all the fellows have agreed to poison me." His wife said to him, "Can't you see the hand of the Lord in this, that He is making you dislike the stuff that has been your ruin?" This word brought conviction to the man's heart and he came to the meeting and got saved. The Lord has still power to set the captives free.

When I was in Australia a lady came to me who was much troubled about her son who was so lazy. I prayed over a handkerchief which was placed on the boy's pillow. He slept that night on the handkerchief and the next morning he got up and went out and secured a position and went to work. Oh, praise the Lord, you can't shut God out, but if you will only believe He will shut the devil out.

Jesus was willing to go and heal the sick one but the centurion said, "Lord, I am not worthy that thou shouldest come under my roof; but speak the word only, and my servant shall be healed." Jesus was delighted with this expression and said to the man, "Go thy way; and as thou hast believed, so be it done unto thee." And his servant was healed the self-same hour.

When I was in Australia a man came up to me. He was leaning on a big stick and said, "I would like you to help me. It will take you half an hour to pray for me." I said, "Believe God and in one moment you will be whole." His faith was quickened to receive an immediate healing and he went away glorifying God for a miraculous healing. The word of the Lord is sufficient today. If you will dare to believe God's Word you will see a performance of His Word that will be truly wonderful. Here we have with the centurion an audacity of faith, a faith that did not limit God. Failures come when we limit the Holy One of Israel. I want to encourage you to a living faith to believe God's Word.

The next healing we read of here is the healing of Peter's wife's mother who was sick of a fever. Luke tells us that Jesus rebuked the fever. The fever could hear. The moment it could hear it went. Jesus had a new method. Today there are a lot of folks who try to sweat out a fever. You can't sweat the devil out. He can stand all the heat that you can apply to him. But if thou canst believe, deliverance is as sure and certain for you as it was for Peter's wife's mother.

I received a telegram once urging me to visit a case about 200 miles from my home. As I went to this place I met the father and mother and found them broken hearted. They lead me up a staircase to a room and I saw a young woman on the floor and five people were holding her down. She was a frail young woman but the power in her was greater than all those young men. As I went into the room the evil powers looked out of her eyes and they used her lips saying, "We are many, you can't cast us out." I said, "Jesus can." He is equal to every occasion. He is waiting for an opportunity to bless. He is ready for every opportunity to deliver souls. When we receive Jesus it is true of us, "Greater is He that is in you than he that is in the world." He is greater than all the powers of darkness. No man can meet the devil in his own strength, but any man filled with the knowledge of Jesus, filled with His presence, filled with His power, is more than a match for the powers of darkness. God has called us to be more than conquerors through Him that loved us.

The living Word is able to destroy Satanic forces. There is power in the name of Jesus. I would that every window in the street had the name of Jesus written large upon it. His name, through faith in His name brought deliverance to this poor, bound soul, and thirty-seven demons came out giving their names as they came forth. The dear woman was completely delivered and they were able to give her back her child. That night there was heaven in that home and the father and mother and son and his wife were all united in glorifying Christ for His infinite grace. The next morning we had a gracious time in the breaking of bread. All things are wonderful with our wonderful Jesus. If you would dare rest your all upon Him, things would take place and He would change the whole situation. In a moment, through the name of Jesus, a new order of things can be brought in.

In the world they are always having new diseases and the doctors cannot locate them. A doctor said to me, "The science of medicine is in its infancy, and really we doctors have no confidence in our medicine. We are always experimenting." But the man of God does not experiment. He knows, or ought to know, redemption in its fullness. He knows, or ought to know, the mightiness of the Lord Jesus Christ. He is not, or should not be, moved by outward observation, but should get divine revelation of the mightiness of the name of Jesus and the power of His blood. If we exercise our faith in the Lord Jesus Christ He will come forth and get glory over all the powers of darkness.

At eventide they brought unto Him many that were possessed with devils; and He cast out the spirits with His word and healed all that were sick: that it might be fulfilled which was spoken by Esaias the prophet, saying, "Himself took our infirmities, and bare our sicknesses." The work is done if you only believe it. It is done. Himself took our infirmities and bare our sicknesses. If you can only see the Lamb of God as He went to Calvary! He took our flesh that He might take upon Himself the full burden of all our sin and all the consequences of sin. There on the cross God laid upon Him the iniquities of us all. There on the cross of Calvary the results of sin were also dealt with. "As the children are partakers of flesh and blood, he also himself took part of the same; that through death he might destroy him that had the power of death, that is, the devil; and deliver them who through fear of death were all their life time subject to bondage." Through His death there is deliverance for you today.

# CHAPTER 7

## Our Risen Christ

---

READ THE FOURTH chapter of Acts.

Today we praise God for the fact that our glorious Jesus is the risen Christ. Those of us who have tasted the power of the indwelling Spirit know something of the manner in which the hearts of those two disciples burned as they walked to Emmaus with their risen Lord as their companion.

Note the words of verse 30, "And when they had prayed, the place was shaken." There are many churches where they never pray the kind of prayer that you read of here. A church that does not know how to pray and to shout will never lie shaken. If you live in a place like that you may as well write "Ichabod - the glory of the Lord has departed" - over the threshold. It is only when men have learned the secret of prayer, of power, and of praise, that God comes forth. Some people say, "Well, I praise God inwardly," but if there is an abundance of praise in your heart, your mouth cannot help speaking it.

There was a man who had a large business in London who was a great church-goer. The church he attended was beautifully decorated, and his pew was delightfully cushioned-just about enough to make it easy to sleep through the sermons. He was a prosperous man in business, but he had no peace in his heart. But there was a boy at his business who always looked happy. He was always jumping and whistling. One day he said to this boy, "I want to see you in my office." When the boy was in his office he asked him, "How is it that you can always whistle and be happy?" "I cannot help it," answered the boy. "Where did you get it?" asked the master. "I got it at the Pentecostal mission." "Where is that?" The boy told him, and the next thing was, that the man was attending. The Lord broke him up there, and in a short while he was entirely changed. One day, shortly after this, he found that, instead of being distracted by his business as he formerly had been, he was actually whistling and jumping. His whole position and his whole life had been changed.

The shout cannot come out unless it is in. There must first be the inner working of the power of God. It is He who changes the heart, and transforms the life, and before there is any real outward evidence there must be the inflow of divine life. Sometimes I say to people, "You weren't at meeting the other night." They reply, "Oh yes, I was there in spirit." I say to them, "Well, come next time with your body also. We don't want a lot of spirit here and no bodies. We want you to come and get filled with God." When all the people will come and pray and praise as did these early disciples there will be something doing. People who come will catch fire and they will want to come again. But they will have no use for a place where everything has become formal, dry, and dead.

The power of Pentecost as it came at first came to loose men. God wants us free on every line. Men and women are tired of imitations; they want reality; they want to see people who have the living Christ within, and are filled with Holy Ghost power.

I received several letters and telegrams about a certain case, but when I arrived I was told I was too late. I said, "That cannot be. God has never sent me too late anywhere." God showed me when I went that something different would happen to anything I had seen previously. The people I went to were all strangers. I was introduced to a young man who lay helpless, and for whom there was no hope. The doctor had been to see him that morning and had declared that he would not live through the day. He lay with his face to the wall, and when I spoke to him he whispered, "I cannot turn over." His mother said that they had had to lift him out of bed on sheets for weeks, and that he was so weak and helpless that he had to stay in one position.

The young man said, "My heart is very weak." I assured him, "God is the strength of thy heart and thy portion forever. If you will believe God, it shall be so today."

Our Christ is risen. He is a living Christ who indwells us. We must not have this truth merely as a theory, Christ must be risen in us by the power of the Spirit. The power that raised Him from the dead must animate us, and as this glorious resurrection power surges through your being, you will be freed from all your weaknesses and you will become strong in the Lord and in the power of His might. There is a resurrection power that God wants you to have and to have it today. Why not? Receive your portion here and now.

I said to these people, "I believe your son will rise today." They only laughed. People do not expect to see signs and wonders today as the disciples saw them of old. Has God changed? Or has our faith waned so that we are not expecting the greater works that Jesus promised? We must not harp on any minor key. Our message must rise to concert pitch, and there must be nothing left out of it that is in the Book.

It was winter time and I said to the parents, "Will you get the boy's suit and bring it here?" They would not listen to the request, for they were expecting the boy to die. But I had gone to that place believing God. In Romans 4:17, we read of Abraham, "(I have made thee a father of many nations,) before him whom he believed, even God, who quickeneth the dead, and calleth those things which be not as though they were." God help us to understand this. It is time people knew how to shout in faith as they contemplate the eternal power of our God to whom it is nothing to quicken and raise the dead. I come across some who would be giants in the power of God but they have no shout of faith. I find everywhere people who go down even when they are praying simply because they are just breathing sentences without uttering speech, and you cannot get victory that way. You must learn to take the victory and shout in the face of the devil, "It is done!" There is no man who can doubt if he learns to shout. When we know how to shout properly, things will be different, and tremendous things will happen. In verse 24 we read, "They lifted up their voice with one accord." It surely must have been a loud prayer. We must know that God means us to have life. If there is anything in the world that has life in it, it is this Pentecostal revival we are in. I believe in the Baptism of the Holy Ghost with the speaking in tongues, and I believe that every man who is baptized in the Holy Ghost will speak in other tongues as the Spirit gives him utterance. I believe in the Holy Ghost. And if you are filled with the Spirit you will be superabounding in life-living waters will flow from you.

At last I persuaded the parents to bring the boy's clothes and lay them on the bed. From the natural viewpoint, the young man lay dying. I spoke to the afflicted one, "God has revealed to me that, as I lay my hands upon you, the place will be filled with the Holy Ghost, the bed will be shaken, you will be shaken and thrown out of bed by the power of the Holy Ghost, you will dress yourself and be strong." I said this to him in faith. I laid hands on him in the name of Jesus and instantly the power of God fell and filled the place. I felt helpless and fell flat on the floor. I knew nothing except that a short while after the place was shaken, I heard the young man walking over me and saying, "For Thy glory, Lord! For Thy glory, Lord!"

He dressed himself and cried, "God has healed me." The father fell, the mother fell, and another who was present fell also. God manifested His power that day in saving the whole household and healing the young man. It is the power of the risen Christ we need. That young man is today preaching the gospel.

For years we have been longing for God to come forth, and, praise Him, He is coming forth. The tide is rising everywhere. I was in Switzerland not long ago, preaching in many places where the Pentecostal message had not been heard, and today there are nine new Pentecostal assemblies in different places going on blessedly for God. All over the world it is the same, this great Pentecostal work is in motion. You can hardly get to a place now where God is not pouring out His Spirit on hungry hearts. God has promised to pour out His

Spirit upon all flesh, and His promises never fail. Our Christ is risen. His salvation was not a thing done in a corner. Truly He was a man of glory who went to Calvary for us, in order that He might free us from all that would mar and hinder, that He might transform us by His grace, and bring us out from under the power of Satan into the glorious power of God. One touch of our risen Christ will raise the dead. Hallelujah!

Oh, this wonderful Jesus of ours! He comes and indwells us. He comes to abide. He it is who baptizes us with the Holy Ghost, and makes everything different. We are to be a kind of firstfruits unto God and are to be like Christ who is the firstfruit, walking in His footsteps, living in His power. What a salvation this is, having this risen Christ in us. I feel that everything else must go to nothingness, helplessness and ruin. Every thought of advantage for ourselves must be on the decrease in order that Christ may increase, that we may live in another state, where all things are under the power of the Spirit.

Dare you take your inheritance from God? Dare you believe God? Dare you stand on the record of His Word? What is the record? If thou shalt believe thou shalt see the glory of God. You will be sifted as wheat. You will be tried as though some strange thing tried you. You will be put in places where you will have to put your whole trust in God. There is no such thing as anyone being tried beyond what God will allow. There is no temptation that will come, but God will be with you right in the temptation to deliver you, and when you have been tried, He will bring you forth as gold. Every trial is to bring you to a greater position in God. The trial that tries your faith will take you on to the place where you will know that the faith of God will be forthcoming in the next test. No man is able to win any victory save through the power of the risen Christ within him. You will never be able to say, "I did this or that." You will desire to give God the glory for everything.

If you are sure of your ground, if you are counting on the presence of the living Christ within, you can laugh when you see things getting worse. God would have you settled and grounded in Christ, and it is only as you are filled with the Holy Ghost that you become steadfast and unmoveable in Him.
The Lord Jesus said, "I have a baptism to be baptized with; and how

am I straitened till it be accomplished." He was assuredly straitened in the way, at Gethsemane, at the judgment hall, and, after that, at the cross, where He, through the eternal Spirit, offered Himself without spot to God. God will take us right on in like manner, and the Holy Spirit will lead every step of the way. God led Him right through to the empty tomb, to the ascension glory, to a place on the throne; and the Son of God will never be satisfied until He has us with Himself, sharing His glory and sharing His throne.

# CHAPTER 8

# Righteousness

---

IT IS WRITTEN of our blessed Lord, "Thou hast loved righteousness, and hated iniquity; therefore God, even thy God, hath anointed thee with the oil of gladness above thy fellows." It is the purpose of God that we, as we are indwelt by the Spirit of His Son, should likewise love righteousness and hate iniquity. I see that there is a place for us in Christ Jesus where we are no longer under condemnation but where the heavens are always open to us. I see that God has a realm of divine life opening up to us where there are boundless possibilities, where there is limitless power, where there are untold resources, where we have victory over all the power of the devil. I believe that, as we are filled with the desire to press on into this life of true holiness, desiring only the glory of God, there is nothing that can hinder our true advancement.

Peter commences his second epistle with these words, "Simon Peter, a servant and an apostle of Jesus Christ, to them that have obtained like precious faith with us through the righteousness of God and our Saviour Jesus Christ." It is through faith that we realize that we have a blessed and glorious union with our risen Lord. When He was on earth Jesus told us, "I am in the Father and the Father in me." "The Father that dwelleth in Me, He doeth the works." And He prayed to His Father, not only for His disciples but for those who should believe on Him through their word; "That they all may be one; as Thou, Father, art in Me, and I in Thee, that they also may be one in us: that the world may believe that Thou hast sent Me." Oh what an inheritance is ours when the very nature, the very righteousness, the very power of the Father and the Son are made real in us. That is God's purpose, and as we by faith lay hold on the purpose we shall be ever conscious of the fact that greater is He that is in us than he that is in the world. The purpose of all Scripture is to move us on to this wonderful and blessed elevation of faith where our constant experience is the manifestation of God's life and power through us.

Peter goes on writing to these who have obtained like precious faith, saying, "Grace and peace be multiplied unto you through the knowledge of God, and of Jesus our Lord." We can have the multiplication of this grace and peace only as we live in the realm of faith. Abraham attained to the place where he became a friend of God, on no other line than that of believing God. He believed God and God counted that to him for righteousness. Righteousness was imputed to him on no other ground than that he believed God. Can this be true of anybody else? Yes, every person in the whole wide world who is saved by faith is blessed with faithful Abraham. The promise which came to him because he believed God was that in Him all the families of the earth should be blessed. When we believe God there is no knowing where the blessing of our faith will end.

Some are tied up because, when they are prayed for, the thing that they are expecting does not come the same night. They say they believe, but you can see that they are really in turmoil of unbelief. Abraham believed God. You can hear him saying to Sarah, "Sarah, there is no life in you and there is nothing in me, but God has promised us a son and I believe God." And that kind of faith is a joy to our Father in heaven.

One day I was having a meeting in Bury, in Lancashire, England. A young woman was present who came from a place called Ramsbottom, to be healed of goiter. Before she came she said, "I am going to be healed of this goiter, mother." After one meeting she came forward and was prayed for. The next meeting she got up and testified that she had been wonderfully healed, and she said, "I shall be so happy to go and tell mother that I have been wonderfully healed." She went to her home and testified how wonderfully she had been healed, and the next year when we were having the convention she came again. To the natural view it looked as though the goiter was just as big as ever; but that young woman was believing God and she was soon on her feet giving her testimony, and saying, "I was here last year and the Lord wonderfully healed me. I want to tell you that this has been the best year of my life." She seemed to be greatly blessed in that meeting and she went home to testify more strongly than ever that the Lord had healed her. She believed God. The third year she was at the meeting again, and some people who looked at her said, "How big that goiter has become." But when the time came for testimony she was up on her feet and testified, "Two years ago the Lord graciously healed me of goiter. Oh I had a most wonderful healing. It is grand to be healed by the power of God." That day someone remonstrated with her and said, "People will think there is something the matter with you. Why don't you look in the glass? You will see your goiter is bigger than ever." That good woman went to the Lord about it and said, "Lord, you so wonderfully healed me two years ago. Won't you show all the people that you healed me?" She went to sleep peacefully that night still believing God and when she came down the next day there was not a trace or a mark of that goiter.

God's word is from everlasting to everlasting. His word cannot fail. God's word is true and when we rest in the fact of its truth what mighty results we can get. Faith never looks in the glass. Faith has a glass into which it can look. It is the glass of the perfect law of liberty. "Whoso looketh into the perfect law of liberty, and continueth therein, he being not a forgetful hearer, but a doer of the work, this man shall be blessed in his deed." To the man who looks into this perfect law of God all darkness is removed and he sees his completeness in Christ. There is no darkness in faith. There is only darkness in nature. Darkness only exists when the natural is put in the place of the divine.

Not only is grace multiplied to us through knowledge of God and of Jesus Christ, but peace also. As we really know our God and Jesus Christ whom He has sent, we will have peace multiplied to us even in the multiplied fires of ten thousand Nebuchadnezzars. It will be multiplied to us even though we are put into the den of lions, and we will live with joy in the midst of the whole thing. What was the difference between Daniel and the king that night when Daniel was put into the den of lions? Daniel knew, but the king was experimenting. The king came around the next morning and cried, “Oh Daniel, servant of the living God, is thy God, whom thou servest continually, able to deliver thee from the lions?” Daniel answered, “My God hath sent His angel, and hath shut the lions’ mouths.” The thing was done. It was done when Daniel prayed with his windows open toward heaven. All our victories are won before we go into the fight. Prayer links us on to our lovely God, our abounding God, our multiplying God. Oh I love Him! He is so wonderful!

You will note, as you read these first two verses of the first chapter of the second epistle of Peter, that this grace and peace is multiplied through the knowledge of God, but that first our faith comes through the righteousness of God. Note that righteousness comes first and knowledge afterwards. It cannot be otherwise. If you expect any revelation of God apart from holiness you will have only a mixture. Holiness opens the door to all the treasures of God. He must first bring us to the place where we, like our Lord, love righteousness and hate iniquity, before He opens up to us these good treasures. When we regard iniquity in our hearts the Lord will not hear us, and it is only as we are made righteous and pure and holy through the precious blood of God’s Son that we can enter into this life of holiness and righteousness in the Son. It is the righteousness of our Lord Himself made real in us as our faith is stayed in Him.

After I was baptized with the Holy Ghost the Lord gave me a blessed revelation. I saw Adam and Eve turned out of the garden for their disobedience and unable to partake of the tree of life, for the cherubim with flaming sword kept them away from this tree. When I was baptized I saw that I had begun to eat of this tree of life and I saw that the flaming sword was all round about. It was there to keep the devil away. Oh, what privileges are ours when we are born of God. How marvelously He keeps us so that the wicked one touches us not. I see a place in God where Satan dare not come. Hidden in God. And He invites us all to come and share this wonderful hidden place where our lives are hid with Christ in God, where we dwell in the secret place of the Most High and abide under the shadow of the Almighty.

God has this place for you in this blessed realm of grace.

Peter goes on to say, "According as His divine power hath given unto us all things that pertain unto life and godliness, through the knowledge of Him that hath called us to glory and virtue." God is calling us to this realm of glory and virtue where, as we feed on His exceeding great and precious promises, we are made partakers of the divine nature. Faith is the substance of things hoped for right here in this life. It is right here that God would have us partake of His divine nature. It is nothing less than the life of the Lord Himself imparted and flowing into our whole beings, so that our very body is quickened, so that every tissue and every drop of blood and our bones and joints and marrow receive this divine life. I believe that the Lord wants this divine life to flow right into our natural bodies, this law of the spirit of life in Christ Jesus that makes us free from the law of sin and death. God wants to estabish our faith so that we shall lay hold on this divine life, this divine nature of the Son of God, so that our spirit and soul and body will be sanctified wholly and preserved unto the corning of the Lord Jesus Christ.

When that woman was healed of the issue of blood, Jesus perceived that power had gone out of Him. The woman's faith laid hold and this power was imparted and immediately the woman's being was surcharged with life and her weakness departed. The impartation of this power produces everything you need; but it comes only as our faith moves out for its impartation. Faith is the victory. If thou canst believe, it is thine.

I suffered for many years from piles, till my whole body was thoroughly weak; the blood used to gush from me. One day I got desperate and I took a bottle of oil and anointed myself. I said to the Lord, "Do what you want to, quickly." I was healed at that very moment. God wants us to have an activity of faith that dares to believe God. There is what seems like faith, and appearance of faith, but real faith believes God right to the end.

What was the difference between Zacharias and Mary? The angel came to Zacharias and told him, "Thy wife Elizabeth shall bear thee a son." Zacharias was there in the holy place, but he began to question this message, saying, "I am an old man, my wife is well stricken in years." Gabriel rebuked him for his unbelief and told him, "Thou shalt be dumb, and not able to speak, until the day that these things shall be performed, because thou believest not my words." But note the contrast when the angel came to Mary. She said, "Behold the handmaid of the Lord; be it unto me according to thy word." And Elizabeth greeted Mary with the words, "Blessed is she that believed: for there shall be a performance of those things which were told her from the Lord." God would have us to lay hold on His word in like manner. He would have us to come with boldness of faith declaring, "You have promised it, Lord. Now do it." God rejoices when we manifest a faith that holds Him to His word. Can we get there?

The Lord has called us to this glory and virtue; and, as our faith lays hold on Him, we shall see this in manifestation. I remember one day I was holding an open-air meeting. My uncle came to that meeting and said, "Aunt Mary would like to see Smith before she dies." I went to see her and she was assuredly dying. I said, "Lord, can't you do something?" All I did was this, to stretch out my hands and lay them on her. It seemed as though there was an immediate impartation of the glory and virtue of the Lord. Aunt Mary cried, "It is going all over my body." And that day she was made perfectly whole.

One day I was preaching and a man brought a boy who was done up in bandages. The boy was in irons and it was impossible for him to walk and it was difficult for them to get him to the platform. They passed him over about six seats. The power of the Lord was present to heal and it entered right into the child as I placed my hands on him. The child cried, "Daddy, it is going all over me." They stripped the boy and found nothing imperfect in him.

The Lord would have us to be walking epistles of His word. Jesus is the Word and is the power in us, and it is His desire to work in and through us His own good pleasure. We must believe that He is in us. There are boundless possibilities for us if we dare to act in God and dare to believe that the wonderful virtue of our living Christ shall be made manifest through us as we lay our hands on the sick in His name.

The exceeding great and precious promises of the Word are given to us that we might be partakers of the divine nature. I feel the Holy Ghost is grieved with us because, when we know these things, we do not do greater exploits for God. Does not the Holy Ghost show us wide-open doors of opportunity? Shall we not let God take us on to greater things? Shall we not believe God to take us on to greater manifestations of His power? His call for us is to forget the things that are behind, and reach forth unto the things which are before and to press toward the mark for the prize of the high calling of God in Christ Jesus.

# CHAPTER 9

# The Words of This Life

---

BIBLE READING -Acts 5:1-20.

Notice this expression that the Lord gives of the Gospel message - "the words of this life." It is the most wonderful life possible - the life of faith in the Son of God. This is the life where God is all the time. He is round about and He is within. It is the life of many revelations and of many manifestations of God's Holy Spirit, a life in which the Lord is continually seen, known, felt and heard. It is a life without death, for "we have passed from death unto life." The very life of God has come within us. Where that life is within in its fullness, disease cannot exist. It would take me a month to tell out what there is in this wonderful life. Everyone can go in and possess and be possessed by this life.

It is possible for you to be within the vicinity of this life and yet miss it. It is possible for you to be in a place where God is pouring out His Spirit and yet miss the blessing that God is so willing to bestow. It all comes through shortness of revelation and through a misunderstanding of the infinite grace of God, and of the "God of all grace," who is willing to give to all who will reach out the hand of faith. This life that He freely bestows is a gift. Some think they have to earn it and they miss the whole thing. Oh, for a simple faith to receive all that God so lavishly offers. You can never be ordinary from the day you receive this life from above. You become extraordinary, filled with the extraordinary power of our extraordinary God.

Ananias and Sapphira were in this thing and yet they missed it. They thought that possibly the thing might fail. So they wanted to have a reserve for themselves in case it did turn out to be a failure. They were in the wonderful revival that God gave to the early church and yet they missed it. There are many people like them today who make vows to God in times of a great crisis in their lives. But they fail to keep their vows and in the end they become spiritually bankrupt. Blessed is the man who will swear to his own hurt and change not; who keeps the vow he has made to God; who is willing to lay his all at God's feet. The man who does this never becomes a lean soul. God has promised to "make fat his bones." There is no dry place for such a man; he is always fat and flourishing, and he becomes stronger and stronger. It pays to trust God with all and to make no reservation.

I wish I could make you see how great a God we have. Ananias and Sapphira were really doubting God and were questioning whether this work that He had begun would go through. They wanted to get some glory for selling their property, but because of their lack of faith they kept back part of the price in reserve in case the work of God should fail.

Many are doubting whether this Pentecostal revival will go through. Do you think this Pentecostal work will stop? Never. For fifteen years I have been in constant revival and I am sure that it will never stop. When George Stephenson made his first engine he took his sister Mary to see it. She looked at it and said to her brother, "George, it'll never go." He said to her, "Get in, Mary." She said again, "It'll never go." He said to her, "We'll see, you get in." Mary at last got in-the whistle blew, there was a puff and a rattle, and the engine started off. Then Mary cried out, "George, it'll never stop! It'll never stop!"

People are looking on at this Pentecostal revival and they are very critical and they are saying, "It'll never go;" but when they are induced to come into the work, they one and all say, "It'll never stop." This revival of God is sweeping on and on and there is no stopping the current of life, of love, of inspiration, and of power.

(Interpretation; It is the living Word who has brought this. It is the Lamb in the midst, the same yesterday, today and forever.)

God has brought unlimited resources for everyone. Do not doubt. Hear with the ear of faith. God is in the midst. See that it is God who hath set forth that which you see and hear today.

I want you to see that in the early church, controlled by the power of the Holy Ghost, it was not possible for a lie to exist. The moment it came into the church, there was instant death. And as the power of the Holy Ghost increases in these days of the Latter Rain, it will be impossible for any man to remain in our midst with a lying spirit. God will purify the church; the Word of God will be in such power in healing and other spiritual manifestations, that great fear will be upon all those who see the same.

It seems to the natural mind a small thing for Ananias and Sapphira to want to have a little to fall back on; but I want to tell you that you can please God, and you can get things from God, only on the line of a living faith. God never fails. God never can fail.

When I was in Bergen, Norway, there came to the meeting a young woman who was employed at the hospital as a nurse. A big cancer had developed on her nose, and the nose was enlarged and had become black and greatly inflamed. She came out for prayer and I said to her, "What is your condition?" She said, "I dare not touch my nose, it gives me so much pain." I said to all the people, "I want you to look at this nurse and notice her terrible condition. I believe that our God is merciful and that He is faithful, and that He will bring to naught this condition that the devil has brought about. I am going to curse this disease in the all-powerful name of Jesus. The pain will go. I believe God will give us an exhibition of His grace and I will ask this young woman to come to the meeting tomorrow night and declare what God has done for her."

Oh, the awfulness of sin! Oh, the awfulness of the power of sin! Oh, the awfulness of the consequences of the fall! When I see a cancer I always know it is an evil spirit. I can never believe it is otherwise. The same with tumors. Can this be the work of God? God help me to show you that this is the work of the devil, and to show you the way out.

I do not condemn people that sin. I don't scold people. I know what is back of the sin. I know that Satan is always going about as a roaring lion, seeking whom he may devour. I always remember the patience and love of the Lord Jesus Christ. When they brought to Him a woman that they had taken in adultery, telling Him that they had caught her in the very act, He simply stooped down and wrote on the ground. Then He quietly said, "He that is without sin among you, let him cast the first stone." I have never seen a man without sin. "All have sinned and come short of the glory of God." But I read in this blessed Gospel message that God hath laid upon Jesus the iniquity of us all; so, when I see an evil condition, I feel that I must stand in my office and rebuke the condition.

I laid my hands on the nose of that suffering nurse and cursed the evil power that was causing her so much distress. The next night the place was packed and the people were jammed together, so that it seemed that there was not room for one more to come into that house. How God's rain fell upon us. How good God is, so full of grace and so full of love. I saw the nurse in the audience and I asked her to come forward. She came and showed everyone what God had done. He had perfectly healed her. Oh, I tell you He is just the same Jesus. He is just the same today. All things are possible if you dare to trust God.

When the power of God came so mightily upon the early church, even in the death of Ananias and Sapphira, great fear came upon all the people. And when we are in the presence of God, when God is working mightily in our midst, there comes a great fear, a reverence, a holiness of life, a purity that fears to displease God. We read that no man durst join them, but God added to the church such as should be saved. I would rather have God add to our Pentecostal church than have all the town join it. God added daily to His own church.

The next thing that happened was that people became so assured that

God was working that they knew that anything would be possible, and they brought their sick into the streets and laid them on beds and couches, that at least the shadow of Peter passing by might overshadow them. Multitudes of sick people and those oppressed with evil spirits were brought to the apostles and God healed them every one. I do not believe that it was the shadow of Peter that healed, but the power of God was mightily present and the faith of the people was so aroused that they joined with one heart to believe God. God will always meet people on the line of faith.

God's tide is rising all over the earth. I had been preaching at Stavanger in Norway, and was very tired and wanted a few hours rest. I went to my next appointment, arriving at about 9:30 in the morning. My first meeting was to be at night. I said to my interpreter, "After we have had something to eat, let us go down to the fjords." We spent three or four hours down by the sea and at about 4:30 returned. We found the end of the street, which has a narrow entrance, just filled with autos, wagons, etc., containing invalids and sick people of every kind. I went up to the house and was told that the house was full of sick people. It reminded me of the scene described in the fifth chapter of Acts. I began praying for the people in the street and God began to heal the people. How wonderfully He healed those people who were in the house. We sat down for a lunch and the telephone bell rang and someone at the other end was saying, "What shall we do? The town hall is already full; the police cannot control things."

In that little Norwegian town the people were jammed together, and oh, how the power of God fell upon us. A cry went up from every one, "Isn't this the revival?"

Revival is coming. The breath of the Almighty is coming. The breath of God shows up every defect, and as it comes flowing in like a river, everybody will need a fresh anointing, a fresh cleansing of the blood. You can depend upon it that that breath is upon us.

At one time I was at a meeting in Ireland. There were many sick carried to that meeting and helpless ones were helped there. There were many people in that place who were seeking for the Baptism of the Holy Ghost. Some of them had been seeking for years. There were sinners there who were under mighty conviction. There came a moment when the breath of God swept through the meeting. In about ten minutes every sinner in the place was saved. Everyone who had been seeking the Holy Spirit was baptized, and every sick one was healed. God is a reality and His power can never fail. As our faith reaches out, God will meet us and the same rain will fall. It is the same blood that cleanseth, the same power, the same Holy Ghost, and the same Jesus made real through the power of the Holy Ghost! What would happen if we should believe God?

Right now the precious blood of the Lord Jesus Christ is efficacious to cleanse your heart and bring this life, this wonderful life of God, within you. The blood will make you every whit whole if you dare believe. The Bible is full of entreaty for you to come and partake and receive the grace, the power, the strength, the righteousness, and the full redemption of Jesus Christ. He never fails to hear when we believe.

At one place where I was, a lame man was brought to me who had been in bed for two years, with no hope of recovery. He was brought thirty miles to the meeting, and he came up on crutches to be prayed for. His boy was also afflicted in the knees and they had four crutches between the two of them. The man's face was filled with torture. There is healing virtue in the Lord and He never fails to heal when we believe. In the name of Jesus-that name so full of virtue-I put my hand down that leg that was so diseased. The man threw down his crutches and all were astonished as they saw him walking up and down without aid. The little boy called out to his father, "Papa, me; papa, me, me, me!" The little boy who was withered in both knees wanted a like touch. And the same Jesus was there to bring a real deliverance for the little captive. He was completely healed.

These were legs that were touched. If God will stretch out His mighty power to loose afflicted legs, what mercy will He extend to that soul of yours that must exist forever? Hear the Lord say, "The Spirit of the Lord is upon me, because he hath anointed me to preach the gospel to the poor; he hath sent me to heal the broken hearted, to preach deliverance to the captive, and recovering of sight to the blind, to set at liberty them that are bruised." He invites you, "Come unto me, all ye that labor and are heavy laden, and I will give you rest." God is willing in His great mercy to touch thy limbs with His mighty vital power, and if He is willing to do this, how much more anxious is He to deliver thee from the power of Satan and to make thee a child of the King. How much more necessary it is for you to be healed of your soul sickness than of your bodily ailments. And God is willing to give the double cure.

I was passing through the city of London one time, and Mr. Mundell, the secretary of the Pentecostal Missionary Union, learned that I was there. He arranged for me to meet him at a certain place at 3:30 p. m. I was to meet a certain boy whose father and mother lived in the city of Salisbury. They had sent this young man to London to take care of their business. He had been a leader in Sunday school work but he had been betrayed and had fallen. Sin is awful and the wages of sin is death. But there is another side-the gift of God is eternal life.

This young man was in great distress; he had contracted a horrible disease and feared to tell anyone. There was nothing but death ahead for him. When the father and mother got to know of his condition they suffered inexpressible grief.

When we got to the house, Brother Mundell suggested, that we get down to prayer. I said, "God does not say so, we are not going to pray yet. I want to quote a scripture, `Fools, because of their transgression, and because of their iniquities, are afflicted: their soul abhorreth all manner of meat; and they draw near unto the gates of death."' The young man cried out, "I am that fool." He broke down and told us the story of his fall. Oh, if men would only repent, and confess their sins, how God would stretch out His hand to heal and to save. The moment that young man repented, a great abscess burst, and God sent virtue into his life, giving him a mighty deliverance.

God is gracious and not willing that any should perish. How many are willing to make a clean breast of their sins ? I tell you that the moment you do this, God will open heaven. It is an easy thing for Him to save your soul and heal your disease if you will but come and shelter today in the secret place of the Most High. He will satisfy you with long life and show you His salvation. In His presence there is fullness of joy, at His right hand there are pleasures forevermore. There is full redemption for all through the precious blood of the Son of God.

# CHAPTER 10

# Life In The Spirit

---

BIBLE READING, 2 Corinthians 3

We are told that we are to leave the first principles of the doctrine of Christ and go on to perfection, not laying again the foundation of repentance from dead works and the doctrine of baptisms and other first principles (Hebrews 6). What would you think of a builder who was everlastingly pulling down his house and putting in fresh foundations? Never look back if you want the power of God in your life. You will find out that in the measure you have allowed yourself to look back you have missed that which God has for you.

The Holy Ghost shows us that we must never look back to the law of sin and death from which we have been delivered. God has brought us into a new order of things, a life of love and liberty in Christ Jesus that is beyond all human comprehension. Many are brought into this new life through the power of the Spirit of God, and then, like the Galatians, who ran well at the beginning, they try to perfect themselves on the lines of legalism. They go back from the life in the Spirit to a life on natural lines. God is not pleased with this, for He has no place for the man who has lost the vision. The only thing to do is to repent. Don't try to cover up anything. If you have been tripped tip on any line, confess it out, and then look to God to bring you to a place of stability of faith where your whole walk will be in the Spirit.

We all ought to have a clear conviction that salvation is of the Lord. It is more than a human order of things. If the enemy can move you from a place of faith, he can get you outside the plan of God. The moment a man falls into sin, divine life ceases to flow, and his life becomes one of helplessness. But this is not God's thought for any of His children. Read the third chapter of John's first epistle and take your place as a son of God. Take the place of knowing that you are a son of God, and remember that, as your hope is set in Christ, it should have a purifying effect on your life. The Holy Spirit says, "Whosoever is born of God doth not commit sin; for His seed remaineth in him: and he cannot sin, because he is born of God." There is life and power in the seed of the Word that is implanted within. God is in that "cannot," and there is more power in that word of His than in any human objections. God's thought for everyone of us is that we shall reign in life by Jesus Christ. You must come to see how wonderful you are in God and how helpless you are in yourself.

God declared Himself more mighty than every opposing power when He cast out the powers of darkness from heaven. I want you to know that the same power that cast Satan out of heaven dwells in every man that is born of God. If you would but realize this, you would reign in life. When you see people laid out under an evil power, when you see the powers of evil manifesting themselves, always put the question, "Did Jesus come in the flesh?" I have never seen an evil power answer in the affirmative. When you know you have an evil spirit to deal with you have power to cast it out. Believe it and act on it, for greater is He that is in you than he that is in the world" (1 John 4:4). God means you to be in a place of overcoming, and has put a force within you whereby you may defeat the devil.

Temptations will come to all. If you are not worth tempting you are not worth powder and shot. Job said: "When He hath tried me, I shall come forth as gold." In every temptation that comes, the Lord lets you be tempted up to the very hilt, but will never allow you to be defeated if you walk in obedience; for right in the midst of the temptation He will always "make a way of escape."

Tongues and Interpretation: "God comes forth and with His power sweeps away the refuge of lies and all the powers of darkness, and causes you always to triumph in Christ Jesus. The Lord loveth His saints and covereth them with His almighty wings."

May God help us to see it. We cannot be to the praise of His glory until we are ready for trials, and are able to triumph in them. We cannot get away from the fact that sin came in by nature, but God comes into our nature and puts it into the place of death, that the Spirit of God may come into the temple in all His power and liberty, that right here in this present evil world Satan may be dethroned by the believer.

Satan is always endeavoring to bring the saints of God into disrepute, bringing against them railing accusations, but the Holy Ghost never comes with condemnation. He always reveals the blood of Christ. He always brings us help. The Lord Jesus referred to Him as the Comforter who would come. He is always on hand to help in the seasons of trial and test. The Holy Ghost is the lifting power of the church of Christ. And Paul tells us that we "are manifestly declared to be the epistle of Christ, . . . written not with ink, but with the Spirit of the living God; not in tables of stone, but in fleshly tables of the heart." The Holy Ghost begins in the heart, right in the depths of human affections. He brings into the heart the riches of the revelation of Christ, implanting purity and holiness there, so that, out of its depths, praises may well up continually.

The Holy Ghost will make us epistles of Christ, ever telling out that Jesus our Lord is our Redeemer and God has never put away that revelation. And because of the perfect atonement of that slain Lamb, there is salvation, healing and deliverance for all. Some people think that they have only to be cleansed once, but as we walk in the light the blood of Jesus Christ is ever cleansing.

The very life of Christ has been put within us, and is moving within us-a perfect life. May the Lord help us to see the power of this life. The years of a man's life are threescore and ten, and so in the natural order of things, my life will be finished in seven years, but I have begun a new life that will never end. "From everlasting to everlasting

Thou art God." This is the life I have come into, and there is no end to this life. In me is working a power stronger than every other power; Christ, the power of God, formed within me. I can see why we need to be clothed upon from above, for the life that is in me is a thousand times bigger than I am outside. There must be a tremendous expansion. I see, and cannot help seeing, that this thing cannot be understood on natural lines; no natural reason can comprehend the divine plan.

"We are not sufficient to think anything as of ourselves, but our sufficiency is of God." If you go back, you miss the plan. We leave the old order of things. We can never have confidence in the flesh; we cannot touch that. We are in a new order, a spiritual order. It is a new life of absolute faith in the sufficiency of our God in everything that pertains to life and godliness.

You could never come into this place and be a Seventh-day Adventist. The law has no place in you. You are set free from everything. At the same time, like Paul, you are "bound in the Spirit" so that you would not do anything to grieve the Lord.
Paul further tells us that He has made us "able ministers of the New Testament, not of the letter, but of the spirit: for the letter killeth, but the spirit giveth life." It is one thing to read this, and another to have the revelation of it and to see the spiritual force of it. Any man can live in the letter and become dry and wordy, limited in knowledge of spiritual verities, and spend his time everlastingly in splitting hairs; but as soon as he touches the realm of the Spirit, all the dryness goes, all the spirit of criticism leaves. There can be no divisions in a life in the Spirit. The Spirit of God brings such pliability and such love! There is no love like the love in the Spirit. It is a pure, a holy, a divine love that is shed in our hearts by the Spirit. It loves to serve and to honor the Lord.

I can never estimate what the Baptism of the Holy Ghost has been to me these past fifteen years. It seems that every year has had three years packed into it, so that I have had forty-five years of happy service since 1907. And it is getting better all the time. It is a luxury to be filled with the Spirit, and at the same time it is a divine command for us, not to be filled with wine wherein is excess, but to be filled with the Spirit. No Pentecostal person ought to get out of bed without being lost in the Spirit and speaking in tongues as the Spirit gives utterance. No one should come into the door of an assembly without speaking in tongues or having a psalm, or a note of praise. We emphasize that at the incoming of the Spirit He should so fill us that the last member in the body is yielded to Him, and that no one is baptized in the Spirit without speaking in tongues as the Spirit gives utterance; and I maintain that, with a constant filling, you will speak in tongues morning, noon and night. As you live in the Spirit, when you walk down the steps of the house where you live, the devil will have to go before you. You will be more than a conqueror over the devil.

I see everything a failure except that which is done in the Spirit. But as you live in the Spirit, you move, act, eat, drink, and do everything to the glory of God. Our message is always this, "Be filled with the Spirit." This is God's place for you, and it is as far above the natural life as the heavens are above the earth. Yield yourselves for God to fill.

Moses had a tremendous trial with the people. They were always in trouble. But as he went up into the mount, and God unfolded to him the ten commandments, the glory fell. He rejoiced to bring those two tables of stone down from the mount, and his very countenance shone with the glory. He was bringing to Israel that which, if obeyed, would bring life.

I think of my Lord coming from heaven. I think all heaven was moved by the sight. The law of the letter was brought by Moses and it was made glorious, but all its glory was dimmed before the excelling glory which Jesus brought to us in the Spirit of life. The glory of Sinai paled before the glory of Pentecost. Those tables of stone with their "Thou shalt not, thou shalt not," are done away; for they never brought life to anyone, and the Lord has brought in a new covenant, putting His law in our minds and writing it in our hearts, this new law of the Spirit of life. As the Holy Ghost comes in, He fills us with such love and liberty that we shout for joy these words of this 11th verse, "Done away! Done away!" Henceforth there is a new cry in our hearts, "I delight to do Thy will, O God." He taketh away the first, the ministration of death, written and engraven in stones, that He might establish the second, this ministration of righteousness, this life in the

Spirit.

You ask, "Does a man who is filled with the Spirit cease to keep the commandments?" I simply repeat what the Spirit of God has told us here, that this ministration of death, written and engraven in stones (and you know that the ten commandments were written on stones) is "DONE AWAY." The man who becomes a living epistle of Christ, written with the Spirit of the living God, has ceased to be an adulterer, or a murderer or a covetous man; the will of God is his delight. I love to do the will of God; there is no irksomeness to it; it is no trial to pray; no trouble to read the Word of God; it is not a hard thing to go to the place of worship. With the psalmist you say, "I was glad when they said unto me, Let us go into the house of the Lord."

How does this new life work out? The thing works out because God works in you to will and to do of His own good pleasure (Phil. 2:13). There is a great difference between a pump and a spring. The law is a pump, the Baptism is a spring. The old pump gets out of order, the parts perish, and the well runs dry. The letter killeth. But the spring is ever bubbling up and there is a ceaseless flow direct from the throne of God. There is life.

It is written of Christ, "Thou lovest righteousness, and hatest wickedness." And in this new life in the Spirit, in this new covenant life, you love the things that are right and pure and holy, and shudder at all things that are wrong. Jesus was able to say, "The prince of this world cometh, and hath nothing in Me," and the moment we are filled with the Spirit of God we are brought into like wonderful condition, and, as we continue to be filled with the Spirit, the enemy cannot have an inch of territory in us.

Do you not believe that you can be so filled with the Spirit that a man who is not living right can be judged and convicted by your presence? As we go on in the life of the Spirit, it will be said of us, "in whose eyes a vile person is contemned" (Psalm 15:4). Jesus lived there and moved in this realm, and His life was a constant reproof to the wickedness around. But He was the Son of God, you say. God, through Him has brought us into the place of sonship, and I believe that if He has a chance with the material, the Holy Ghost can make something of us, and bring us to the same place.

I don't want to boast. If I glory in anything, it is only in the Lord who has been so gracious to me. But I remember one time stepping out of a railroad carriage to wash my hands. I had a season of prayer, and the Lord just filled me to overflowing with His love. I was going to a convention in Ireland, and I could not get there fast enough. As I returned, I believe that the Spirit of the Lord was so heavily upon me that my face must have shone. (No man can tell himself when the Spirit transforms his very countenance.) There were two clerical men sitting together, and as I got into the carriage again, one of them cried out, "You convince me of sin." Within three minutes every one in the carriage was crying to God for salvation. This thing has happened many times in my life. It is this ministration of the Spirit that Paul speaks of, this filling of the Spirit, that will make your life effective, so that even the people in the stores where you trade will want to leave your presence because they are brought under conviction.

We must move from everything of the letter. All that we do must be done under the anointing of the Spirit. The trouble has been that we as Pentecostal people have been living in the letter. Believe what the Holy Spirit says through Paul-that all this ministration of condemnation that has hindered your liberty in Christ is done away. The law is DONE AWAY! As far as you are concerned, all that old order of things is forever done away, and the Spirit of God has brought in a new life of purity and love. The Holy Ghost takes it for granted that you are finished with all the things of the old life when you become a new creation in Christ. In the life in the Spirit, the old allurements have lost their power. The devil will meet you at every turn, but the Spirit of God will always lift up a standard against him.

O, if God had His way, we should be like torches, purifying the very atmosphere wherever we go, moving back the forces of wickedness.

Tongues and Interpretation: "The Lord is that Spirit. He moves in your heart. He shows you that the power within you is mightier than all the powers of darkness."

Done away! What do I mean? Will you be disloyal? You will be more than loyal. Will you grumble when you are treated badly? No, you will turn the other cheek. This is what you will always do when God lives in you. Leave yourselves in God's hands. Enter into rest. "He that is entered into His rest, he also hath ceased from his own works, as God did from His" (Hebrews 4). O this is a lovely rest! The whole life is a Sabbath. This is the only life that can glorify God. It is a life of joy, and every day is a day of heaven on earth.

There is a continued transformation in this life. Beholding the Lord and His glory we are changed into the same image from glory to glory, even by the Spirit of the Lord. There is a continued unveiling, a constant revelation, a repeated clothing upon from above. I want you to promise God never to look back, never to go back to that which the Spirit has said is "done away." I made this promise to the Lord that I would never allow myself to doubt His Word.

There is one thing about a baby, it takes all that comes to it. A prudent man lets his reason cheat him out of God's best. But a baby takes all that its mother brings, and tries to swallow the bottle and all. The baby can't walk, but the mother carries it; the baby cannot dress itself, but the mother dresses it. The baby can't even talk. So in the life of the Spirit, God undertakes to do what we cannot do. We are carried along by Him, He clothes us, and He gives us utterance. Would that we all had the simplicity of the babes.

# CHAPTER 11

## What It Means to Be Full of the Spirit

---

BIBLE READING -Acts 6.

In the days when the number of disciples began to be multiplied there developed a situation which caused the twelve to make a definite decision not to occupy themselves with serving tables, but to give themselves continually to prayer and to the ministry of the Word. How important it is for all God's ministers to be continually in prayer, and constantly feeding on the Scriptures of Truth. I often offer a reward to anyone who can catch me anywhere without my Bible or my Testament.

None of you can be strong in God unless you are diligently and constantly hearkening to what God has to say to you through His Word. You cannot know the power and the nature of God unless you partake of His inbreathed Word. Read it at morn and at night, and at every opportunity you get. After every meal, instead of indulging in unprofitable conversation round the table, read a chapter from the Word and then have a season of prayer. I endeavour to make a point of doing this no matter where or with whom I am staying.

The Psalmist said that he had hid God's Word in his heart, that he might not sin against Him; and you will find that the more of God's Word you hide in your heart, the easier it is to live a holy life. He also testified that God's Word quickened him; and, as you receive God's Word into your being, your whole physical being will be quickened and you will be made strong. As you receive with meekness the Word, you will find faith upspringing within. And you will have life through the Word.

The twelve told the rest to look out seven men to look after the business end of things. They were to be men of honest report and filled with the Holy Ghost. These were just ordinary men who were chosen, but they were filled with the Holy Spirit, and this infilling always lifts a man to a plane above the ordinary. It does not take a cultured or a learned man to fill a position in God's church; what God requires is a yielded, consecrated, holy life, and He can make of such a flame of fire. Baptized with the Holy Ghost and fire!

The multitude chose out seven men to serve tables. They were doubtless faithful in their appointed tasks, but we see that God soon had a better choice for two of them. Philip was so full of the Holy Ghost that he could have a revival wherever God put him down. Man chose him to serve tables, but God chose him to win souls. O, if I could only stir you up to see that as you are faithful in performing the humblest office, God can fill you with His Spirit and make you a chosen vessel for Himself, and promote you to a place of mighty ministry in the salvation of souls and in the healing of the sick. There is nothing impossible to a man filled with the Holy Ghost. It is beyond all human comprehension. When you are filled with the power of the Holy Ghost, God will wonderfully work wherever you go.

When you are filled with the Spirit you will know the voice of God. I want to give you one illustration of this. When I was going out to Australia recently, our boat stopped at Aden and at Bombay. In the first place the people came round the ship selling their wares, beautiful carpets and all sorts of oriental things. There was one man selling some ostrich feathers. As I was looking over the side of the ship watching the trading, a gentleman said to me, "Would you go shares with me in buying that bunch of feathers?" What did I want with feathers? I had no use for such things and no room for them either. But the gentleman put the question to me again, "Will you go shares with me in buying that bunch?" The Spirit of God said to me, "Do it."

The feathers were sold to us for three pounds, and the gentleman said, "I have no money on me, but if you will pay the man for them, I will send the cash down to you by the purser." I paid for the feathers and gave the gentleman his share. He was travelling first, and I was travelling second class. I said to him, "No, please don't give that money to the purser, I want you to bring it to me personally to my cabin." I said to the Lord, "What about these feathers?" He showed me that He had a purpose in my purchasing them.

At about 10 o'clock the gentleman came to my cabin and said, "I've brought the money." I said to him, "It is not your money that I want, it is your soul that I am seeking for God." Right there he opened up the whole plan of his life and began to seek God; and that morning he wept his way through to God's salvation.

You have no conception what God can do through you when you are filled with His Spirit. Every day and every hour you can have the divine leading of God. To be filled with the Holy Ghost means much in every way. I have seen some who have been suffering for years, and when they have been filled with the Holy Ghost everything of their sickness has passed away. The Spirit of God has made real to them the life of Jesus and they have been completely liberated of every sickness and infirmity.

Look at Stephen. He was just an ordinary man chosen to serve tables. But the Holy Ghost was in him and he was full of faith and power, and did great wonders and miracles among the people. There was no resisting the wisdom and the spirit by which he spake. How important it is that every man shall be filled with the Holy Spirit.

Tongues and Interpretation: "The divine will is that you should be filled with God; for the power of the Spirit to fill you with the mightiness of God. There is nothing God will withhold from a man filled with the Holy Ghost."

I want to impress the importance of this upon you. It is not healing that I am presenting to you-it is the living Christ. It is a glorious fact that the Son of God came down to bring liberty to the captives.

How is it that the moment you are filled with the Holy Ghost persecution starts? It was so with the Lord Jesus Himself. We do not read of any persecutions before the Holy Spirit came down like a dove upon Him. Shortly after this we find that, after preaching in His home town, they wanted to throw Him over the brow of a hill. It was the same with the twelve disciples. They had no persecution before the day of Pentecost; but after they were filled with the Spirit, they were soon in prison. The devil and the priests of religion will always get stirred when a man is filled with the Spirit and does things in the power of the Spirit. And persecution is the greatest blessing to a church. When we have persecution we will have purity. If you desire to be filled with the Spirit you can count on one thing, and that is persecution. The Lord came to bring division, and even in your own household you may find three against two.

The Lord Jesus came to bring peace; and soon after you get peace within, you get persecution without. If you remain stationary, the devil and his agents will not disturb you much. But when you press on and go the whole length with God the enemy has you as a target. But God will vindicate you in the midst of the whole thing.

At a meeting I was holding, the Lord was working and many were being healed. A man saw what was taking place and remarked, "I'd like to try this thing." He came up for prayer and told me that his body was broken in two places. I laid my hands on him in the name of the Lord, and said to him, "Now, you believe God." The next night he was at meeting and he got up like a lion. He said, "I want to tell you people that this man here is deceiving you. He laid his hands on me last night for rupture in two places, but I'm not a bit better." I stopped him and said, "You are healed, your trouble is that you won't believe it."

He was at meeting the next night and when there was opportunity for testimony this man arose. He said, "I'm a mason by trade. Today I was working with a labourer and he had to put a big stone in place. I helped him and did not feel any pain. I said to myself, `How have I done it?' I went away to a place where I could strip, and found that I was healed." I told the people, "Last night this man was against the Word of God, but now he believes it. It is true that these signs shall follow them that believe, they shall lay hands on the sick and they shall recover. And all through the power that is in the name of Christ." It is the Spirit who has come to reveal the Word of God, and to make it spirit and life to us.

You people who are seeking the Baptism are entering a place where you will have persecution. Your best friends will leave you-or those you may esteem your best friends. No good friend will ever leave you. But it is worth while. You enter into a realm of illumination, or revelation by the power of the Holy Ghost. He reveals the preciousness and the power of the blood of Christ. I find by the revelation of the Spirit that there is not one thing in me that the blood does not cleanse. I find that God sanctifies me by the blood and reveals that efficacy of the work by the Spirit.

Stephen was just an ordinary man clothed with the divine. He was full of faith and power, and great wonders and miracles were wrought by him. Oh, this life in the Holy Ghost! This life of deep, inward revelation, of transformation from one state to another, of growing in grace and in all knowledge and in the power of the Spirit, the life and the mind of Christ being renewed in you, and of constant revelations of the might of His power. It is the only kind of thing that will enable us to stand.

In this life, the Lord puts you in all sorts of places, and then reveals His power. I had been preaching in New York, and sailed one day for England on the Lusitania. As soon as I got on board I went down to my cabin. Two men were there, and one of them said, "Well, will I do for company?" He took out a bottle and poured out a glass of whiskey and drank it, and then he filled it up for me. "I never touch that stuff," I said. "How can you live without it?" he asked. "How could I live with it?" I asked. He admitted, "I have been under the influence of this stuff for months, and they say my `inside is all shrivelled up,' and I know that I am dying. I wish I could be delivered, but I just have to keep on drinking. Oh, if I could only be delivered! My father died in England and has given me his fortune, but what will the good of it be to me except to hasten me to my grave?"

I said to this man, "Say the word, and you will be delivered." He enquired, "What do you mean?" I said, "Say the word, show that you are willing to be delivered and God will deliver you." But it was just as if I was talking to this platform for all the comprehension he showed. I said to him, "Stand still," and I laid my hands on his head in the name of Jesus and cursed that drink demon that was taking his life. He cried out, "I'm free! I'm free! I know I'm free!" He took two bottles of whiskey and threw them overboard, and God saved, sobered and healed him. I was preaching all the way across. He sat beside me at the table. Previous to this he had not been able to eat; but at every meal he went right through the menu. You only have to have a touch from Jesus to have a good time. The power of God is just the same today. To me, He's lovely. To me, He's saving health. To me, He's the lily of the valley. O this blessed Nazarene, this King of kings! Hallelujah! Will you let Him have your will? Will you let Him have you? If you will, all His power is at your disposal.

They were not able to resist the wisdom and spirit by which Stephen spake, and so, full of rage, they brought him to the council. And God filled his face with a ray of heaven's light. It is worth being filled with the Spirit, no matter what it costs. Read the seventh chapter, the mighty prophetic utterance by this holy man. Without fear he tells them, "Ye stiffnecked and uncircumcised in heart, ye do always resist the Holy Ghost." And when they heard these things they were cut to the heart. There are two ways of being affected at the heart. Here they gnashed their teeth and cast him out of the city and stoned him. On the day of Pentecost, when they were pricked at the heart they cried out, "What shall we do?" They took the opposite way. The devil, if he can have his way, will cause you to commit murder. If Jesus has His way, you will repent.

And Stephen, full of the Holy Ghost, looked up steadfastly into heaven, and saw the glory of God, and the Son of man standing on the right hand of God. O, this being full of the Holy Ghost! How much it means. I was riding for sixty miles one summer day and as I looked up in the heavens I had an open vision of Jesus all the way. It takes the Holy Ghost to give this.

Stephen cried out, "Lord, lay not this sin to their charge." As he was full of the Spirit he was full of love, and he manifested the very same compassion for his enemies that Jesus did at Calvary. This being filled with the Holy Ghost means much in every way. It means constant filling, quickening, and a new life continually. Oh, it's lovely! We have a wonderful gospel and a great Saviour! If you will but be filled with the Holy Ghost you will have a constant spring within, yea, as your faith centres in the Lord Jesus, from within you shall flow rivers of living water.

# CHAPTER 12

# The Bible Evidence of the Baptism of The Holy Spirit

---

THERE IS MUCH CONTOVERSY today as regards the genuineness of this Pentecostal work, but there is nothing so convincing as the fact that over fifteen years ago a revival on Holy Ghost lines began and has never ceased. You will find that in every clime throughout the world God has poured out His Spirit in a remarkable way in a line parallel with the glorious revival that inaugurated the church of the first century. People, who could not understand what God was doing when He kept them concentrated in prayer, wondered as these days were being brought about by the Holy Ghost, and found themselves in exactly the same place and entering into an identical experience as the Apostles on the day of Pentecost.

Our Lord Jesus said to His disciples, "Behold, I send the promise of My Father upon you: but tarry ye in the city of Jerusalem, until ye be endued with power from on high" (Luke 24:49). God promised through the prophet Joel, "I will pour out My Spirit upon all flesh... Upon the servants and upon the handmaids in those days will I pour out My Spirit." As there is a widespread misconception concerning this receiving of the Holy Spirit, I believe the Lord would have us examine the Scriptures on this subject.

You know, beloved, it had to be something on the line of solid facts to move me. I was as certain as possible that I had received the Holy Ghost, and was absolutely rigid in this conviction. When this Pentecostal outpouring began in England I went to Sunderland and met with the people who had assembled for the purpose of receiving the Holy Ghost. I was continually in those meetings causing disturbances until the people wished I had never come. They said that I was disturbing the whole conditions. But I was hungry and thirsty for God, and had gone to Sunderland because I heard that God was pouring out His Spirit in a new way. I heard that God had now visited His people, had manifested His power and that people were speaking in tongues as on the day of Pentecost.

When I got to this place I said, "I cannot understand this meeting. I have left a meeting in Bradford all on fire for God. The fire fell last night and we were all laid out under the power of God. I have come here for tongues, and I don't hear them-I don't hear anything."

"Oh!" they said, "when you get baptized with the Holy Ghost you will speak in tongues." "Oh, is that it?" said I, "when the presence of God came upon me, my tongue was loosened, and really I felt as I went in the open air to preach that I had a new tongue." "Ah no," they said, "that is not it." "What is it, then?" I asked. They said, "When you get baptized in the Holy Ghost-" "I am baptized," I interjected, "and there is no one here who can persuade me that I am not baptized." So I was up against them arid they were up against me.

I remember a man getting up and saying, "You know, brothers and sisters, I was here three weeks and then the Lord baptized me with the Holy Ghost and I began to speak with other tongues." I said, "Let us hear it. That's what I'm here for." But he would not talk in tongues. I was doing what others are doing today, confusing the 12th of I Corinthians with the 2nd of Acts. These two chapters deal with different things, one with the gifts of the Spirit, and the other with the Baptism of the Spirit with the accompanying sign. I did not understand this and so I said to the man, "Let's hear you speak in tongues." But he could not. He had not received the "gift" of tongues, but the Baptism.

As the days passed I became more and more hungry. I had opposed the meetings so much, but the Lord was gracious, and I shall ever remember that last day-the day I was to leave. God was with me so much that last night. They were to have a meeting and I went, but I could not rest. I went to the Vicarage, and there in the library I said to Mrs. Boddy, "I cannot rest any longer, I must have these tongues." She replied, "Brother Wigglesworth, it is not the tongues you need but the Baptism. If you will allow God to baptize you, the other will be all right." "My dear sister, I know I am baptized," I said. "You know that I have to leave here at 4 o'clock. Please lay hands on me that I may receive the tongues."

She rose up and laid her hands on me and the fire fell. I said, "The fire's falling." Then came a persistent knock at the door, and she had to go out. That was the best thing that could have happened, for I was ALONE WITH GOD. Then He gave me a revelation. Oh, it was wonderful! He showed me an empty cross and Jesus glorified. I do thank God that the cross is empty, that Christ is no more on the cross. It was there that He bore the curse, for it is written, "Cursed is everyone that hangeth on a tree." He became sin for us that we might be made the righteousness of God in Him, and now, there He is in the glory. Then I saw that God had purified me. It seemed that God gave me a new vision, and I saw a perfect being within me with mouth open, saying, "Clean! Clean! Clean!" When I began to repeat it I found myself speaking in other tongues. The joy was so great that when I came to utter it my tongue failed, and I began to worship God in other tongues as the Spirit gave me utterance.

It was all as beautiful and peaceful as when Jesus said, "Peace, be still!" and the tranquillity of that moment and the joy surpassed anything I had ever known up to that moment. But, Hallelujah these days have grown with greater, mightier, more wonderful divine manifestations and power. That was but the beginning. There is no end to this kind of beginning. You will never get an end to the Holy Ghost till you are landed in the glory-till you are right in the presence of God forever. And even then we shall ever be conscious of His presence.

What had I received? I had received the Bible evidence. This Bible evidence is wonderful to me. I knew I had received the very evidence of the Spirit's incoming that the Apostles received on the day of Pentecost. I knew that everything I had up to that time was in the nature of an anointing bringing me in line with God in preparation, but now I knew I had the Biblical Baptism in the Spirit. It had the backing of the Scriptures. You are always right when you have the backing of the Scriptures and you are never right if you have not a foundation for your testimony in the Word of God.

For many years I have thrown out a challenge to any person who can prove to me that he has the Baptism without speaking in tongues as the Spirit gives utterance-to prove it by the Word that he has been baptized in the Holy Ghost without the Bible evidence, but so far no one has accepted the challenge. I only say this because so many were as I was; they have a rigid idea that they have received the Baptism without the Bible evidence. The Lord Jesus wants those who preach the Word to have the Word in evidence. Don't be misled by anything else. Have a Bible proof for all you have, and then you will be in a place where no man can move you.

I was so full of joy that I wired home to say that I had received the Holy Ghost. As soon as I got home, my boy came running up to me and said, "Father, have you received the Holy Ghost?" I said, "Yes, my boy." He said, "Let's hear you speak in tongues." But I could not. Why? I had received the Baptism in the Spirit with the speaking in tongues as the Bible evidence according to Acts 2:4, and had not received the gift of Tongues according to 1 Corinthians 12. I had received the Giver of all gifts. At some time later when I was helping some souls to seek and receive the Baptism of the Spirit, God gave me the gift of Tongues so that I could speak at any time. I could speak, but will not - no never! I must allow the Holy Ghost to use the gift. It should be so, so that we shall have divine utterances only by the Spirit. I would be very sorry to use a gift, but the Giver has all power to use the whole nine gifts.

I want to take you to the Scriptures to prove my position. There are business men here, and they know that in cases of law, where there are two clear witnesses they could win a case before any judge in Australia. On the clear evidence of two witnesses any judge will give a verdict. What has God given us? Three clear witnesses on the Baptism in the Holy Spirit-more than are necessary in law courts.

The first is in Acts 2:4, "They were all filled with the Holy Ghost, and began to speak with other tongues, as the Spirit gave them utterance." Here we have the original pattern. And God gave to Peter an eternal word that couples this experience with the promise that went before. "This is that." And God wants you to have nothing less than that. He wants you to receive the Baptism in the Holy Spirit according to this original Pentecostal pattern.

In Acts 10 we have another witness. Peter is in the house of Cornelius. Cornelius had had a vision of a holy angel and had sent for Peter. A person said to me one day, "You don't admit that I am filled and baptized with the Holy Ghost. Why, I was ten days and ten nights on my back before the Lord and He was flooding my soul with joy." I said, "Praise the Lord, sister, that was only the beginning." The disciples were tarrying that time, and they were still, and the mighty power of God fell upon them then and the Bible tells what happened when the power fell. And that is just what happened in the house of Cornelius. The Holy Ghost fell on all them which heard the word. "And they of the circumcision which believed were astonished, as many as came with Peter, because that on the Gentiles was poured out the gift of the Holy Ghost." What convinced these prejudiced Jews that the Holy Ghost had come? "For they heard them speak with tongues and magnify God." There was no other way for them to know. This evidence could not be contradicted. It is the Bible evidence.

We have heard two witnesses, and that is sufficient to satisfy the world. But God goes one better. Let us look at Acts 19:6, "And when Paul had laid his hands upon them, the Holy Ghost came on them; and they spake with tongues and prophesied." These Ephesians received the identical Bible evidence as the Apostles at the beginning and they prophesied in addition. Three times the Scriptures show us this evidence of the Baptism in the Spirit. I do not magnify tongues. No, by God's grace, I magnify the Giver of tongues. And I magnify above all Him whom the Holy Ghost has come to reveal to us, the Lord Jesus Christ. He it is who sends the Holy Spirit and I magnify Him because He makes no difference between us and those at the beginning.

But what are tongues for? Look at the 2nd verse of 1 Cor. 14 and you will see a very blessed truth. Oh, Hallelujah! Have you been there, beloved? I tell you, God wants to take you there. “He that speaketh in an unknown tongue, speaketh not unto men, but unto God: for no man understandeth him; howbeit in the spirit he speaketh mysteries.” It goes on to say, “He that speaketh in an unknown tongue edifieth himself.”

Enter into the promises of God. It is your inheritance. You will do more in one year if you are really filled with the Holy Ghost than you could do in fifty years apart from Him.

# CHAPTER 13

## Concerning Spiritual Gifts

IN 1 COR. 12:1 WE READ, "Now concerning spiritual gifts, brethren, I would not have you ignorant." There is a great weakness in the church of Christ because of an awful ignorance concerning the Spirit of God and the gifts He has come to bring. God would have us powerful on all lines because of the revelation of the knowledge of His will concerning the power and manifestation of His Spirit. He would have us ever hungry to receive more and more of His Spirit. In times past I have arranged many conventions, and I have found that it is better to have a man on my platform who has not received the Baptism but who is hungry for all that God has for him, than a man who has received the Baptism and is satisfied and has settled down and become stationary and stagnant. But of course I would prefer a man that is baptized with the Holy Ghost and is still hungry for more of God. A man who is not hungry to receive more of God is out of order in any convention.

It is impossible to overestimate the importance of being filled with the Spirit. It is impossible for us to meet the conditions of the day, to walk in the light as He is in the light, to subdue kingdoms and work righteousness and bind the power of Satan unless we are filled with the Holy Ghost.

We read that in the early church they continued steadfastly in the apostles' doctrine and fellowship, and in breaking of bread, and in prayers. It is important for us also to continue steadfastly in these same things. For some years I was associated with the Plymouth Brethren. They are very strong on the Word, and are sound on water baptism, and they do not neglect the breaking of bread service, but have it every Lord's Day morning as they had it in the early church. These people seem to have everything except the match. They have the wood, but they need the fire and then they would be all ablaze. Because they lack the fire of the Holy Spirit there is no life in their meetings. One young man who attended their meetings received the Baptism with the speaking in other tongues as the Spirit gave utterance. The brethren were very upset about this and came to the father and said to him, "You must take your son aside and tell him to cease." They did not want any disturbance. The father told the son and said, "My boy, I have been attending this church for twenty years and have never seen anything of this kind. We are established in the truth and do not want anything new. We won't have it." The son replied, "If that is God's plan I will obey, but somehow or other I don't think it is." As they were going home the horse stood still; the wheels were in deep ruts. The father pulled at the reins but the horse did not move. He asked, "What do you think is up?" The son answered, "It has got established." God save us from becoming stationary.

God would have us to understand concerning spiritual gifts and to covet earnestly the best gifts, and also to enter into the more excellent way of the fruit of the Spirit. We must beseech God for these gifts. It is a serious thing to have the Baptism and yet be stationary; to live two days in succession on the same spiritual plane is a tragedy. We must be willing to deny ourselves everything to receive the revelation of God's truth and to receive the fullness of the Spirit. Only that will satisfy God, and nothing less must satisfy us. A young Russian received the Holy Spirit and was mightily endued with power from on High. Some sisters were anxious to know the secret of his power. The secret of his power was continuous waiting upon God. As the Holy Ghost filled him it seemed as though every breath became a prayer and so all his ministry was on an increasing line.

I know a man who was full of the Holy Ghost and would preach only when he knew that he was mightily unctionized by the power of God. He was asked to preach at a Methodist church. He was staying at the minister's house and he said, "You go on to church and I will follow." The place was packed with people and this man did not turn up and the Methodist minister, becoming anxious, sent his little girl to inquire why he did not come. As she came to the bedroom door she heard him crying out three times, "I will not go." She went back and reported that she heard the man say three times that he would not go. The minister was troubled about it, but almost immediately after this the man came in, and, as he preached that night, the power of God was tremendously manifested. The preacher asked him, "Why did you tell my daughter that you were not coming?" He answered, "I know when I am filled. I am an ordinary man and I told the Lord that I dared not go and would not go until He gave me a fresh filling of the Spirit. The moment the glory filled me and overflowed I came to the meeting."

Yes, there is a power, a blessing, an assurance, a rest in the presence of the Holy Ghost. You can feel His presence and know that He is with you. You need not spend an hour without this inner knowledge of His holy presence. With His power upon you there can be no failure. You are above par all the time.

"Ye know that ye were Gentiles, carried away unto these dumb idols, even as ye were led." This is the Gentile day. When the Jews refused the blessings of God He scattered them, and He has grafted the Gentiles into the olive tree where the Jews were broken off. There never has been a time when God has been so favorable to a people who were not a people. He has brought in the Gentiles to carry out His purpose of preaching the gospel to all nations and to receive the power of the Holy Ghost to accomplish this task. It is of the mercy of God that He has turned to the Gentiles and made us partakers of all the blessings that belong to the Jews; and here under this canopy of glory, because we believe, we get all the blessings of faithful Abraham.

"Wherefore I give you to understand, that no man speaking by the Spirit of God calleth Jesus accursed: and that no man can say that

Jesus is the Lord, but by the Holy Ghost." There are many evil, deceiving spirits sent forth in these last days who endeavor to rob Jesus of His Lordship and of His rightful place. Many are opening the doors to these latest devils, such as New Theology and New Thought and Christian Science. These evil cults deny the fundamental truths of God's Word. They all deny eternal punishment and all deny the deity of Jesus Christ. You will never see the Baptism of the Holy Ghost come upon a man who accepts these errors. Neither will you see a Romanist receive. They put Mary in the place of the Holy Ghost. I would like you to produce a Romanist who knows that he is saved. No man can know he is saved by works. If you ever speak to a Romanist you will know that he is not definite on the line of the new birth. He cannot be. Another thing, you will never find a Russellite baptized in the Holy Ghost; nor a member of any other cult that does not put the Lord Jesus Christ pre-eminent above all.

The all important thing is to make Jesus Lord. Men can grow lopsided by emphasizing the truth of divine healing. Man can get wrong by all the time preaching on water baptism. But we never go wrong in exalting the Lord Jesus Christ, giving Him the preeminent place and magnifying Him as both Lord and Christ, yes, as very God of very God. As we are filled with the Holy Ghost our one desire is to magnify Him. We need to be filled with the Spirit to get the full revelation of the Lord Jesus Christ.

God's command is for us to be filled with the Spirit. We are no good if we have only a full cup; we need to have an overflowing cup all the time. It is a tragedy not to live in the fullness of overflowing. See that you never live below the overflowing tide.

"Now there are diversities of gifts but the same Spirit." Every manifestation of the Spirit is given that we might "profit withal." When the Holy Spirit is moving in an assembly and His gifts are in operation, everyone will receive profit. I have seen some who have been terribly switched. They believe in gifts, in prophecy, and they use these gifts apart from the power of the Holy Ghost. We must look to the Holy Spirit to show us the use of the gifts, what they are for, and when to use them, so that we may never use them without the power of the Holy Ghost. I do not know of anything which is so awful today as people using a gift without the power. Never do it, God save us from doing it.

A man who is filled with the Holy Ghost, while he may not be conscious of having any gift of the Spirit, can have the gifts made manifest through him. I have gone to many places to help and have found that under the unction of the Holy Spirit many wonderful things have happened in the midst when the glory of the Lord was upon the people. Any man who is filled with God and filled with His Spirit might at any moment have any of the nine gifts made manifest through him without knowing that he has a gift. Sometimes I have wondered whether it was better to be always full of the Holy Ghost and to see signs and wonders and miracles without any consciousness of possessing a gift or whether it was better to know one has a gift. If you have received the gifts of the Spirit and they have been blessed, you should never under any circumstances use them without the power of God upon you pressing the gift through. Some have used the prophetic gift without the holy touch, and they have come into the realm of the natural, and it has brought ruin, caused dissatisfaction, broken hearts, upset assemblies. Do not seek the gifts unless you are purposed to abide in the Holy Spirit. They should be manifested only in the power of the Holy Spirit.

The Lord will allow you to be very drunk in His presence, but sober among people. I like to see people so filled with the Spirit that they are drunk like the 120 on the Day of Pentecost, but I don't like to see people drunk in the wrong place. That is what troubles us, somebody being drunk in a place of worship where a lot of people come in that know nothing about the Word. If you allow yourself to be drunk there you send people away; they look at you instead of seeing God. They condemn the whole thing because you have not been sober at the right time. Paul writes, "For whether we be beside ourselves, it is to God: or whether we be sober, it is for your cause" (2 Cor. 5:13). You can be beside yourself. You can go a bit further than being drunk. You can dance, if you will do it at the right time. So many things are commendable when all the people are in the Spirit. Many things are very foolish if the people round about you are not in the Spirit. We must be careful not to have a good time at the expense of somebody else. When you have a good time you must see that the spiritual conditions in the place lend themselves to help you and that the people are falling in line with you. Then you will find it always a blessing.

While it is right to covet earnestly the best gifts, you must recognize that the all important thing is to be filled with the power of the Holy Ghost Himself. You will never have trouble with people who are filled with the power of the Holy Ghost, but you will have a lot of trouble with people who have the gifts and have no power. The Lord wants us to come behind in no gift, but at the same time He wants us to be so filled with the Holy Ghost that it will be the Holy Spirit manifesting Himself through the gifts. Where the glory of God alone is desired you can look for every needed gift to be made manifest. To glorify God is better than to idolize gifts. We prefer the Spirit of God to any gift; but we can look for the Trinity in manifestation, different gifts by the same Spirit, different administrations but the same Lord, diversities of operation but the same God working all in all. Can you conceive of what it will mean for our Triune God to be manifesting Himself in His fullness in our assemblies?

Watch that great locomotive boiler as it is filled with steam. You can see the engine letting off some of the steam as it remains stationary. It looks as though the whole thing might burst. You can see saints like that. They start to scream, but that is not to edification. But when the locomotive moves on, it serves the purpose for which it was built, and pulls along much traffic with it. It is wonderful to be filled with the power of the Holy Ghost, and for Him to serve His own purposes through us. Through our lips divine utterances flow, our hearts rejoice and our tongue is glad. It is an inward power within which is manifested in outward expression. Jesus Christ is glorified. As your faith in Him is quickened, from within you will flow rivers of living water. The Holy Spirit will pour through you like a great river of life and thousands will be blessed because you are a yielded channel through whom the Spirit may flow.

The most important thing, the one thing that counts, is to see that we are filled with the Holy Spirit, filled to overflowing. Anything less than this is displeasing to God. We are commanded by God to be filled with the Spirit, and in the measure you fail of this you are that far short of the plan of God. The Lord would have us moving on from faith to faith, from glory to glory, from fullness to overflowing. It is not good for us to be ever thinking in the past tense, but we should be moving on to the place where we dare believe God. He has declared that after the Holy Ghost is come upon us we shall have power. I believe there is an avalanche of power from God to be apprehended if we will but catch the vision.

Paul wrote at one time, "I will now come to visions and revelations." God has put us in a place where He expects us to have His latest revelation, the revelation of that marvelous fact, CHRIST IN US, and what this really means. We can apprehend Christ fully only as we are filled and overflowing with the Spirit of God. Our only safeguard from dropping back into our natural mind from which we can never get anything, is to be filled and yet filled again with the Spirit of God and to be taken on to visions and revelations on a new line. The reason why I emphasize the importance of the fullness of the Holy Ghost is that I want to get you beyond all human plans and thoughts into the fullness of vision, into the full revelation of the Lord Jesus Christ. Do you want rest? It is in Jesus. Do you want to be saved from everything the devil is bringing up in these last times? Receive and continue in the fullness of the Holy Ghost, and He will be ever revealing to you that all you need for all times is in Christ Jesus your Lord.

I desire to emphasize the importance of the Spirit's ministration and of the manifestation of the Spirit which is given to every man to profit withal. As you yield to the Spirit of the Lord He has power over your intellect, over your heart, and over your voice. The Holy Spirit has power to unveil Christ and to project the vision of Christ upon the canvas of your mind, and then He uses your tongue to glorify and magnify Him in a way that you could never do apart from the Spirit's power.

Never say that when you are filled with the Holy Ghost you are "obliged" to do this or that. When people say that they are "obliged" to do this or that I know it is not the Spirit of God, but their own spirit moving them on to do that which is unseemly and unprofitable. Lots of people spoil meetings because they scream. If you want to do that kind of thing you had better get into some cellar. That is not to edification. I believe that, when the Spirit of God is upon you and moving you to speak as He gives utterance, it will always be to edification. But don't spoil the prayer meeting because when you ought to stop you go on. Who spoils the prayer meeting? The man who starts in the Spirit and finishes in the flesh. Nothing is more lovely than prayer, but a prayer meeting is killed if you will go on and on in your own spirit when the Spirit of God is through with you. You say as you come from some meetings, "That was a lovely message if the preacher only had stopped half an hour before he did." Learn to cease immediately when the unction of the Spirit lifts. The Holy Ghost is jealous. Your body is the temple, the office of the Holy Ghost, but He does not fill the temple for human glorification, but only for the glory of God. You have no license to continue beyond a "Thus saith the Lord."

There is another side to this. God would have the assembly as free as possible, and you must not put your hand upon the working of the Spirit or it will surely bring trouble. You must be prepared to allow a certain amount of extravagance in young and newly baptized souls. You must remember that when you were brought into this life of the Spirit you had as many extravagances as anybody, but you have now become somewhat sobered down. It is a pity that some do get sobered down, for they are not where they were in the early days. We have to look to God for wisdom that we do not interfere or dampen the Spirit or quench the power of God when He is manifested in our meetings. If you want to have an assembly full of life you must have an assembly full of manifestation. Nobody will come if there is no manifestation. We need to look to God for special grace that we do not move back to looking at things from a natural viewpoint.

The preacher, after he loses his unction, should inwardly repent and get right with God and get the unction back. We are no good without the unction of the Spirit of God. If you are filled with the grace of God you will not be judging everybody in the assembly, you will rather be trusting everybody, you will not be frightened at what is being done, you will have a heart to believe all things, and to believe that though there may be some extravagances, the Spirit of God will take control of things and will see that the Lord Jesus Christ Himself is exalted, glorified, and revealed to hungry hearts that desire to know Him. The Lord would have us wise unto that which is good and simple concerning evil, free from distrust, entering into a divine likeness to Jesus, that dares believe that God Almighty will surely watch over all. Hallelujah!

The Holy Ghost is the One who magnifies the Lord Jesus Christ, the One who gives illumination of Him. If you are filled with the Holy Ghost, it is impossible to keep your tongue still. Talk about a dumb baptized soul! It is not to be found in the Scriptures or outside of the Scriptures. We are filled with the Spirit in order that we may magnify the Lord, and there should be no meeting in which the saints do not glorify, magnify, praise, and worship the Lord in Spirit and in truth.

I would like to give one word of caution, for failure often comes through our not recognizing the fact that we are always in the body. We will need our bodies as long as we live. But our body is to be used and controlled by the Spirit of God. We are to present our bodies, holy and acceptable unto God, which is our reasonable service. Every member of our body must be so sanctified that it works in harmony with the Spirit of God. Our very eyes must be sanctified. God hates the winking of the eye. From the day that I read in the Proverbs what God had to say about the winking of the eye (Prov. 6:13 and 10:10) I have never winked. I desire that my eyes may be so sanctified that they can always be used for the Lord. The Spirit of God will bring within us a compassion for souls that will be seen in our very eyes.

God has never changed the order of things - that first, there comes the natural, and then the spiritual. For instance, when it is on your heart to pray, you begin in the natural and your second word will probably be under the power of the Spirit. You begin and God will end. It is the same in giving forth utterances under the Spirit's power. You feel the moving of the Spirit within and you begin to speak and the Spirit of God will give forth utterance. Thousands have missed wonderful blessings because they have not had faith to move out and begin in the natural, in faith that the Lord would take them into the realm of the supernatural. When you receive the Holy Ghost you receive God's Gift, in whom are all the gifts of the Spirit. Paul counsels Timothy to stir up the gift that was within. You have power to stir up God's executive within you. The way you stir up the gift within you is by beginning in faith, and then He gives forth what is needed for the occasion. You would never begin unless you were full of God. When we yield to timidity and fear we simply yield to Satan. Satan whispers, "It is all self." He is a liar. I have learned this, If the Spirit of God is stirring me up, I have no hesitation in beginning to speak in tongues, and the Spirit of God gives me utterance and gives me the interpretation. I find that every time I yield to the Lord on this line I get a divine touch, I get a leading thought from the Spirit of God and the meeting is moved up on the line of faith.

You attend a meeting in faith, believing that the Lord is going to meet you there. But perhaps the evangelist is not in harmony with God. The people in the assembly are not getting what God wants. The Lord knows it. He knows His people are hungry. What happens? He will take perhaps the smallest vessels and put His power upon them. As they yield to the Spirit they break forth in a tongue. Another yields to the Spirit and there comes forth the interpretation. The Lord's church has to be fed, and the Lord will take this means of speaking to His people. Pentecostal people cannot be satisfied with the natural message. They are in touch with heavenly things and cannot be satisfied with anything less. They feel when there is something lacking in a meeting, and they look to God and He supplies that which is lacking.

When a man is filled with the Spirit he has no conception of what he has. We are so limited in our conception of what we have received. The only way we can know the power that has been given is through the ministration and manifestation of the Spirit of God. Do you think that Peter and John knew what they had when they went up to the temple to pray? They were limited in thought, and limited in their expression. The nearer we get to God the more conscious we are of the poverty of the human and we cry with Isaiah, "I am undone, I am unclean." But the Lord will bring the precious blood and the flaming coals for cleansing and refining and send us out to labor for Him empowered by His Spirit.

God has sent forth this outpouring that we may all be brought into a revelation of our sonship - that we are sons of God, men of power, that we are to be like the Lord Jesus Christ, that we are to have the powers of sonship, the power to lay hold of that which is weak and to quicken it. The Baptism of the Spirit is to make us sons of God with power. We shall be conscious of our human limits, but we shall not limit the Holy One who has come to dwell within. We must believe that since the Holy Ghost has come upon us we are indeed sons of God with power. Never say that you can't. All things are possible to them that believe. Launch out into the deep and believe that God has His all for you, and that you can do all things through Him who, strengthens you.

Peter and John knew that they had been in the upper room, they had felt the glory, they had been given divine utterances. They had seen conviction on the people. They knew that they had come into a wonderful thing. They know that what they had would be ever increasing and that it would be ever needful to cry, "Enlarge the vessel that the Holy Ghost may have more room within." They knew that all the old things were moved away and they had entered into an increasing and ever increasing knowledge of God, and that it was their Master's wish that they should be filled with the Spirit of God and with power every day and every hour. The secret of power is the unveiling of Christ, the all-powerful One within, the revelation of God who comes to abide within us. As they looked upon the crippled man at the Beautiful Gate they were filled with compassion. They were prompted by the Spirit to stop and speak with him. They said to the lame man, "Look on us." It was God's plan that the man should open his eyes with expectation. Peter said, "Of silver and gold we have none. But we have something and we will give it to you. We don't know what it is, but we give it to you. It is all in the name of Jesus." And then began the ministry of God. You begin in faith and you see what will happen. It is bidden from us at the beginning, but as we have faith in God He will come forth. The coming forth of the power is not of us but of God. There is no limit to what He will do. It is all in a nutshell as you believe God. And so Peter said, "Such as I have I give to thee: in the name of Jesus Christ of Nazareth rise up and walk." And the man who had been in that way for forty years stood up, and began to leap, and entered into the temple walking and leaping and praising God.

"For to one is given by the Spirit the word of wisdom." I want you to keep in mind the importance of never expecting the gifts of the Spirit apart from the power of the Spirit. In coveting the best gifts, covet to be so full of God and His glory that the gifts in manifestation will always glorify Him. We do not know all and we cannot know all that can be brought forth in the manifestation of the word of wisdom. One word of wisdom from God, one flash of light on the Word of God, is sufficient to save us from a thousand pitfalls. People have built without a word from God, they have bought things without a word from God, and they have been ensnared. They have lacked that word of wisdom which will bring them into God's plan for their lives. I have been in many places where I have needed a word of wisdom from God and this has been vouchsafed.

I will give you one instance. There is one thing I am very grateful to the Lord for, and that is that He has given me grace not to have a desire for money. The love of money is a great hindrance to many; and many a man is crippled in his ministry because he lets his heart run after financial matters. I was walking out one day when I met a godly man who lived opposite me and he said, "My wife and I have been talking together about selling our house and we feel constrained to sell it to you." As we talked together he persuaded me to buy his place, and before we said good-by I told him that I would take it. We always make big mistakes when we are in a hurry. I told my wife what I had promised, and she said, "How will you manage it?" I told her that I had managed things so far, but I did not know how I was going to get through this. I somehow knew that I was out of divine order. But when a fellow gets out of divine order it seems that the last person he goes to is God. I was relying on an architect to help me, but that scheme fell through. I turned to my relations and I certainly had a wet shirt as one after another turned me down. I tried my friends and managed no better. My wife said to me, "Thou hast never been to God Yet." What could I do?

I have a certain place in our house where I go to pray. I have been there very often. As I went I said, "Lord, if You will get me out of this scrape, I will never trouble Thee on this line again." As I waited on the Lord He just gave me one word. It seemed a ridiculous thing, but it was the wisest counsel. There is divine wisdom in every word He speaks. I came down to my wife, saying, "What do you think? The Lord has told me to go to Brother Webster." I said, "It seems very ridiculous, for he is one of the poorest men I know." He was the poorest man I knew, but he was also the richest man I knew, for he knew God. My wife said, "Do What God says, and it will be right."

I went off at once to see him, and he said as he greeted me, "Smith, what brings you so early?" I answered, "The word of God." I said to him, "About three weeks ago I promised to buy a house of a man, and

I am short 100 pounds ($500). I have tried to get this money, but somehow I seem to have missed God." "How is it," he asked, "that you have come to me only now?" I answered, "Because I went to the Lord about it only last night." "Well," he said, "it is a strange thing; three weeks ago I had 100 pounds. For years I have been putting money into a co-operative system and three weeks ago I had to go and draw 100 pounds out. I hid it under the mattress. Come with me and you shall have it. Take it. I hope it will bring as great a blessing to you as it has been a trouble to me." I had had a word from God, and all my troubles were ended. This has been multiplied in a hundred ways since that time. If I had been walking along filled with the Holy Ghost, I would not have bought that house and would not have had all that strain. I believe the Lord wants to loose us from things of earth. But I am ever grateful for that word from God. There have been times in my life when I have been in great crises and under great weight of intercession. I have gone to the meeting without the knowledge of what I would say, but somehow or other God would vouchsafe the coming forth under the power of the Spirit of some word of wisdom, just what some souls in that meeting needed. As we look to God His mind will be made known, and His revelation and His word of wisdom will be forth coming.

# CHAPTER 14

## The Word of Knowledge and Faith

---

"TO ANOTHER THE WORD of knowledge, by the same Spirit; to another faith, by the same Spirit" (1 Cor. 12:8, 9).

We have not passed this way hitherto. I believe that Satan has many devices and that they are worse today than ever before; but I also believe that there is to be a full manifestation on the earth of the power and glory of God to defeat every device of Satan.

In Ephesians 4 we are told to endeavor to keep the unity of the Spirit in the bond of peace, for there is one body, and one Spirit, one Lord, one faith, one baptism, and one God and Father of all. The Baptism of the Spirit is to make us all one. Paul tells us in 1 Cor. 12:13 that by one Spirit we are all baptized into one body, and have been all made to drink into one Spirit. It is God's thought that we speak the same thing. If we all have the full revelation of the Spirit of God we shall all see the same thing. Paul asked these Corinthians, "Is Christ divided?" When the Holy Ghost has full control, Christ is never divided, His body is not divided, there is no division. Schism and division are the products of the carnal mind.

How important it is that we shall have the manifestation of "the word of knowledge" in our midst. It is the same Spirit who brings forth the word of wisdom that brings forth the word of knowledge. The revelation of the mysteries of God comes by the Spirit, and we must have a supernatural word of knowledge in order to convey to others the things which the Spirit of God has revealed. The Spirit of God reveals Christ in all His wonderful fullness, and He shows Him to us from the beginning to the end of the Scriptures. It is the Scriptures that make us wise unto salvation, that open to us the depths of the kingdom of heaven, which reveal all the divine mind to us.

There are thousands of people who read and study the Word of God. But it is not quickened to them. The Bible is a dead letter except by the Spirit. The Word of God can never be vital and powerful in us except by the Spirit. The words that Christ spoke were not just dead words but they were spirit and life. And so it is the thought of God that a living word, a word of truth, the word of God, a supernatural word of knowledge, shall come forth from us through the power of the Spirit of God. It is the Holy Ghost who will bring forth utterances from our lips and a divine revelation of all the mind of God.

The child of God ought to thirst for the Word. He should know nothing else but the Word, and should know nothing among men save Jesus. "Man shall not live by bread alone, but by every word which proceedeth out of the mouth of God." It is as we feed on the Word and meditate on the message it contains, that the Spirit of God can vitalize that which we have received, and bring forth through us the word of knowledge that will be as full of power and life, as when He, the Spirit of God, moved upon holy men of old and gave them these inspired Scriptures. They were all inbreathed of God as they came forth at the beginning, and through the same Spirit they should come forth from us vitalized, living, powerful and sharper than any two-edged sword.

With the gifts of the Spirit should come the fruit of the Spirit. With wisdom we should have love, with knowledge we should have joy, and with the third gift, faith, we should have the fruit of peace. Faith is always accompanied by peace. Faith always rests. Faith laughs at impossibilities. Salvation is by faith, through grace, and it is the gift of God. We are kept by the power of God through faith. God gives faith and nothing can take it away. By faith we have power to enter into the wonderful things of God. There are three positions of faith; saving faith, which is the gift of God; the faith of the Lord Jesus; and the gift of faith. You will remember the word of the Lord Jesus Christ given to Paul, to which he refers in the 26th of Acts, where the Lord commissioned him to go to the Gentiles, "to open their eyes, and to turn them from darkness unto light, and from the power of Satan unto God, that they may receive forgiveness of sins, and inheritance among them ''WHICH ARE SANCTIFIED BY FAITH THAT IS IN ME."

Oh, this wonderful faith of the Lord Jesus. Your faith comes to an end. How many times I have been to the place where I have had to tell the Lord, "I have used all the faith I have," and then He has placed His own faith within me.

One of our workers said to me at Christmas time, "Wigglesworth, I never was so near the end of my purse in my life." I replied, "Thank God, you are just at the opening of God's treasures." It is when we are at the end of our own, that we can enter into the riches of God's resources. It is when we possess nothing, that we can possess all things.

The Lord will always meet you when you are on the line of living faith. I was in Ireland at one time and went to a house and said to the lady who came to the door, "Is Brother Wallace here?" She replied, "Oh, he has gone to Bangor, but God has sent you here for me. I need you. Come in." She told me her husband was a deacon of the Presbyterian Church. She had herself received the Baptism while she was a member of the Presbyterian Church, but they did not accept it as from God. The people of the church said to her husband, "This thing cannot go on. We don't want you to be deacon any longer, and your wife is not wanted in the church." The man was very enraged and he became incensed against his wife. It seemed as though an evil spirit possessed him, and the home that had once been peaceful became very terrible: At last he left home and left no money behind him, and the woman asked me what should she do.

We went to prayer and before we had prayed five minutes the woman was mightily filled with the Holy Ghost. I said to her, "Sit down and let me talk to you. Are you often in the Spirit like this?" She said.

"Yes, and what could I do without the Holy Ghost now?" I said to her, "The situation is yours. The Word of God says that you have power to sanctify your husband. Dare to believe the Word of God. Now the first thing we must do is to pray that your husband come back tonight." She said, "I know he won't." I said, "If we agree together, it is done." She said, "I will agree." I said to her, "When he comes home show him all possible love, lavish everything upon him. If he won't hear what you have to say, let him go to bed. The situation is yours. Get down before God and claim him for the Lord. Get into the glory just as you have got in today, and as the Spirit of God prays through you, you will find that God will grant all the desires of your heart."

A month later I saw this sister at a convention. She told how her husband came home that night and that he went to bed, but she prayed right through to victory and then laid her hands upon him. The moment she laid hands upon him he cried out for mercy. The Lord saved him and baptized him in the Holy Spirit. The power of God is beyond all our conception. The trouble is that we do not have the power of God in a full manifestation because of our finite thoughts, but as we go on and let God have His way, there is no limit to what our limitless God will do in response to a limitless faith. But you will never get anywhere except you are in constant pursuit of all the power of God.

One day when I came home from our open-air meeting at eleven o'clock I found that my wife was out. I asked, "Where is she?" I was told that she was down at Mitchell's. I had seen Mitchell that day and knew that he was at the point of death. I knew that it was impossible for him to survive the day unless the Lord undertook.

There are many who let down in sickness and do not take hold of the life of the Lord Jesus Christ that is provided for them. I was taken to see a woman who was dying and said to her, "How are things with you?" She answered, "I have faith, I believe." I said, "You know that you have not faith, you know that you are dying. It is not faith that you have, it is language." There is a difference between language and faith. I saw that she was in the hands of the devil. There was no possibility of life until he was removed from the premises. I hate the devil, and I laid hold of the woman and shouted, "Come out, you devil of death. I command you to come out in the name of Jesus." In one minute she stood on her feet in victory.

But to return to the case of Brother Mitchell, I hurried down to the house, and as I got near I heard terrible screams. I knew that something had happened. I passed Mrs. Mitchell on the staircase and asked, "What is up?" She replied, "He is gone! He is gone!" I just passed her and went into the room, and immediately I saw that Mitchell had gone. I could not understand it, but I began to pray. My wife was always afraid that I would go too far, and she laid hold of me and said, "Don't, Dad! Don't you see that he is dead?" I continued to pray and my wife continued to cry out to me, "Don't, Dad. Don't you see that he is dead?" But I continued praying. I got as far as I could with my own faith, and then God laid hold of me. Oh, it was such a laying hold that I could believe for anything. The faith of the Lord Jesus laid hold of me and a solid peace came into my heart. I shouted, "He lives! He lives! He lives!" And he is living today. There is a difference between our faith and the faith of the Lord Jesus. The faith of the Lord Jesus is needed. We must change faith from time to time. Your faith may get to a place where it wavers. The faith of Christ never wavers. When you have that faith the thing is finished. When you have that faith you will never look at things as they are, you will see the things of nature give way to the things of the Spirit, you will see the temporal swallowed up in the eternal.

I was at a camp meeting in Cazadero, California, several years ago, and a remarkable thing happened. A man came there who was stone deaf. I prayed for him and I knew that God had healed him. Then came the test. He would always move his chair up to the platform, and every time I got up to speak he would get up as close as he could and strain his ears to catch what I had to say. The devil said, "It isn't done." I declared, "It is done." This went on for three weeks and then the manifestation came and he could hear distinctly sixty yards away. When his ears were opened he thought it was so great that he had to stop the meeting and tell everybody about it. I met him in Oakland recently and he was hearing perfectly. As we remain steadfast and unmovable on the ground of faith, we shall see what we believe for in perfect manifestation.

People say to me, "Have you not the gift of faith?" I say that it is an important gift, but what is still more important is for us every moment to be making an advancement in God. Looking at the Word of God today I find that its realities are greater to me today than they were yesterday. It is the most sublime, joyful truth that God brings an enlargement. Always an enlargement. There is nothing dead, dry or barren in this life of the Spirit; God is always moving us on to something higher, and as we move on in the Spirit our faith will always rise to the occasion as different circumstances arise.

This is how the gift of faith is manifested. You see an object and you know that your own faith is nothing in the case. The other day I was in San Francisco. I sat on a car and saw a boy in great agony on the street. I said, "Let me get out." I rushed to where the boy was. He was in agony through cramp of the stomach. I put my hands on his stomach in the name of Jesus. The boy jumped, and stared at me with astonishment. He found himself instantly free. The gift of faith dared in the face of everything. It is as we are in the Spirit that the Spirit of God will operate this gift anywhere and at any time.

When the Spirit of God is operating this gift within a man, He causes him to know what God is going to do. When the man with the withered hand was in the synagogue, Jesus got all the people to look to see what would happen. The gift of faith always knows the results. He said to the man, "Stretch forth thine hand." His word had creative force. He was not living on the line of speculation. He spoke and something happened. He spake at the beginning and the world came into being. He speaks today and these things have to come to pass. He is the Son of God and came to bring us into sonship. He was the firstfruit of the resurrection and He calls us to be firstfruits, to be the same kind of fruit like to Himself.

There is an important point here. You cannot have the gifts by mere human desire. The Spirit of God distributes them severally as He will. God cannot trust some with the gift, but some who have a lowly, broken, contrite heart He can trust. One day I was in a meeting where there were a lot of doctors and eminent men, and many ministers. It was at a convention, and the power of God fell on the meeting. One humble little girl that waited at table opened her being to the Lord and was immediately filled with the Holy Ghost and began to speak in tongues. All these 'big men stretched their necks and looked up to see what was happening and were saying, "Who is it?" Then they learned it was "the servant!" Nobody received but "the servant!" These things are hidden and kept back from the wise and prudent, but the little children, the lowly ones, are the ones that receive. We cannot have faith if we have honor one of another. A man who is going on with God won't accept honor from his fellow beings. God honors the man of a broken, contrite spirit. How shall I get there? So many people want to do great things, and to be seen doing them, but the one that God will use is the one that is willing to be hidden. My Lord Jesus never said He could do things, but He did them. When that funeral procession was coming up from Nain with the widow's son carried upon the bier, He made them lay it down. He spoke the word, "Arise!" and gave the son back to the widow. He had compassion for her. And you and I will never do anything except on the line of compassion. We shall never be able to remove the cancer until we are immersed so deeply into the power of the Holy Ghost, that the compassion of Christ is moving through us.

I find that, in all my Lord did, He said that He did not do it, but that another in Him did the work. What a holy submission! He was just an instrument for the glory of God. Have we reached a place where we dare to be trusted with the gift? I see in 1 Corinthians 13 that if I have faith to remove mountains and have not charity, all is a failure. When my love is so deepened in God that I only move for the glory of God, that I only seek the glory of God, then the gifts can be made manifest. God wants to be manifested, and to manifest His glory to humble spirits.

A faint heart can never have a gift. There are two things essential; first, love, and second, determination, a boldness of faith that will cause God to fulfill His word. When I was baptized I had a wonderful time and had utterance in the Spirit, but for some time afterwards I did not again speak in tongues. But one day as I was helping another, the Lord again gave me utterances in the Spirit. I was one day going down the road and speaking in tongues a long while. There were some gardeners doing their work, and they stuck their heads out to see what was going on. I said, "Lord, you have something new for me. You said that when a man speaks in tongues, he should ask for the interpretation. I ask for the interpretation, and I'll stay right here till I get it." And from that hour the Lord gave me interpretation.

At one time I was in Lincolnshire in England and came in touch with the old pastor of an Episcopalian Church. He became much interested and asked me into his library. I never heard anything sweeter than the prayer the old man uttered as he got down to pray. He began to pray, "Lord, make me holy. Lord, sanctify me." I called out, "Wake up! Wake up now! Get up and sit in your chair." He sat up and looked at me. I said to him, "I thought you were holy." He answered, "Yes." "Then what makes you ask God to do what He has done for you?" He began to laugh and then to speak in tongues. Let us move into the realm of faith, and live in the realm of faith, and let God have His way.

# CHAPTER 15

# Gifts of Healings and Miracles

---

GOD HAS GIVEN US MUCH in these last days, and where much is given much will be required. The Lord has said to us, "Ye are the salt of the earth: but if the salt have lost his savor, wherewith shall it be salted? It is thenceforth good for nothing, but to be cast out, and to be trodden under foot of men." We see a thought on the same line when our Lord Jesus says, "If a man abide not in Me, he is cast forth as a branch, and is withered; and men gather them, and cast them into the fire, and they are burned." On the other hand He tells us, "If ye abide in Me, and My words abide in you, ye shall ask what ye will, and it shall be done unto you." If we do not move on with the Lord these days, and do not walk in the light of revealed truth, we shall become as the savorless salt, as a withered branch. This one thing we must do, forgetting those things that are behind, the past failures and the past blessings, we must reach forth for those things which are before, and press toward the mark for the prize of our high calling of God in Christ Jesus.

For many years the Lord has been moving me on and keeping me from spiritual stagnation. When I was in the Wesleyan Methodist Church I was sure I was saved and was sure I was all right. The Lord said to me, "Come out," and I came out. When I was with the people known as the Brethren I was sure I was all right now. But the Lord said, "Come out." Then I went into the Salvation Army. At that time it was full of life and there were revivals everywhere. But the Salvation Army went into natural things and the great revivals that they had in those early days ceased. The Lord said to me, "Come out," and I came out. I have had to come out three times since. I believe that this Pentecostal revival that we are now in is the best thing that the Lord has on the earth today, and yet I believe that God has something out of this that is going to be still better. God has no use for any man who is not hungering and thirsting for yet more of Himself and His righteousness.

The Lord has told us to covet earnestly the best gifts, and we need to be covetous for those that will bring Him most glory. We need to see the gifts of healing and the working of miracles in operation today. Some say that it is necessary for us to have the gift of discernment in operation with the gifts of healing, but even apart from this gift I believe the Holy Ghost will have a divine revelation for us as we deal with the sick. Most people seem to have discernment, or think they have, and if they would turn it on themselves for twelve months they would never want to discern again. The gift of discernment is not criticism. I am satisfied that in Pentecostal circles today that our paramount need is more perfect love.

Perfect love will never want the preeminence in everything, it will never want to take the place of another, it will always be willing to take the back seat. If you go to a convention there is always someone who wants to give a message, who wants to be heard. If you have a desire to go to a convention you should have three things settled in your mind. Do I want to be heard? Do I want to be seen? Do I want anything on the line of finances? If I have these things in my heart I have no right to be there. The one thing that must move us must be the constraining love of God to minister for Him. A preacher always loses out when he gets his mind on finances. It is well for Pentecostal preachers to avoid making much of finances except to stir up people to help our missionaries on financial lines. A preacher who gets big collections for the missionaries need never fear, the Lord will take care of his finances. A preacher should not land at a place and say that God had sent him. I am always fearful when I hear a man advertising this. If he is sent of God, the saints will know it. God has His plans for His servants and we must so live in His plans that He will place us where He wants us. If you seek nothing but the will of God, He will always put you in the right place at the right time. I want you to see that the gifts of healing and the working of miracles are part of the Spirit's plan and will come forth in operation as we are working along that plan. I must know the movement of the Spirit and the voice of God. I must understand the will of God if I am to see the gifts of the Spirit in operation.

The gifts of healing are so varied. You may go and see ten people and every case is different. I am never happier in the Lord than when I am in a bedroom with a sick person. I have had more revelations of the Lord's presence when I have ministered to the sick at their bedsides than at any other time. It is as your heart goes out to the needy ones in deep compassion that the Lord manifests His presence. You are able to locate their position. It is then that you know that you must be filled with the Spirit to deal with the conditions before you.

Where people are in sickness you find frequently that they are dense about Scripture. They usually know three scriptures though. They know about Paul's thorn in the flesh, and that Paul told Timothy to take a little wine for his stomach's sake, and that Paul left someone sick somewhere; they forget his name, and don't remember the name of the place, and don't know where the chapter is. Most people think they have a thorn in the flesh. The chief thing in dealing with a person who is sick is to locate their exact position. As you are ministering under the Spirit's power the Lord will let you see just that which will be more helpful and most faith-inspiring to them.

When I was in the plumbing business I enjoyed praying for the sick. Urgent calls would come and I would have no time to wash, and with my hands all black I would preach to these sick ones, my heart all aglow with love. Ah, you must have your heart in the thing when you pray for the sick. You have to get right to the bottom of the cancer with a divine compassion and then you will see the gifts of the Spirit in operation.

I was called at 10 o'clock one night to pray for a young person given up by the doctor who was dying of consumption. As I looked, I saw that unless God undertook it was impossible for her to live. I turned to the mother and said, "Well, mother. you will have to go to bed." She said, "Oh, I have not had my clothes off for three weeks." I said to the daughters, "You will have to go to bed," but they did not want to go. It was the same with the son. I put on my overcoat and said, "Good-bye, I'm off." They said, "Oh, don't leave us." I said, "I can do nothing here." They said, "Oh, if you will stop, we will all go to bed." I knew that God would move nothing in an atmosphere of mere natural sympathy and unbelief.

They all went to bed and I stayed, and that was surely a time as I knelt by that bed face to face with death and with the devil. But God can change the hardest situation and make you know that He is almighty.

Then the fight came. It seemed as though the heavens were brass. I prayed from 11 to 3:30 in the morning. I saw the glimmering light on the face of the sufferer and saw her pass away. The devil said, "Now you are done for. You have come from Bradford and the girl has died on your hands." I said, "It can't be. God did not send me here for nothing. This is a time to change strength." I remembered that passage which said, "Men ought always to pray and not to faint." Death had taken place but I knew that my God was all-powerful, and He that had split the Red Sea is just the same today. It was a time when I would not have "No," and God said "Yes." I looked at the window and at that moment the face of Jesus appeared. It seemed as though a million rays of light were coming from His face. As He looked at the one who had just passed away, the color came back to the face. She rolled over and fell asleep. Then I had a glorious time. In the morning she woke early, put on a dressing gown and walked to the piano. She started to play and to sing a wonderful song. The mother and the sister and the brother had all come down to listen. The Lord had undertaken. A miracle had been wrought.

The Lord is calling us along this way. I am thanking God for difficult cases. The Lord has called us into heart union with Himself; He wants His bride to have one heart and one Spirit with Him and to do what He Himself loved to do. That case had to be a miracle. The lungs were gone, they were just in shreds, but the Lord restored lungs that were perfectly sound.

There is a fruit of the Spirit that must accompany the gift of healing and that is longsuffering. The man who is going through with God to be used in healing must be a man of longsuffering. He must be always ready with a word of comfort. If the sick one is in distress and helpless and does not see everything eye to eye with you, you must bear with him. Our Lord Jesus Christ was filled with compassion and lived and moved in a place of longsuffering, and we will have to get into this place if we are to help needy ones.

There are some times when you pray for the sick and you are apparently rough. But you are not dealing with a person, you are dealing with the Satanic forces that are binding the person. Your heart is full of love and compassion to all, but you are moved to a holy anger as you see the place the devil has taken in the body of the sick one, and you deal with his position with a real forcefulness. One day a pet dog followed a lady out of her house and ran all round her feet. She said to the dog, "My dear, I cannot have you with me today." The dog wagged its tail and made a big fuss. She said, "Go home, my dear." But the dog did not go. At last she shouted roughly, "Go home," and off it went. Some people deal with the devil like that, The devil can stand all the comfort you like to give him. Cast him out! You are dealing not with the person, you are dealing with the devil. Demon power must be dislodged in the name of the Lord. You are always right when you dare to deal with sickness as with the devil. Much sickness is caused by some misconduct, there is something wrong, there is some neglect somewhere, and Satan has had a chance to get in. It is necessary to repent and confess where you have given place to the devil, and then he can be dealt with.

When you deal with a cancer case, recognize that it is a living evil spirit that is destroying the body. I had to pray for a woman in Los Angeles one time who was suffering with cancer, and as soon as it was cursed it stopped bleeding. It was dead. The next thing that happened was that the natural body pressed it out, because the natural body had no room for dead matter. It came out like a great big ball with tens of thousands of fibers. All these fibers had been pressing into the flesh. These evil powers move to get further hold of the system, but the moment they are destroyed their hold is gone. Jesus said to His disciples that He gave them power to loose and power to bind. It is our privilege in the power of the Holy Ghost to loose the prisoners of Satan and to let the oppressed go free.

Take your position in the first epistle of John and declare, "Greater is He that is in me than he that is in the world." Then recognize that it is not yourself that has to deal with the power of the devil, but the Greater One that is in you. Oh, what it means to be filled with Him. You can do nothing of yourself, but He that is in you will win the victory. Your being has become the temple of the Spirit. Your mouth, your mind, your whole being becomes exercised and worked upon by the Spirit of God.

I was called to a certain town in Norway. The hall seated about 1500 people. When I got to the place it was packed, and hundreds were trying to get in. There were some policemen there. The first thing I did was to preach to the people outside the building. Then I said to the policemen, "It hurts me very much that there are more people outside than inside and I feel I must preach to the people. I would like you to get me the market place to preach in." They secured for me a great park and a big stand was erected and I was able to preach to thousands. After the preaching we had some wonderful cases of healing. One man came a hundred miles bringing his food with him. He had not been passing anything through his stomach for over a month as he had a great cancer on his stomach. He was healed at that meeting, and opening his parcel, he began eating before all the people. There was a young woman there with a stiff hand. Instead of the mother making the child use her arm she had allowed the child to keep the arm dormant until it was stiff, and she had grown up to be a young woman and was like the woman that was bowed down with the spirit of infirmity. As she stood before me I cursed the spirit of infirmity in the name of Jesus. It was instantly cast out and the arm was free. Then she waved it all over. At the close of the meeting the devil laid out two people with fits. When the devil is manifesting himself, then is the time to deal with him. Both of these people were delivered, and when they stood up and thanked and praised the Lord what a wonderful time we had.

We need to wake up and be on the stretch to believe God. Before God could bring me to this place He has broken me a thousand times. I have wept, I have groaned, I have travailed many a night until God broke me. It seems to me that until God has mowed you down you never can have this longsuffering for others. We can never have the gifts of healing and the working of miracles in operation only as we stand in the divine power that God gives us and we stand believing God, and having done all we still stand believing.

We have been seeing wonderful miracles these last days and they are only a little of what we are going to see. I believe that we are right on the threshold of wonderful things, but I want to emphasize that all these things will be through the power of the Holy Ghost. You must not think that these gifts will fall upon you like ripe cherries. There is a sense in which you have to pay the price for everything you get. We must be covetous for God's best gifts, and say Amen to any preparation the Lord takes us through, in order that we may be humble, usable vessels through whom He Himself can operate by means of the Spirit's power.

# CHAPTER 16

# The Gift of Prophecy

---

IN 1 COR. 12:10, speaking of the diversities of gifts by the same Spirit, Paul writes, "To another prophecy." We see the importance of this gift from 1 Cor. 14:1, where we are told to follow after charity, and desire spiritual gifts, but rather that we may prophesy. We see also that he that prophesieth speaketh unto man to edification, and exhortation and comfort. How important it is then that we should have this gift in manifestation in the church in order that the saints might be built up and made strong and filled with the comfort of God. But with this as all other gifts we should see that it is operated by the Spirit's power and brought forth in the unction of the Spirit; so that everyone who shall hear prophecy, as it is brought forth by the Spirit of God, shall know that it is GOD who is bringing forth that which is for the edification of those who hear. It is the Spirit of God who takes of the deep things of God and reveals them, and unctionizes the prophet to give forth that which is a revelation of the things of God.

Utterance in prophecy has a real lifting power and gives real light on the truth to those who hear. Prophecy is never a mind reflection, it is something far deeper than this. By means of prophecy we receive that which is the mind of the Lord; and as we receive these blessed, fresh utterances through the Spirit of the Lord the whole assembly is lifted into the realm of the spiritual. Our hearts and minds and whole bodies receive a quickening through the Spirit given word. As the Spirit brings forth prophecy we find there is healing and salvation and power in every line. For this reason it is one of the gifts that we ought to covet.

While we appreciate true prophecy, we must not forget that the Scriptures warn us in no uncertain manner concerning that which is false. In 1 John 4:1 we are told, "Beloved, believe not every spirit, but try the spirits whether they are of God: because many false prophets are gone out into the world." And John tells us how we can tell the difference between the true and the false, "Hereby know ye the Spirit of God: every spirit that confesseth that Jesus Christ is come in the flesh is of God: and every spirit that confesseth not that Jesus Christ is come in the flesh is not of God; but this is that spirit of antichrist, whereof ye have heard that it should come." There are voices which seem like prophecy and some have got into terrible darkness and bondage through listening to these counterfeits of the true gift of prophecy. True prophecy is always Christ-exalting, magnifying the Son of God, exalting the blood of Jesus Christ, encouraging the saints to praise and worship the true God. False prophecy deals with things that do not edify and is designed to puff up its hearers and to lead them into error.

Many picture Satan as a great, ugly monster with great ears, eyes and a tail; but the Scriptures give us no such picture of him. He was a being of great beauty whose heart became lifted up. He is manifesting himself everywhere today as an angel of light. He is full of pride, and if you don't watch he will try to make you think you are somebody. This is the weakness of most preachers and most men-the idea of being somebody! There are none of us who are anything, and the more we know we are nothing, the more God can make us a channel of His power. May the dear Lord save us from all these pride side-lines they are the devil's traps. True prophecy will show you that Christ is all in all, and that you are in yourself less than nothing and vanity. False prophecy will not magnify Christ but will make you think that after all you are going to be some great one. You may be sure that such is inspired by "the chief of the sons of pride."

I want to warn you against the foolishness of continually seeking to hear voices. Look in the Bible. Here we have the voice of God, who at sundry times and in divers manners, spake in time past unto the fathers by the prophets, and hath in these last days spoken unto us by His Son. Don't run away with anything else. If you hear the voice of God it will be on the line of the Scriptures of truth given in the inspired Word. In Rev. 22:18, 19 we see the danger of attempting to add to or take from the prophecy of this Book. True prophecy, as it comes forth in the power of the Spirit of God, will neither take from nor add to the Scriptures, but will intensify and quicken that which already has been given to us of God. The Holy Ghost will bring to our remembrance all the things that Jesus said and did. True prophecy will bring forth things new and old out of the Scriptures of truth and will make them living and powerful to us.

Some may ask, "If we have the Scriptures, why do we need prophecy?" The Scriptures themselves answer this question. God has said that in the last days He will pour out of His Spirit upon all flesh, "and your sons and your daughters shall prophesy." The Lord knew that in these last days prophecy would be a real means of blessing to us, and that is why we can count on Him giving us, by means of the Spirit, through His servants and His handmaids, true prophetic messages.

I want to give you a warning concerning listening to voices. I was at a meeting in Paisley in Scotland and came in touch with two young women. One of them wore a white blouse but it was smeared with blood. They were in a great state of excitement. These two girls were telegraph operators and were precious young women, having received the Baptism in the Spirit. They were both longing to be missionaries. But whatever our spiritual state is we are subject to temptations. An evil power came to one of these young women and said, "If you will obey me, I will make you one of the most wonderful missionaries that ever went out." This was just the devil or one of his agents acting as an angel of light. One of these young women was captured immediately and she became so excited that her sister saw there was something wrong and asked the overseer to allow them to be free for a time.

As she took her into a room, the power of Satan, endeavoring to imitate the Spirit of God, manifested itself in a voice, and led this young woman to believe that the missionary enterprise would be unfolded that night if she would obey. This evil spirit said, “Don’t tell anybody but your sister.” I reckon that everything of God can be told everybody. If you cannot preach what you live, your life is wrong. If you are afraid of telling what you do in secret, some day it will be told from the housetop. Don’t think you will get out of it. That which is pure cometh to the light He that doeth truth cometh to the light that his deeds may be made manifest, that they are wrought in God.

The evil power went on to say to this girl, “You go to the railroad station tonight, and there will be a train coming in at 7:32. Buy a ticket for yourself and your sister. Then you will have six pence left. You will find a woman in a carriage dressed as a nurse, and opposite her will be a gentleman who has all the money you need.” She bought her ticket and had just six pence left. The first thing came right. Next, the train came in at exactly 7:32. But the next thing did not come. They ran from the top to the bottom of that railroad train before it moved out and nothing turned out as they had been told. As soon as the train moved out the same voice came and said, “Over on the other platform.” All that night until 9:30 these two young women were rushed from platform to platform. As soon as it was 9:30 this same evil power said, “Now that I know you will obey me, I will make you the greatest missionaries.” Always something big! They might have known it was all wrong. This evil power said, “This gentleman will take you to a certain bank at a certain corner in Glasgow where he will put all that money in for you.” Banks are not open at that time of night in Glasgow. If she had gone to the street this evil spirit mentioned, there probably would not have been a bank there. All they needed was a little common sense and they would have seen that it was not the Lord. If you have your heart open for these kind of voices you will soon get into a trap. We must ever remember that there are many evil spirits in the world.

Were these two people delivered? Yes, after terrible travail with God, they were perfectly delivered. Their eyes were opened to see that this thing was not of God but of the devil. These two sisters are now laboring for the Lord in China and doing a blessed work for Him. If you do get into error on these lines, praise God there is a way out. I praise God that He will break us down till all pride leaves us. The worst pride we can have is the pride of exaltation of self.

Paul wrote at the commandment of the Lord, "Let the prophets speak two or three, and let the others judge. If anything be revealed to another that sitteth by, let the first hold his peace. For ye may all prophesy one by one, that all may learn, and all may be comforted." If you are not humble enough to allow your prophecy to be judged, it is as surely wrong as you are wrong. Prophecy has to be judged. A meeting such as this one that Paul suggests would certainly be the greatest meeting you ever had. Praise God, the tide will rise to this. It will all come into perfect order when the church is bathed and lost in the great ideal of only glorifying Jesus. Then things will come to pass that will be worth while.

Coupled with prophecy you will have the fruit of the Spirit that is goodness. They were holy men who spoke in prophecy in days of old as the Holy Ghost prompted them, and so today the prophet who can be trusted is a man that is full of goodness, that goodness which is the fruit of the Spirit. But when he gets out of this position, and rests upon his own individuality, he is in danger of being puffed up and becoming an instrument for the enemy.

I knew some people who had a wonderful farm, very productive, in a very good neighborhood. They listened to voices telling them to sell everything and go to Africa. These voices so unhinged them that they had scarcely had time to sell out. They sold their property at a ridiculous price. The same voices told them of a certain ship they were to sail on. When they got to the port they found there wasn't a ship of that name. The difficulty was this, to get them not to believe these false voices. They said perhaps it was the mind of the Lord to give them another ship, and the voice soon gave them the name of another ship. When they reached Africa they knew no language that was spoken there. But the voice did not let them stop. They had to come back, brokenhearted, shaken through, and having lost all confidence in everything. If these people had had sense to go to some men of God who were filled with the Spirit and seek their counsel, they would soon have been persuaded that these voices were not of God. But listeing to these voices always brings about a spiritual pride that makes a man or woman think that they are superior to their brethren, and that they are above taking counsel of men who they think are not so filled with the Spirit as they are. If you hear any voices that make you think that you are superior to those whom God has put in the church to rule the church, watch out, that is surely the devil.

We read in the Revelation that the testimony of Jesus is the spirit of prophecy. You will find that true prophetic utterance always exalts the Lamb of God.

No prophetic touch is of any good unless there is fire in it. I never expect to be used of God till the fire burns. I feel that if I ever speak, it must be by the Spirit. At the same time remember that the prophet must prophesy according to the measure of faith. If you rise up in your weakness, but rise up in love because you want to honor God, and just begin, you will find the presence of the Lord upon you. Act in faith and the Lord will meet you.

May God take us on and on into this glorious fact of faith, that we may be so in the Holy Ghost that God will work through us on the line of the miraculous and on the lines of prophecy, where we shall always know that it is no longer we but He who is working through us, bringing forth that which is in His own divine good pleasure.

# CHAPTER 17

## The Discerning of Spirits

"TO ANOTHER DISCERNING of spirits" (1 Cor. 12:10). There is a vast difference between natural discernment and spiritual. When it comes to natural discernment you will find many people loaded with it, and they can see so many faults in others. To such the words of Christ in the sixth chapter of Luke surely apply, "Why beholdest thou the mote that is in thy brother's eye, but perceivest not the beam that is in thine own eye?" If you want to manifest natural discernment, focus the same on yourself for at least twelve months and you will see so many faults in yourself that you will never want to fuss about the faults of another. In the sixth of Isaiah we read of the prophet being in the presence of God and he found that even his lips were unclean and everything was unclean. But praise God, there is the same live coal for us today, the baptism of fire, the perfecting of the heart, the purifying of the mind, the regeneration of the spirit. How important it is that the fire of God shall touch our tongues.

In 1 John 4:1 we are told, "Beloved, believe not every spirit, but try the spirits whether they are of God." We are further told, "And every spirit that confesseth not that Jesus Christ is come in the flesh is not of God: and this is that spirit of antichrist, whereof ye have heard that it should come; and even now already is it in the world." From time to time as I have seen a person under the power of evil, or having a fit, I have said to the power of evil, or Satanic force that is within the possessed person, "Did Jesus Christ come in the flesh?" and straightway they have answered, "No." They either say, "No," or hold their tongues, refusing altogether to acknowledge that the Lord Jesus Christ came in the flesh. It is then, remembering that further statement of John's, "Greater is He that is in you than he that is in the world," that you can in the name of the Lord Jesus Christ deal with the evil powers and command them to come out. We as Pentecostal people must know the tactics of the evil one and must be able to displace and dislodge him from his position.

I was preaching in Doncaster, England, at one time on the line of faith and a number of people were delivered. There was a man present who was greatly interested and moved by what he saw. He was suffering himself with a stiff knee and had yards and yards of flannel wound around it. After he got home he said to his wife, "I have taken in Wigglesworth's message and now I am going to act on it and get deliverance. Wife, I want you to be the audience." He took hold of his knee and said, "Come out, you devil, in the name of Jesus." Then he said, "It is all right, wife." He took the yards and yards of flannel off and found he was all right without the bandage. The next night he went to the little Primitive Methodist Church where he worshiped. There were a lot of young people who were in bad plight there and Jack had a tremendous business delivering his friends through the name of Jesus. He had been given to see that a great many ills to which flesh is heir are nothing else but the operation of the enemy, but his faith had risen and he saw that in the name of Jesus there was a power that was more than a match for the enemy.

I arrived one night at Gottenberg in Sweden and was asked to hold a meeting there. In the midst of the meeting a man fell full length in the doorway. The evil spirit drew him down, manifesting itself and disturbing the whole meeting. I rushed to the door and laid hold of this man and cried out to the evil spirit within him, "Come out, you devil! In the name of Jesus we cast you out as an evil spirit." I lifted him up and said, "Stand on your feet and walk in the name of Jesus." I don't know whether anybody in the meeting understood me except the interpreter, but the devils knew what I said. I talked in English but these devils in Sweden cleared out. A similar thing happened in Christiania.

The devil will endeavor to fascinate through the eyes and through the mind. At one time there was brought to me a beautiful young woman who had been fascinated with some preacher, and just because he had not given her satisfaction on the line of courtship and marriage, the devil took advantage and made her fanatical and mad. They brought her 250 miles in that condition. She had previously received the Baptism in the Spirit. You ask, "Is there any place for the enemy in one that has been baptized in the Holy Ghost?" Our only safety is in going on with God and in constantly being filled with the Holy Ghost. You must not forget Demas. He must have been baptized with the Holy Ghost for he appears to have been a right-hand worker with Paul, but the enemy got him to the place where he loved this present world and he dropped off. When they brought this young woman to me the evil power was immediately discerned and immediately I cast the thing out in the name of Jesus. It was a great joy to present her before all the people in her right mind again.

There is a life of perfect deliverance, and this is where God wants you to be. If I find my peace is disturbed on any line, I know it is the enemy who is trying to work. How do I know this? Because the Lord has promised to keep your mind in perfect peace when it is stayed on Him. Paul tells us to present our bodies a living sacrifice, holy, acceptable unto God, which is our reasonable service; the Holy Spirit breathes through him, "And be not conformed to this world; but be ye transformed by the renewing of your mind, that ye may prove what is that good, and acceptable, and perfect will of God." He further tells us in Phil. 4, "Finally, brethren, whatsoever things are true, whatsoever things are honest, whatsoever things are just, whatsoever things are pure, whatsoever things are of good report; if there be any virtue, if there be any praise, think on these things." As we think about that which is pure, we become pure. As we think about that which is holy, we become holy. And as we think about our Lord Jesus Christ, we become like Him. We are changed into the likeness of the object on which our gaze is fixed.

To discern spirits we must dwell with Him who is holy, and He will give the revelation and unveil the mask of Satanic power on all lines.

In Australia I went to one place where there were disrupted and broken homes. The people were so deluded by the evil power of Satan that men had left their wives, and wives had left their husbands, and had gotten into spiritual affinity with one another. That is the devil ! May God deliver us from such evils in these days. There is no one better than the companion God has given you. I have seen so many broken hearts and so many homes that have been wrecked. We need a real revelation of these evil seducing spirits which come in and fascinate by the eye and destroy lives, and bring the work of God into disrepute. But there is always flesh behind it. It is never clean; it is unholy, impure, Satanic, devilish, and hell is behind it. If the enemy comes in to tempt you on any line like this, I beseech you to look instantly to the Lord Jesus. He can deliver you from any such Satanic power. You must be separated on all lines if you are going to have faith.

The Holy Ghost will give us this gift of discerning of spirits if we desire it so that we may perceive by revelation this evil power which comes in to destroy. We can reach out and get this unction of the Spirit that will reveal these things unto us.

You will have people come to meetings who are spiritists. You must be able to deal with spiritist conditions. You can so deal with them that they will not have any power in the meetings. If you ever have Theosophists or Christian Scientists, you must be able to discern them and settle them. Never play with them; always clear them out. They are better with their own company always, unless they are willing to be delivered from the delusion they are in. Remember the warning of the Lord Jesus, "The thief cometh not, but for to steal, and to kill, and to destroy."

Before Satan can bring his evil spirits there has to be an open door. Hear what the Scriptures say

"That wicked one toucheth him not" (1 John 5:18).

"The Lord shall preserve thee from all evil: He shall preserve thy soul" (Psa. 121:7). How does Satan get an opening? When the saint ceases to seek after holiness, purity, righteousness, truth; when he ceases to pray, stops reading the Word and gives way to carnal appetites, then it is that Satan comes. So often sickness comes as a result of disobedience. David said, "Before I was afflicted, I went astray." Seek the Lord and He will sanctify every thought, every act, till your whole being is ablaze with holy purity and your one desire will be for Him who has created you in holiness. Oh, this holiness! Can we be made pure? We can. Every inbred sin must go. God can cleanse away every evil thought. Can we have a hatred for sin and a love for righteousness? Yes, God will create within thee a pure heart. He will take away the stony heart out of the flesh. He will sprinkle thee with clean water and thou shalt be cleansed from all thy filthiness. When will He do it? When you seek Him for such inward purity.

# CHAPTER 18

# The Gift of Tongues

"FOLLOW AFTER CHARITY, and desire spiritual gifts, but rather that ye may prophesy. For he that speaketh in an unknown tongue, speaketh not unto men, but unto God: for no man understandeth him; howbeit in the spirit he speaketh mysteries" (1 Cor. 14:1, 2).

It is necessary that we have a great desire for spiritual gifts. We must thirst after them and covet them earnestly because the gifts are necessary and important, that we, by the grace of God having received the gifts, may be used for God's glory.

God has ordained this speaking in an unknown tongue unto Himself as a wonderful, supernatural means of communication in the Spirit. As we speak to Him in the unknown tongue we speak wonderful mysteries in the Spirit. In Rom. 8:27 we read, "He that searcheth the hearts knoweth what is the mind of the Spirit, because he maketh intercession for the saints according to the will of God." Many times as we speak unto God in an unknown tongue we are in intercession and as we pray thus in the Spirit we pray according to the will of God. And there is such a thing as the Spirit making intercession with groanings which cannot be uttered.

On this line I want to tell you about Willie Burton, who is laboring for God in the Belgium Congo. Brother Burton is a mighty man of God and is giving his life for the heathen in Africa. He took fever and went down to death. They said; “He has preached his last; what shall we do?” All their hopes seemed to be blighted, and there they stood, with broken hearts, wondering what was going to take place. They left him for dead; but, in a moment, without any signal, he stood right in the midst of them; and they could not understand it. The explanation he gave was this, that, when he came to himself, he realized a warmth going right through his body; and there wasn’t one thing wrong with him. How did it come about? It was a mystery until he went to London and was telling the people how he was left for dead, and then was raised up. A lady came up and asked for a private conversation with him, and arranged a time. She asked, “Do you keep a diary?” He answered, “Yes.” She told him, “It happened on a certain day that I went to pray; and as soon as I knelt, I had you on my mind. -The Spirit of the Lord took hold of me and prayed through me in an unknown tongue. A vision came before me in which I saw you laid out helpless; and I cried out in the unknown tongue till I saw you rise up and go out of that room.” She had kept a note of the time and when he turned to his diary he found that it was exactly the time when he was raised up. There are great possibilities as we yield to the Spirit and speak unto God in quiet hours in our bedrooms. God wants you to be filled with the Holy Ghost so that everything about you shall be charged with the dynamic of heaven.

“He that speaketh in an unknown tongue edifieth himself; but he that prophesieth edifieth the church” (Verse 4). I want you to see that he that speaketh in an unknown tongue edifieth himself or builds himself up. We must be edified before we can edify the church. I cannot estimate what I, personally, owe to the Holy Ghost method of spiritual edification. I am here before you as one of the biggest conundrums in the world. There never was a weaker man on the platform. Language? None. Inability-full of it. All natural things in my life point exactly opposite to my being able to stand on the platform and preach the gospel. The secret is that the Holy Ghost came and brought this wonderful edification of the Spirit. I had been reading this Word continuallv as well as I could, but the Holy Ghost came and took hold of it, for the Holy Ghost is the breath of it, and He illuminated it to me. And He gives me language that I cannot speak fast enough; it comes too fast; and it is there because God has given it. When the Comforter is come He shall teach you ALL things; and He has given me this supernatural means of speaking in an unknown tongue to edify myself, so that, after being edified, I can edify the church.

In 1 John 2:20 we read, "But ye have an unction from the Holy One, and ye know all things." In verse 27 we read, "But the anointing which ye have received of him abideth in you, and ye need not that any man should teach you; but as the same anointing teacheth you of all things, and is truth, and is no lie, and even as it hath taught you, ye shall abide in him." Even, when you are baptized in the Spirit you may say, "I seem so dry, I don't know where I am." The Word says you have an unction. Thank God you have received an anointing. The Holy Ghost here says that He is abiding and that He teaches you of all things. These are great and definite positions for you. The Holy Ghost would have you stir up your faith to believe that this word is true that you have the unction and that the anointing abideth. As you rise up in the morning believe this wonderful truth, and as you yield to the Spirit's presence and power you will find yourself speaking unto God in the Spirit and you will find that you are personally being edified by doing this. Let everything about you be a lie, but let this word of God be true. The devil will say you are the driest person and that you will never do anything, but you believe God's word, that the anointing which ye have received of Him abideth in you.

"I would that ye all spake with tongues, but rather that ye prophesied: for greater is he that prophesieth than he that speaketh with tongues, except he interpret, that the church may receive edification." You must understand that God would always have you to be in the place of prophecy, for everyone who has received the Holy Ghost has a right to prophesy. In verse 31 we read, "Ye may all prophesy one by one." Now prophecy is far in advance of speaking in tongues, except that you have the interpretation of the speaking in tongues, and then God gets an equivalent to prophecy. In verse 13 we read, "Let him that speaketh in an unknown tongue, pray that he may interpret." This is an important word.

After receiving the Baptism in the Holy Ghost and speaking in tongues as the Spirit gave utterance, I did not speak with tongues again for nine months. I was troubled about it because I went up and down laying hands upon people that they might receive the Holy Ghost, and they were speaking in tongues, but I did not have the joy of speaking myself. God wanted to show me that the speaking in tongues as the Spirit gave utterance, which I received when I received the Baptism, was distinct from the gift of tongues which I subsequently received. When I laid hands on other people and they received the Holy Ghost, I used to think, "Oh, Lord Jesus, it would be nice if You would let me speak." He withheld the gift from me, for He knew that I would meet many who would say that the Baptism of the Holy Ghost can be received without the speaking in tongues, and that people simply received the gift of tongues when they received the Baptism. I did not receive the gift of tongues at that time, but nine months later I was going out of the door one morning, speaking to the Lord in my own heart, when there came a volume of tongues. When the tongues stopped I said to the Lord, "Now, Lord, I did not do it, and I wasn't seeking it; so You have done it, and I am not going to move from this place until you give me interpretation." And then came an interpretation which has been fulfilled all the world over. Is it the Holy Ghost who speaks? Then the Holy Ghost can interpret. Let him that speaks in a tongue pray that he may interpret, and God will give it. We must not rush through without getting a clear understanding of what God has to say to us.

"What is it then? I will pray with the spirit, and I will pray with the understanding also: I will sing with the spirit, and I will sing with the understanding also" (Verse 15) . If you pray in an unknown tongue in the Spirit you do not know what you are praying; you have no understanding of it. It is unfruitful to those round about you; but you have the same power to pray with the understanding under the unction of the Spirit as you have to pray in an unknown tongue. Some say, "Oh, I could do that, but it would be myself doing it." If YOU pray, it is yourself, and everything you do in the beginning is yourself. I kneel down to pray and the first and second sentences may be in the natural; but as soon as I have finished, the Spirit begins to pray through me. The first may be yourself. Granted. The next will be the Holy Ghost, and the Holy Ghost will take you through, praise the Lord. Everything but faith will say, "That isn't right." Faith says, "It is right." The natural man says, "It isn't right." Faith says, "It is right." Paul says, "I will pray with the spirit, and I will pray with the understanding also;" and he does it in faith. The devil is against it and your own self-life is against it. May God the Holy Ghost bring us into the blessed place where we may live, walk, pray and sing in the Spirit, and pray and sing with the understanding also. Faith will do it. Faith has a deaf ear to the devil and to the working of the natural mind, and a big ear to God. Faith has a deaf ear to yourself and an open ear to God. Faith won't take any notice of feelings. Faith says, "You are complete in Him."

It is a wonderful thing to pray in the Spirit and to sing in the Spirit, praying in tongues and singing in tongues as the Spirit of God gives you utterance. I never get out of bed in the morning without having communion with God in the Spirit. It is the most wonderful thing on earth. It is most lovely to be in the Spirit when you are dressing and you come out to the world and the world has no effect on you. You begin the day like that and you will be conscious of the guidance of the Spirit right through the day.

"I thank my God, I speak with tongues more than ye all: yet in the church I had rather speak five words with my understanding, that by my voice I might teach others also, than ten thousand words in an unknown tongue" (Ver. 18, 19). Many people will come round and say that Paul said he would rather speak five words with the known tongue than ten thousand words without understanding. Then will always leave out that part of the sentence, "I thank my God, I speak with tongues more than ye all." Paul was here correcting the excessive speaking in tongues without interpretation, which was not for the edification of the assembly. If there was no interpreter present, they were simply to speak to themselves and to God. Suppose we had someone preaching and we had twenty or thirty people all up and down in tongues, it would be very serious. There would be confusion. The people who attend the meeting would rather have five words of edification, consolation and comfort than ten thousand words without understanding.

Because you feel a touch of the Spirit you are not obliged to speak in tongues. The Lord will give you a sound mind so that you will hold your body in perfect order for the edification of the church. But Paul here says that he spake in tongues more than they all; and, as it is evident that the Corinthian church was given to this thing very considerably, he certainly must have been speaking tremendously in tongues both day and night. He was so edified by this wonderful, supernatural means of being built up, that he could go to the church, and preaching in a manner so that they could all understand him, he would marvelously edify the saints.

"In the law it is written, With men of other tongues and other lips will I speak unto this people; and yet for all that will they not hear me, saith the Lord. Wherefore tongues are for a sign, not to them that believe, but to them that believe not" (Verses 21, 22). There are many who call themselves believers who are extremely unbelieving. One of the unbelieving "believers" was a Methodist minister who lived in Sheffield, England. A man gave him a check and told him to go and take a rest. This man also gave him my name and address; so, when he got to Bradford, he began to inquire about me. He was warned against me as one of the "tongues people," and was told to be very careful and not to be taken in, for the whole thing was of the devil. He said, "They will not take ME in; I know too much for them to take me in."

He was quite run down and needed rest; and when he came he said, "A friend of yours sent me, is it all right?" I replied, "Yes, you are welcome." But we could do nothing with that man. It was impossible. Talk? You never heard anyone talk like him. It was talk, talk, talk, talk. I said, "Let him alone, he will surely finish some day." We had dinner, and he talked through dinner time; we had the next meal and he talked through that.

It was our Friday night meeting for those seeking the Baptism and the room began to fill with people and still he talked. No one could get an edge in. He lodged himself in a place where he could not be disturbed by those coming in. I said, "Brother, you will have to stop now, we are going to pray." As a general thing we had some singing before going to prayer; but this time it was different. It was God's order. We got straight to prayer and as soon as we began to pray two young women, one on this side and the other on the other side began speaking in tongues. And this minister-it was all so strange to him-moved from one to the other to hear what they were saying. In a little while he said, "May I go to my room?" I said, "Yes, brother, if you wish." So he went to his room and we had a wonderful time.

We went to bed about eleven o'clock or so and at half- past three in the morning this man came to the bedroom door. Knock, knock, "May I come in?" "Yes, come in." He opened the door and said, "He is come, He is come"- holding his mouth, for he could hardly speak in English. I said, "Go back to bed, tell us tomorrow." Tongues are for the unbeliever, and this man was an unbeliever, an unbelieving "believer." Again and again I have seen conviction come upon people through the speaking in tongues.

The next morning he came down to breakfast and said, "Oh, was not that a wonderful night?" He said, "I know Greek and Hebrew, and those two young women were speaking these languages, one was saying in Greek, `Get right with God,' and the other was saying the same thing in Hebrew. I knew it was God speaking, and I knew it was not they. I first had to repent. I came in an unbeliever, but I found that God was here. - In the night God laid me on the floor for about two hours. I was helpless. Then God broke through." Here he began again to speak in tongues, right over the breakfast table.

God will have witnesses of His mighty power that no man can gainsay. You will have to see that the Holy Ghost will speak through you in tongues and interpretation which will bring conviction to the unbeliever in the open air; and you will find that God will convict by this means.

I will explain to you the most perfect way to receive the gift. Come with me to the second chapter of 2 Kings and I will show you a man receiving a gift. Elijah had been mightily used of God in calling down fire and in other miracles; and Elisha is moved with a great spirit of covetousness to have this man's gifts. You can be very covetous for the gifts of the Spirit and God will allow it. When Elijah said to him, "I want you to stop at Gilgal," Elisha said, "As the Lord liveth and as thy soul liveth, I will not leave thee." There was no stopping him. When Elijah wanted Elisha to stop at Jericho he said in substance, "I am not stopping." The man that stops gets nothing. O, don't stop at Jericho; don't stop at Jordan; don't stop anywhere when God would have you move on into all of His fullness that He has for you.

They came to Jordan and Elijah took his mantle and smote the waters. They divided; and Elijah and Elisha went over on dry ground. Elijah turned to Elisha and said in substance, "Look here, what do you want?" Elisha was wanting what he was going to have, and you may covet all that God says that you shall have. Elisha said, "I pray thee, let a double portion of thy spirit be upon me." This was the plow-boy, who had washed the hands of his master; but his spirit got so big that he purposed in his heart that, when Elijah stepped off the scene, he would be put into his place.

Elijah said, "Thou hast asked a hard thing: nevertheless, if thou see me when I am taken from thee, it shall be so unto thee." May God help you never to stop persevering till you get what you want. Let your aspiration be large and your faith rise until you are wholly on fire for God's best.

Onward they go, and as one steps, the other steps with him. He purposed to keep his eye on his master until the last. It took a chariot of fire and horses of fire to part them asunder, and Elijah went up by a whirlwind into heaven. I can fancy I hear Elisha crying out, "Father Elijah, drop that mantle!" And it came down. Oh, I can see it lowering, lowering and lowering. Elisha took all of his own clothes and rent them in two pieces, and then he took up the mantle of Elijah. I do not believe that, when he put on that other mantle, he felt any difference in himself; but when he came to Jordan, he took the mantle of Elijah and smote the waters and said, "Where is the Lord God of Elijah?" And the waters parted and he went over on dry ground. And the sons of the prophets said, "The spirit of Elijah doth rest upon Elisha."

It is like receiving a gift; you don't know that you have it till you act in faith. Brothers and sisters, as you ask, BELIEVE.

Made in United States
Orlando, FL
04 January 2023

28186227R00157